RALLY ROUND THE FLAG

Uniforms of the Union Volunteers of 1861

HARTFORD CITY GUARD,
Organized, Jan. 8th, 1861.

The New England States

Vermont.

FREEDOM AND UNITY.

For the Union.

RON FIELD

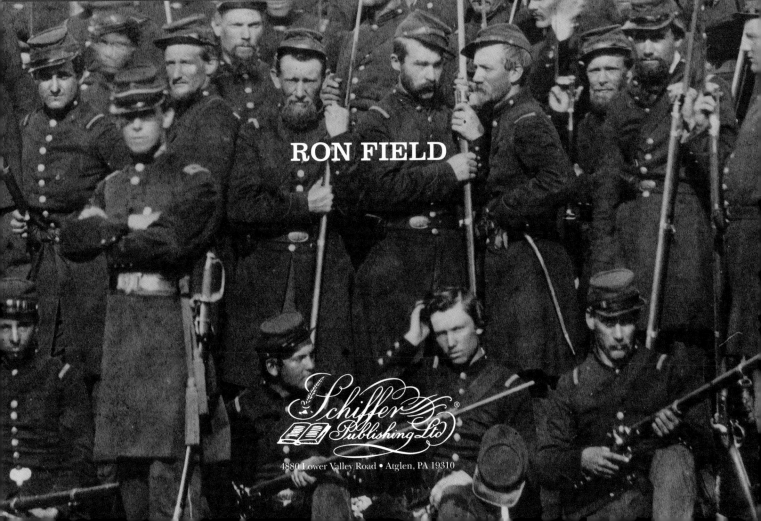

Schiffer Publishing Ltd

4880 Lower Valley Road • Atglen, PA 19310

Other Schiffer titles by Ron Field
Bluejackets
ISBN: 978-0-7643-3375-0

Copyright © 2015 by Ron Field

Library of Congress Control Number: 2015943021

Cover designed by Molly Shields
Type set in Clarendon BT/Minion Pro

ISBN: 978-0-7643-4908-9
Printed in the United States of America

Published by Schiffer Publishing, Ltd.
4880 Lower Valley Road
Atglen, PA 19310
Phone: (610) 593-1777; Fax: (610) 593-2002
E-mail: Info@schifferbooks.com

For our complete selection of fine books on this and related subjects,
please visit our website at www.schifferbooks.com. You may also write for a free catalog.

This book may be purchased from the publisher. Please try your bookstore first.

We are always looking for people to write books on new and related subjects.
If you have an idea for a book, please contact us at proposals@schifferbooks.com.

Schiffer Publishing's titles are available at special discounts for bulk purchases for sales promotions or premiums. Special editions, including personalized covers, corporate imprints, and excerpts can be created in large quantities for special needs. For more information, contact the publisher.

DEDICATION

Washington, DC, 2014

To Whom it May Concern:

The Company of Military Historians takes great pride in endorsing *Rally Round the Flag: Uniforms of the Union Volunteers of 1861—The New England States* as a standard reference in American Military History.

David M. Sullivan
Administrator

RALLY ROUND THE FLAG

Uniforms of the Union Volunteers of 1861

The New England States

RON FIELD

CONTENTS

Introduction. 8

Acknowledgments 10

Massachusetts. 13

Rhode Island 47

New Hampshire 65

Connecticut 83

Vermont 97

Maine 111

Bibliography. 122

Endnotes 130

Index 150

INTRODUCTION

When the volunteers of 1861 rallied around the flag to defend the Union at the beginning of the Civil War, they wore a great variety of uniforms. This volume explores the efforts of the six New England States—Massachusetts, Rhode Island, New Hampshire, Connecticut, Vermont, and Maine—to prepare their troops for the conflict. The clothing and equipping of these troops was anything but straightforward. Uniforms were one of the first major needs of the men. The textile industry in New England had to gear up to the demands of war and the work force, and some mills worked around the clock to meet contract deadlines. There was also a great reliance on volunteer help to turn the cloth into uniforms. Many tailors charged minimum rates for cutting and sewing coats, jackets, and pants, while the womenfolk in hundreds of communities gathered in church halls and other public places to make shirts, blankets, and Havelock head coverings for the troops. An important port and manufacturing center in Boston, Massachusetts, provided much that its own volunteers, plus its neighboring states, required. Large firms such as Whiting, Galloupe, Bliss & Co., and Haughton, Sawyer & Co., supplied uniform suits, overcoats, headgear, and shirts, in vast quantities. The latter company also had offices and stores in New York, Philadelphia, Chicago, and Columbus, Ohio, and clothed and equipped tens of thousands of Union volunteers across the North.

The Salem Light Infantry, or Salem Zouaves, 8th MVM, pose for the camera in front of New York City Hall during a drill display on City Hall Park on April 30, 1861. Three of the officers wear fezzes, while second from right stands Capt. Arthur F. Devereux in a red cap similar to that worn by the enlisted men who wear overcoats over their blue-trimmed red uniforms. This company arrived at the Brooklyn Navy Yard aboard the frigate U.S.S. *Constitution* on April 28, 1861, after that vessel had been towed from the Naval Academy at Annapolis, Maryland, where Secessionists were preparing to seize her. The *Frank Leslie's Illustrated Newspaper* building is seen at rear right. *Anne S. K. Brown collection, Brown University.*

Although the simplicity and coarse cut of the uniforms alarmed many men used to finer, well-tailored prewar militia uniforms, some observers were more realistic. On April 26, 1861, the Annapolis correspondent of the *New York Times* commented, "This war is destined to create an entire revolution in uniforms. What looks very pretty on parade is very absurd when men have to cut their way through."[1] The plain dress supplied to most of the Union volunteers of 1861 greatly echoed this view.

The shortcomings of some poorly made uniform clothing, known as "shoddy," quickly became apparent as certain unscrupulous entrepreneurs took advantage of the urgency of the times. Garments were either too small or too large for volunteers eager to adopt a military appearance. Also, after only a few days or weeks in camp or on campaign, trousers began to fall apart, and caps, jackets, and coats began to fade. The one exception came from Rhode Island whose troops were initially clothed in substantially made blouses, or hunting shirts, over 1,000 of which were produced by the womenfolk of Providence within a few days of the commencement of hostilities.

Usually made of more substantial cloth, the overcoat was essential issue for volunteers during the cold New England spring of 1861. In Massachusetts, this was the first item of clothing produced, 6,000 yards of cloth for overcoats having been purchased by the state before the outbreak of war, although volunteers soon discarded them when the season changed and they reached the warmer climes of Virginia. The exception, once again, was Rhode Island, which adopted red poncho blankets for use as wearing apparel and as bed covering at night.

Regarding the color of the cloth, a gray semi-chasseur uniform was initially chosen for both three-month and some three-year Massachusetts regiments. Those forming the early regiments in Maine and Vermont were similarly clothed in gray, while dark blue was predominantly the chosen color in Connecticut and Rhode Island. The first efforts at the standardization of uniform color did not occur until August 1861, following confusion, mistaken identity, and incidents of friendly fire during the battles of Big Bethel and First Bull Run. On the twenty-first of that month, General George Brinton McClellan, commanding the Military Division of the Potomac, issued an order forbidding "the purchase of gray uniforms," which he called "the rebels' color."[2] During November 1861, US Quartermaster General Montgomery C. Meigs invited proposals from contractors to uniform much of the Union army stating categorically, "Light or dark blue cloths preferred, and light greys will not be considered."[3] Thus, by the end of the year, much of the Union army was wearing "Army Blue."

AUTHOR NOTE

The notation "&c." within the text of this book is the mid-nineteenth century version of "etcetera" (etc.) meaning unspecified additional items or odds and ends.

ACKNOWLEDGMENTS

A study such as this could never have been completed in isolation, and I am immensely grateful to numerous individuals and institutions for providing images and sharing knowledge and information. For years, my mentor and inspiration, Michael J. McAfee, curator of uniforms at the United States Military Academy, New York, provided numerous images from his extensive collection. Peter Harrington, curator at the Anne S. K. Brown Military Collection, gave generously of his services during my examination of the Frederick Todd Collection at the John Hay Library, Brown University, Rhode Island, during 2010. Dr. Michael R. Cunningham of the University of Louisville shared generously of his collection and vast knowledge of the period. I am also grateful to Paul Boag, field sales executive at Cengage Learning, for generously providing access to the extensive collection of Civil War period newspapers held in the Gale Digital Collections. To Robert Biondi, senior editor at Schiffer Publishing, I owe a great debt of gratitude for his patience and encouragement during the long period of time this project was in preparation. For further help, I am indebted to Martha Mayo at the Center for Lowell History, University of Massachusetts Lowell; Anthony Douin, Maine State Archives; Donna Gilbreth, supervisor at the New Hampshire State Library, Concord, New Hampshire; Denise LaFrance, reference librarian at the Dover Public Library, New Hampshire; James DaMico, Special Collections curator; and J.D. Kay, Digital Imaging specialist and Rights & Reproductions manager at the Rhode Island Historical Society; Richard C. Malley, head of Research & Collections, and Sierra Dixon, Research & Collections associate, Connecticut Historical Society, Hartford, Connecticut; Marilyn Labbe, Killingly Historical & Genealogical Society, Connecticut; Deborah Shapiro, executive director, Middlesex County Historical Society, Connecticut. Clifton P. Hyatt, former curator of photography at the United States Army Heritage and Education Center at Carlisle, Pennsylvania; Carol Johnson, curator of photography, Library of Congress, Prints and Photographs Division, Washington, DC; Harry Ridgeway, The Civil War Relicman; Janet and Bedford Hayes of Maine Legacy; plus Don Troiani; Alan Thrower, Daniel Miller; Jason Puckett; Martin Schoenfeld; Monte Akers; C. Paul Loane; Dave Morin; Dave Nelson; Jeremy Rowe; Ron Swanson; Robert Grandchamp; Debbie Weaver; Marius B. Peladeau, Kris VanDenBossche, Daniel J. Binder, Stephen Osman, Buck Zaidel, and Thomas Arliskas. Lastly, my thanks go to Dinah Roseberry whose patience, advice, and editorial expertise guided *Rally Round the Flag* to final fruition.

Ron Field, 2015

Yes we'll rally round the flag, boys,
we'll rally once again,
Shouting the battle cry of freedom,
We will rally from the hillside,
we'll gather from the plain,
Shouting the battle cry of freedom!

Mayer. 316 Chesnut St. Phila

ARMS OF

ENSE PETIT PLACIDAM

MASSACHUSETTS

Death before Dissolut

MASSACHUSETTS

MASSACHUSETTS

At the outbreak of Civil War in 1861, the volunteer militia system within the Commonwealth of Massachusetts consisted of a series of undersized regiments, plus numerous independent companies and battalions, many of which maintained their own distinctive uniforms in defiance of regulations issued by the state adjutant general in the early 1850s.[1] Hence, when the state was requested to provide twenty companies of infantry for Federal service on April 15, 1861, the regiments with the most complete organization, consisting of the 3rd, 4th, 6th, and 8th Massachusetts Volunteer Militia (MVM), were ordered out. After assembly at Boston, the 6th followed by 8th regiment was dispatched to Washington, DC, while the other two units were sent to Fortress Monroe on the Virginia Peninsula.

The companies making up these regiments were variously attired in prewar dress uniforms mixed with civilian clothing, some of the latter being hastily altered to lend a military appearance. According to the *New York Herald*, the Union Guards of Lynn (Co. I), 3rd MVM, commanded by Capt. William D. Chamberlain, wore "a handsome uniform furnished by the city, consisting of blue coats and light pants, with stripes. The officers were furnished uniforms by private subscription, more showy than that of the privates, and including black pants. All wear the army requisition hats, similar to the Kossuth hat."[2] According to regimental Chaplain Hanson, each company of the 6th MVM was:

> an independent one in apparel. Company A had changed its name to the National Greys, and its uniforms were being made, but they were unfinished, and the men left for Washington with blue frocks and black pantaloons, tall round caps, and white pompons. Company B wore the United States regulation uniform; that is, dark blue frocks, and light blue trousers. Company C wore gray dress coats, caps, and pantaloons, and yellow trimmings. Company D, wore the same as C, with buff trimmings. Companies E and F were dressed like B, and Company G wore blue dress coats; Company H, gray throughout; Company I, caps, and dark blue frocks and red pants, in the French style. Company K wore gray, and Company L was dressed in blue.[3]

Born in Alexandria, New Hampshire, on December 22, 1843, Luther C. Ladd was a machinist when he enlisted in the Lowell City Guard on January 21, 1861. One of three men of the 6th Massachusetts Volunteer Militia killed by Southern sympathizers as his regiment passed through Baltimore on April 19, 1861, he was shot in the thigh and, according to a contemporary account, "probably bled to death at once." This albumen was produced by Fowler & Winslow, photographers at 28 Merrimac Street, Lowell, from an ambrotype taken on the day his regiment departed for the federal capital. He wears the full-dress uniform still used by the 6th Massachusetts after re-organization from the 5th Regiment of Light Infantry, MVM in 1855. This consisted of a dark-blue coatee, light blue trousers, and Pattern-1851 cap with pompon, "Eagle" plate, and "Looped" Horn insignia. Characteristic of Massachusetts troops, his "body" or waist belt is black leather, while his "cross," or shoulder belt, is white buff leather. *Centre for Lowell History, University of Massachusetts, Lowell.*

Volunteering in the Warren Light Guards (Co. F), 4th MVM on April 16, 1861, James L. Sherman was provided with "a uniform coat (never tailor fitted) and a leather hat (rather too large), then on went the white cross belts, with other required equipments, and last a musket with which I expected to lay out any rebel I should meet, then I was a fully fledged soldier, ready for action."[4] Arriving at the arsenal at North Easton for service with the Easton Light Infantry (Co. B), Robert Dollard recalled:

> It was the work of a few minutes to…have our white stripes, about an inch wide, sewed down the outer seams of our black doeskin Sunday trousers and slip them on with our blue uniform dress coats, ornamented with white epaulets, adjust our white belts, which passed over each shoulder and crossed in front and rear, running down to the roundabout [waist belt] to hold the bayonet scabbard on one side and the cartridge box on the other, and to place the large brass breastplate in position to ward off cannon balls, bullets, bayonet thrusts, etc., I suspect, and adjust our hats, as tall as the ordinary stovepipe article, and, except the visor, much like the form of a bean baking-pot turned bottom side up.…A short staff grew up near the front and top of this hat about a couple of inches which had a white ball, a pompon, on it.[5]

The state supplemented this by providing each man with additional items of clothing and equipage in preparation for the forthcoming campaign. According to the *Boston Herald*, the 6th MVM was marched to the State House in Boston, and in the Doric Hall each man was furnished with "two blue flannel shirts, one pair of socks, and one pair of drawers."[6] The 4th and 8th MVM proceeded to Faneuil Hall where, according to Robert Dollard, they were given "haversacks loaded with fresh boiled beef and soft bread, and canteens filled with tea or coffee." They were then marched to the State House where they exchanged their "old and despised militia guns for Harper's Ferry rifled muskets [*sic*], received gun slings, knapsacks, rubber and woolen blankets, overcoats and each one [a] pair of woolen shirts and two pairs of drawers,"[7] plus "one pair of boots and a Guernsey frock."[8] The latter was described by Dollard as "a gray woolen shirt" worn outside the trousers as "a frock coat, similar to Gen. Burnside's regiment in the early part of the war, and… equipments were put on over this shirt."[9]

Regarding the overcoats, the state had purchased 6,000 yards of medium iron-gray beaver cloth during February 1861 in anticipation of "the inevitable conflict," which it had made based on a pattern obtained after consultation with the US Army quartermaster department. On April 17, the *Boston Herald* reported that the volunteers had the new garments "speedily fitted to their backs" under the supervision of Maj. George Clark Jr., of the 2nd Brigade Staff, and continued, "The coats are made of dark grey cloth, and look very neat and serviceable. They are of the army pattern, and comprise three sizes only—'large,' 'small,' and 'middling.'"[10] With the stocks of these overcoats running low by the end of the day, the state contracted with Whitten, Hopkins & Co. of Boston to supply 1,500 more, with 1,000 to be completed by April 23. The *Herald* advised, "The firm have 4,000 yards of the cloth in store, and the balance needed will soon be manufactured."[11]

Preserved in the collection of the Essex Institute at Salem, this overcoat is one of the original single-breasted infantry overcoats ordered by Governor Andrews in February 1861 and issued to the Massachusetts three-month volunteers. Although patterned after US army regulations, it was made from closely-woven wool of medium iron-gray color, and had a loosely-woven red wool lining. Note the adjustable belt on the rear waist. *Anne S. K. Brown collection, Brown University.*

The poor quality of much of the clothing worn off to war by many of the three-month volunteers, and particularly the trousers, quickly became apparent. According to Capt. Luther Stephenson, commanding the Lincoln Light Infantry (Co. I), 4th MVM, it was "poorly fitted to sustain the rough usage to which it was subjected, and the results were oftentimes ludicrous and amusing." At regular Sunday inspection, he continued, some of the men "commenced to appear in overcoats, although the weather was warm and bright. This was to conceal their tattered clothing, and, in some instances, the fact that they had no trousers, and only their drawers to hide their nakedness. The contrast in appearance between our militia, with their torn, worn-out uniforms, and the companies of regulars who still remained in the fort [Monroe], was very marked and striking."[12]

A citizen of Lowell visiting the camp of the 6th MVM at the Relay House in Maryland at the beginning of May reported in the *Lowell Daily Courier* that "the uniform coats of our men will soon be laid by for the season; besides cramping the motions of the body, at all times, so as to add to the fatigue, they are such hot garments that they cannot be endure[d]!"[13] Reported to be sadly in want of a change of clothing by the middle of May, some companies of the 6th MVM received frock coats for fatigue wear made by the ladies of Lowell and Lawrence, which were variously described as consisting of "blue flannel, trimmed with black, and the eagle button;" and "grey flannel frocks trimmed with black, with large buttons."[14] On June 5, the 6th MVM was presented with Havelocks, "the material for which was purchased and sent to Washington by the congregation of prominent abolitionist Rev. H. Ward Beecher's church, Brooklyn, and the work of making them performed by the Sewing Society attached to the Fourth Presbyterian Church."[15]

As the 8th MVM passed through New York City en route for the federal capital, the Allen Guard (Co. K), of Pittsfield, Massachusetts, were described as wearing a gray dress uniform "nearly a copy" of the "National Guard," or 7th New York State Militia. However, twenty-five as yet un-uniformed recruits with this company "appeared with bundles and carpet bags in hand, evidently having come off in great haste."[16] When this regiment arrived at Annapolis, Maryland, on April 21, 1861, a Baltimore correspondent stated that "the majority of their uniforms consist of woven and working pants and coats, some with black and

Buttons worn by Massachusetts volunteers featured the crest of the state coat of arms, which consisted of an arm, bent at the elbow, holding a sword. Curved around this was the designation "MASS. VOLUNTEER MILITIA." The back mark on this example shows it was made by Benedict & Burnham, who became the Waterbury Button Company in 1849. *The Civil War Relicman.*

drab slouch hats, others with old cloth and oil caps, and a few with military hats, resembling the old hat worn by the Baltimore police, here and there a plume. In fact, the only thing about them to designate them from citizens is a dark steel mixed overcoat and knapsack, and some have not even that."[17]

The gray dress uniform of Allen Guard was trimmed and faced in a style worn by numerous Massachusetts antebellum militia companies, and was indeed probably inspired by that of the 7th New York State Militia. Both the Mechanic Phalanx (Co. C) and Washington Light Guard (Co. K), 6th MVM wore this pattern of uniform, as did the Richardson Light Guard (Co. B) and Summerville Light Infantry (Co. I), 5th MVM. Shortly after arrival in the federal capital, several members of the 5th Regiment were apprehended by the officer of the day attempting to regain entrance to

This detail from a stereoview by E. & H. T. Anthony shows enlisted men of the Allen Guard (Co. K), 8th MVM, encamped in Washington, DC. Three of the men wear federal-issue clothing and caps, which are probably part of that issued to the regiment by special order of Abraham Lincoln on May 17, 1861. The man at left wears the full-dress gray uniform of the Allen Guard, which was formed in Pittsfield, Massachusetts, in August, 1860. Consisting of a heavily trimmed gray tail-coat and matching pants, it is a similar pattern to that worn by companies in regiments such as the 5th and 6th MVM. Before reorganization in April 1861, the Allen Guard was Co. A, 1st Battalion of Infantry, MVM, hence the letter "A" is still attached to the cap front of the man at left. Note the sign "Allen Guard" attached to the front of their tent. *Anne S. K. Brown collection, Brown University.*

This unidentified enlisted man of the Beverly Light Infantry, Co. E, 8th MVM., was photographed by "Ambrotypist and Photographer" George K. Proctor, of Beverly, Massachusetts. His headgear consists of a European-style forage cap of possibly French or Austrian design with a small pompom on metal loop sewn to an oval cloth patch attached to its front. His frock coat possibly conforms to that adopted in 1852 by both the 6th and 7th Light Infantry Regiments, MVM, from which the 8th MVM was created in 1855. This was dark blue with black pants bearing a white seam stripe. Buttons with state coat of arms fasten his coat, which is faced with white collar and cuffs. Full-dress epaulets with .125-inch worsted fringe adorn his shoulders. Popular amongst Massachusetts militia, his ornate two-piece belt plate bears on its tongue an eagle with star in a shield. *Ninth-plate ambrotype—author's collection.*

According to the lettering on his militia-style belt plate, this unidentified gray-clad volunteer belonged to the Boston-based Washington Light Guard. Commanded by Capt. Walter S. Sampson, this company was originally Co. C, 1st MVM, but was added to the 6th MVM as Co. K as the regiment departed Boston on April 16, 1861. He wears the uniform in which his company left for the front, which was described in a letter written by Capt. Sampson from the Relay House, in Maryland, on May 9, 1861, as "not a suitable one for *active* service…. It was made more for a dress parade suit, and is not suitable for this hot climate." *Carte de visite without back mark—author's collection.*

Photographed at the studio of Sewell Shattuck, of Lowell, Massachusetts, this unidentified private holding a spear-pointed knife probably belonged to the Mechanic Phalanx, Co. C, 6th MVM, who wore a uniform consisting of a gray dress coat, cap, and pantaloons, with either orange or yellow trimmings. Acquired during the summer of 1860, this uniform was made by Edwin C. Leslie, a "well-known tailor" in Boston, from cloth procured from the mill at Pittsfield, Massachusetts. On May 18, 1861, the Union army received orders that enlisted men should lay revolvers and knives aside, to be "properly labelled, until they go into action, if they ever do." *Ninth plate ambrotype—collection of Jason Puckett.*

This unidentified enlisted man wears the dress uniform of either the Richardson Light Guard (Co. B) or the Summerville Light Infantry (Co. I), 5th MVM. Resting on the table by his side, his dress cap, or shako, has a gilt star-burst plate with "raised arm bearing a sword" inset, above which is a small shield bearing the arms of the state that is surmounted by a white wool pompon. *Anne S. K. Brown collection, Brown University.*

Camp Andrew after being absent without leave and, according to the regimental historian, "their gray uniforms with three rows of buttons were very conspicuous."[18]

Although the facing color of this uniform appears to have varied from unit to unit, it consisted of a gray tail-coat, sometimes referred to as a "rifle jacket," with two-inch standing collar bearing two small buttons each side; nine rows of three buttons at the front connected by either double or single bar of braid, or tape; a cuff panel with four small buttons; and tails with colored facings on turn-backs, four small buttons attached to facings on false pockets each side, and two buttons at the hip. Matching gray pants had broad seam stripes. Both the Lynn Light Infantry (Co. D) and Beverly Light Infantry (Co. E), 8th MVM appear to have worn tall bearskin hats for full dress, and the volunteers of these companies were reported by the *Daily Evening Traveller* of Boston to be wearing them when they mustered for three months' service at Boston on April 15, 1861.[19]

Many Massachusetts volunteers received gray or blue pullover fatigue shirts. While the records of the state Quartermaster's Department indicate that it provided only seventy-six "Blue Flannel Shirts" to the three-month volunteers, the womenfolk throughout the commonwealth made many more. A pattern for these shirts appears to have been provided for them by the authorities as, on April 22, 1861, a short report in the *Evening Traveller* advised that it had to be followed closely, as "misfits" were "useless to the soldiers."[20] On May 6, the *Lowell Daily Citizen* published "directions for making flannel fatigue shirts" as follows:

> The front strip must project three-fourths of an inch beyond the collar, in order that the buttons upon the strip may be directly under the collar button—seven buttons in all—one upon the collar, two upon the front strip, one upon each pocket, and one upon each sleeve; black metal buttons should be used, and the button hole in front cut to correspond with the collar button; button hole in the pocket cut the lengthwise of the shirt.[21]

Dimensions for two sizes were specified, namely the "Largest Size" and "Second Size," with only an inch difference in body and sleeve length. According to 3rd Lt. Horace P. Williams, of Wardwell's Tigers (Co. F), 5th MVM, clothier George Lane of Dock Square, Boston, provided each man of his company with a blue flannel shirt with a small Bible and handkerchief in the pocket.[22] On April 29, 1861, Col. George Clark's Regiment of Boston Volunteers later designated the 11th Massachusetts Volunteer Infantry (Boston Volunteers), advertised in the *Boston Herald* for "600 Red Flannel Shirts."[23]

Several companies of the 8th MVM received fatigue shirts trimmed around collar, cuffs, pockets, and five-buttoned front. Two members of the American Guard (Co. G), of Gloucester, were photographed wearing this style of shirt under gray zouave jackets, complete with matching chasseur-pattern trousers and cap, with brass shoulder scales and gaiters. Due to a lack of uniforms, only thirty-nine volunteers from this company initially responded to the requisition for troops on April 16.[24] Detached with his company to provide protection aboard the training ship USS *Constitution* as she was towed from the Naval Academy to New York City, an enlisted man of the American Guard wrote, "I am dressed in a blue shirt under my coat, and, as a uniform, another outside my

A fatigue shirt was the simplest and cheapest form of uniform for ladies' sewing groups and other volunteer associations to produce during the first few months of the war. Identified as William H. Cook, Cushing Guards (Co. A), 8th MVM, this man wears a five-button shirt with narrow trim around the pockets and front opening. The function of the two buttons above the pockets is not known. He has matching pants and holds a cap made of cloth of a darker hue. One of a number of Massachusetts men by this name is listed in the 1860 census; this is probably William Cook. Born in Prussia in 1837, he lived in Boston Ward 9 and worked as a book keeper until he enlisted on April 15, 1861. *Carte de visite by "J. White, Photographic Artist, 224 Essex Street, Salem, Mass."—Michael J. McAfee collection.*

Both of these volunteers belonged to the American Guard, Co. G, 8th MVM. First organized as the Gloucester Artillery at Gloucester, Massachusetts, in 1788, disbanded in 1849, and reformed in 1852, the American Guard adopted a zouave uniform in 1860-61 consisting of a light-colored jacket, and chasseur-pattern pants and cap. The man at left wears United States Marine Corps-pattern fringed shoulder scales, and has a waist sash under his belt, which may indicate that he is an officer. He carries a light cavalry saber. A small crossed cannon artillery insignia is attached to the front of his cap, which may be a reminder of the unit's original branch of service. Another unidentified volunteer, the man at right wears the same zouave uniform, although his pants are tucked into leather leggings and he has brass scales attached to his shoulders. He also holds a cavalry saber, which may have been one of the arms carried by this unit before the war. Note that both men wear under their jackets the fatigue shirt received by some, if not all, companies of the 8th M.V.M *Carte de visite without backmark; Carte de visite by "Black & Batchelder, 173 Washington Street, Boston"—Michael J. McAfee collection.*

Cpl. Adolph F. Lindberg, American Guard (Co. G), 8th MVM wears a five-button shirt of similar style to William Cook, but more heavily trimmed around collar, cuffs, front and single pocket. A small pin with an unidentified portrait (possibly of Abraham Lincoln) is attached to his right breast. A cap of darker hue rests on the table with the brass company letter "G" pinned to its front. He has a Colt revolver tucked in a belt fastened by an 1839-Pattern "US" plate. A socket bayonet rests in its scabbard on his left hip. Resident at Gloucester, Massachusetts, Lindberg was 22 when he enlisted on April 15, 1861. He was mustered-out at Boston on August 1, 1861. *U.S. Army Heritage and Education Center.*

The jacket and vest worn by officers of the Salem Zouaves was trimmed with gold, in contrast with the red trim on the uniforms of enlisted men. *www.historicalimagebank.com*.

Sgt. Charles S. Emmerton wears the blue uniform with red trim worn by the Salem Light Infantry (also known as the Salem Zouaves), Co. I, 8th MVM when they arrived in Washington, DC, on May 8, 1861. Resident at Salem, Massachusetts, Emmerton was an 18-year-old clerk when mustered-in during April 1861. He was promoted to First Lieutenant on October 8, 1861, and was appointed regimental adjutant on March 18, 1862. He served as assistant aide-de-camp on the staff of General Charles A. Heckman in North Carolina from December 8, 1862, and was on the staff of General George J. Stannard when mustered-out on October 13, 1864, at the end of his term of service. *U.S. Army Heritage and Education Center.*

coat; have great heavy thick boots on, and a glazed fatigue cap. My over coat, which a grateful country provided for me in Boston, is folded up before me, also a heavy coarse grey blanket."[25] By May 3, the ladies of Gloucester had provided "Jackets, Drawers, bandages, &c." for those who had subsequently joined this company without uniforms. In a letter of thanks, company commander Capt. Addison Center added, "We would like pants as they are most likely to wear out, and would suggest, if the ladies are desirous of continuing their favors, that they make us a loose kind of pants to match the jackets, with a red cord or welt in the side seam," which indicates that the jackets were also trimmed red.[26]

Assigned to the 8th MVM from the 7th MVM as Co. I/J in April 1861, the Salem Light Infantry, or Salem Zouaves, initially wore a blue, nine-button jacket with standing collar, shoulder straps, and nine double rows of scarlet braid across the chest. Their pants were the same color with narrow scarlet piping down the outer seams. On arrival at Washington, DC, on May 9, 1861, they were described as being "armed with the Minie musket

Frederick William Smith was a clerk residing in Salem, Massachusetts, when he enlisted in the Salem Light Infantry/Salem Zouaves, aged 24, on April 15, 1861. Mustered-out at Boston on August 1, 1861, he reenlisted in Capt. Brewster's Zouaves (Co. A), 23rd Massachusetts, on September 28, 1861, being promoted to full sergeant the same day, following which this image was struck. Organized by other ex-members of the Salem Zouaves, and commanded by Capt. E. A .P. Brewster, this company adopted the same dark-blue, trimmed with red, uniform of the original Salem Zouaves. He was discharged for promotion on November 29, 1863, and received a commission as Second Lieutenant, Co. G, 1st U.S. Colored Cavalry, with which unit he served until finally mustered-out on February 4, 1866. *U.S. Army Heritage and Education Center—Ron Beifuss collection*.

Taken from a stereo view by E. & H. T. Anthony of volunteers in camp near The Relay House on the Baltimore and Ohio Railroad, this detail shows six members of the 8th MVM wearing federal-issue sack coats, which were part of a uniform received by special order of Abraham Lincoln at the end of April 1861. The seventh man seated, second from the left, appears to be wearing the gray trousers and red fez as part of the state-issue uniform received by the regiment on May 19, 1861. Note the combination of white shoulder belts and black leather waist belts typical of Massachusetts volunteers. *Michael J. McAfee collection.*

This M1850 Foot Officer's sword was presented to Lt. Hannibal D. Norton of the 5th MVM on April 18, 1861, and was carried at First Bull Run, where its owner was wounded. Resident as a bookkeeper at Charlestown, Massachusetts, Norton was commissioned Third Lieutenant of the Charlestown Artillery, Co. D, 5th MVM on June 13, 1860 and was mustered-in for three months' state service within Co. C, 5th M.V.M with the same rank on May 1, 1861, being mustered-out with his regiment on July 31, 1861. He received a commission as captain of Co. I, 32nd Massachusetts Volunteers on July 28, 1862, but resigned and was discharged on Surgeon's Certificate of Disability on March 18, 1863. On December 10, 1863, he was appointed a captain in the Veteran Reserve Corps and brevetted a major of US Volunteers on March 13, 1865. *Dr. Michael R. Cunningham collection.*

and uniformed in dark blue jackets and pants, trimmed with scarlet braid, and red fatigue caps."[27] By the beginning of June, the Salem Zouaves had worn this uniform out and received a plain gray jacket and pants similar in cut to their blue ones, "which served admirably as a working-suit." Adopted on July 9, 1861, their zouave-style uniform was made in Baltimore, Maryland, and was worn for the first time on July 23, on which date Cpl. Fredcrick Smith, of the Allen Guard, noted in his journal, "The Salem Zouaves have come out in a new and tasty uniform, which takes well, and draws for them, in connection with their good drilling, considerable praise."[28] Made of navy blue woollen twill, the jacket and pants were trimmed with crimson braid, while the collar of the vest was edged with red leather. Vest buttons were of plain brass ball pattern. The kepi had a scarlet woollen top with a dark-blue band, quartered with gold braid. Completing the uniform was a scarlet woollen sash with plum red tassels, and gaiters of a coarsely woven, white cotton duck material complete with white porcelain buttons to secure the lace-up outer seams.

Considered an "honored" company during its three-month period of service, the Salem Zouaves provided the model for two further companies of Massachusetts volunteers, plus a Drill Corps. Formed by several ex-members of the unit, a company commanded by E.A.P. Brewster, and also known as the Salem Zouaves, or Capt. Brewster's Zouaves, was provided by Senator Henry Wilson with the same style of zouave uniform, and eventually enlisted for three years' service during September 1861 as Co. A, 23rd Massachusetts Infantry.[29] A third company wearing this uniform and recruited by Capt. Charles U. Devereux, brother of the captain of the original Salem Zouaves, enlisted in the 19th Massachusetts during December of that year.[30] By the beginning of June 1861, the Salem Zouave Drill Corps, commanded by Capt. Isaiah Woodbury, had been formed in Salem wearing "the red military cap" and "a very neat military jacket."[31]

With the Allen Guard (Co. K), and other companies in the 8th MVM, looking noticeably the worse for wear in appearance while encamped at Washington, DC, the whole regiment, with the exception of the Salem Zouaves, received federal-issue clothing on May 17, 1861, by special order of Abraham Lincoln. Cpl. Fred Smith of the Allen Guard recorded in his journal three days later, "This afternoon we have been furnished with the army fatigue uniform, which consists of blue satinet pants, a loose sack of flannel and fatigue cap of blue cloth. It is perfectly easy, and well-adapted to camp wear. The boys look rather comical in them, and not as dressy as in their Grey suit. But the captain [Henry S. Briggs] informs me it is his intention to have the old suits kept with the company, which can be donned when necessary."[32]

Wearing an "invisible green," or very dark green, tail-coat and "Black German doe skin" trousers, 22-year-old Nathaniel S. Liscomb enlisted on April 19, 1861, and was promoted sergeant major of the 3rd Battalion of Riflemen from the ranks of Co. A, Worcester City Guard, on July 1, 1861. He was mustered-out with his unit on August 3, 1861. Rank is indicated via the chevrons and arc on his upper sleeves, and non-commissioned officer's sword, belt and waist sash. Also note his shoulder scales, which formed part of the dress uniform of the 3rd Battalion. Liscomb was born in Fairhaven, Massachusetts, in 1839 and moved to Worcester in 1854, where he was employed in the hat and furnishing business by F. A. Eldred. In 1861 he became a partner in that concern and twelve years later owned it. By that time, he was known as "Liscomb the Hatter." He also wrote the unit history of the 3rd Battalion of Riflemen, published in 1910. *Carte de visite by "C. R. B. Claflin, Photographic Artist, 188 Main Street, Worcester, Mass."—author's collection.*

Following a visit to camp by several friends from Pittsfield on July 20, Smith again referred to the question of uniform stating "had we been apprised of their intended approach we might have donned our store cloths [*sic*], but as it was we received them in our ungainly but comfortable blues, furnished by the US."[33] However, Capt. Briggs clearly kept his word regarding the gray dress uniforms of the Allen Guard as, on July 21, 1861, Cpl. Charles R. Strong, wrote, "Received the grey uniform, which we have not worn since joining the 8th regiment at the Relay House. We now look and feel like civilized beings. As long as we had the Government blouses and pants, we 'looked like thunder!'"[34]

Earlier on June 4, a member of the American Guard (Co. G) wrote:

An edict was recently issued commanding us to wear that horrid blue suit Old Abe gave us at Washington. But yesterday we were allowed to put on the new clothes Mr. B. brought, and handsome we looked (as a Company, for personally we don't boast of our beauty now) attending Divine service at our temple in the grove. The Salem Zouaves and the Marblehead Companies also came out in new suits, the latter being made of shirting stripes entire. Very cool and comfortable they looked in them. We hope to be allowed to wear our suits half the time at least, the regulation uniforms being excessively uncomfortable in comparison.[35]

The latter reference indicates that the Sutton Light Infantry (Co. C) and Glover Light Guards (Co. H) received service uniforms of striped ticking material.

With a call for more troops on April 16, 1861, Governor John A. Andrew ordered out the 5th MVM, supplemented by companies from the 1st and 7th MVM, plus the 3rd Battalion of Riflemen and Boston Light Artillery—all of which left for Washington, DC, five days later. With stocks of State overcoats depleted, some of these volunteers received "United States garments," or federal-issue overcoats, which the *Boston Herald* of April 22 described as being of "the infantry pattern, blue in color, and…heavier and of better quality than the state coats."[36] State overcoats were furnished to the remaining troops even as they were "on their march to the [railroad] cars," the tailors at Whitten, Hopkins & Co. having worked day and night to cut and sew them. According to the *Herald*, it was impossible to provide these troops with knapsacks, these also having been "exhausted in fitting out the 3rd, 4th, 6th, and 8th Regiments, and their blankets and other baggage was sent on in chests."[37]

When the 5th MVM marched through the northern and western streets of Washington, DC, after arrival on April 29, the *Evening Star* reported, "A want of uniformity in their uniforms, detracts… from their appearance on parade."[38] By May 29, this regiment was encamped at Four Mile Run, near Alexandria, Virginia, where it performed the duty of provost guard and received federal-issue clothing. Of this occasion, a member of the regiment wrote:

> We have just received our army uniforms, which we have sadly needed ever since we started from Boston. It was rather hard to send off a regiment so poorly equipped as we were, each company in its own uniform, and some of them utterly unfit for anything but holiday parades, besides being the most uncomfortable things a man can wear on a long march. Our present uniform is a sort of blouse jacket of blue cashmeret [*sic*], with pants of large dimensions, all very loose and comfortable.[39]

The 5th MVM was dubbed the "Steady Fifth" when reviewed by Lincoln and his cabinet on June 14, 1861.[40] This regiment also wore state-issue "seamless, light blue overcoats," which were considered to be "cheaper, stronger, more durable and comfortable than the ordinary overcoats." When two members of the regiment passed through Philadelphia to join their regiment during mid-May, their overcoats were described as being "seamless with long capes woven into the body of the coat at the neck. The material was water-proof cloth. The button-holes were stitched with silk galloon and every part of the raiment was of the most durable character."[41]

Three companies of the 3rd Battalion Riflemen (Deven's Battalion), of Worcester, Massachusetts, also left for the front in heavy dress militia uniforms consisting of "invisible green," or very dark green, tail-coats and "Black German doe skin" trousers.[42] So urgent was the call for more serviceable clothing for the unit that notice was given from most of the church pulpits in Worcester inviting "the ladies to meet in the afternoon, with their needles, &c." Within four days, the local womenfolk had produced "400 pairs of pants, 196 jackets, 25 uniform jackets [or coats]…40 flannel shirts, 71 white shirts…" On May 27, a member of the Emmett Guards (Co. C) wrote, "The boys look finely since they have got their new coats and pants. The ladies of Worcester are deserving of great praise."[43] However, when inspected at Fort McHenry, Baltimore, on June 10, 1861, three companies of the 3rd Battalion were described as being "without haversacks, canteens, tents, and uniforms suitable for hot weather."[44] When ordered to the federal capital from Fortress Monroe, the fourth company of this battalion, known as Dodd's Rifles (Co. D), commanded by Capt. Albert Dodd, arrived "without any expense to their State" wearing "light blue pants, red shirt, dark grey overcoat, and fatigue cap."[45] Due to the saber bayonets attached to their M1841 Whitney contract rifles this unit was also nick-named "Dodd's Carvers."[46]

Commanded by Maj. Asa Cook, the officers of the Boston Light Artillery wore for full-dress a uniform adopted in 1859 consisting of a double-breasted frock coat of cadet grey cloth with seven buttons in each row, and standing collar and cuffs of red cloth. Pants were also grey with red seam stripes. Headgear consisted of the cap or shako adopted by the US Corps of Cadets in 1853, but with "artillery ornaments" and red pompon.[47] Enlisted men also wore a double-breasted coat, but with eight buttons in each row. Undress for officers consisted of a single-breasted gray frock coat of US Army regulation cut, while enlisted men wore dark-blue forage caps, and dark-blue shirts and the ubiquitous gray overcoat provided by the state.[48]

The uniform adopted by the volunteer artillery corps, known as Cobb's Light Battery, that later became the 2nd Massachusetts Independent Battery, during April and May, 1861, was reported on May 14, 1861, as being entirely different from anything seen in that city. The *Boston Evening Transcript* continued that it was "blue, with red trimmings. The cap is of the zouave pattern, such as is commonly worn by the military of the present day; the jacket or coatee (coming to the hips only) is buttoned at the top only and trimmed with red, showing the

Officers and men of the Boston Light Artillery pose in their double-breasted gray frock coats with the Thomas Viaduct carrying the Baltimore & Ohio Railroad in the background. Headgear consists of undress caps, which were probably dark blue. Enlisted men wear brass shoulder scales, while two officers minus epaulets stand at left. All are armed with an M1840 Light Artillery saber and most carry revolvers. *Detail from a stereoview—Michael J. McAfee collection.*

John Marter was a twenty-five-year-old Britannia metal spinner from Dorchester, Massachusetts, when he enlisted as a private in Co. A, 1st MVM on May 23, 1861. He was killed at Second Bull Run on August 29, 1862. He wears an example of the semi-chasseur-style gray uniform supplied by the state to Massachusetts regiments in May 1861. Trim appears to be evident only on the cuffs of his otherwise plain coat. Note the broad-crowned cap held by his side. *Carte de visite with pencil inscription—Michael J. McAfee collection.*

Officers and men of the Boston Light Artillery pose in their double-breasted gray frock coats with the Thomas Viaduct carrying the Baltimore & Ohio Railroad in the background. Headgear consists of undress caps, which were probably dark blue. Enlisted men wear brass shoulder scales, while two officers minus epaulets stand at left. All are armed with an M1840 Light Artillery saber and most carry revolvers. *Detail from a stereoview—Michael J. McAfee collection.*

light grey shirt with trimmed bosom and military button. The pantaloons are very loose, buttoning at the bottom on the zouave style, with laced or Balmoral boot."[49]

By April 26, 1861, the Committee of the City Council on Military Supplies in Boston had met to choose a pattern of uniform for the volunteers from that city, having appropriated $100,000 to assist in outfitting, equipping, and arming them.[50] After examining several patterns, they chose a semi-chasseur uniform described in the *Boston Herald* as "a sort of Garibaldi suit, made of heavy gray doeskin, and trimmed with red cord. The jacket is to be long bodied and short tailed, with regular military collar, and well-lined throughout. The cap [or hat] is of gray turned up with red, and the whole thing is neat and serviceable. Its cost is but about ten dollars."[51] The next day the *Daily Evening Traveller* observed, "Jackets and pants, the former of 'Garibaldi,' and the latter of 'Cadet mixed,' are contracted for 1,000 men."[52] The firm charged with "making and trim'g" these "Uniform Suits" was Whitten, Hopkins & Co. who supplied 1,035 of "Garibaldi" woolen cloth, which was basically gray in color with strands of red, white, and blue woven into it.[53] Once completed, this clothing was delivered to the Military Equipment Depot, 132 Congress Street, Boston, for distribution to the troops.

Established in Boston as early as 1849, the firm of Haughton, Sawyer, & Co. was a major supplier of "Army Equipments" in 1861. It clothed at least five regiments of Massachusetts volunteers in gray, semi-chasseur uniforms, referred to in the *Pennsylvania Daily Telegraph* of Harrisburg on May 14, 1861, as "Garibaldi Zouave," or "Flannel Suits for a warm climate." Also available was "the famous Military Hat" designed by General Benjamin F. Edmands, commander of the MVM during the 1850s. The firm sold its wares across the Northern states, having stores at Astor House, in New York; Continental House, in Philadelphia; Briggs House, in Chicago; and Neil House, at Columbus, Ohio. *Author's collection.*

An example of the uniform clothing produced by Haughton, Sawyer, & Co., of Boston, the blue-gray semi-chasseur style jacket worn by Pvt. John E. Bickford, South Abington Light Infantry (Co. E), 4th MVM is trimmed with red piping along the front and top edges of the collar, both sides of the lapels, the bottom edges of the skirt including the side slits, and the bottom edges of the cuffs. It is fastened by seven staff cut "Mass. Volunteer Militia" buttons, the top three of which are back-marked "W.[aterbury] Button Co. * Extra *," and the bottom three of which have the back-mark "Steele & Johnson." The middle is a badly corroded replacement. The sleeves are lined with brown cotton, and an inside pocket of the same material is attached to the left breast. There is no body lining. Bickford was a 23-year-old shoemaker and a member of the 4th MVM when his company was the first to report for duty in Boston on April 16, 1861. The regiment garrisoned Fortress Monroe, Virginia, on April 20, 1861; occupied Newport, Virginia on May 27, 1861; and fought at Big Bethel on June 10, 1861. Bickford was mustered-out with his regiment at Long Island in Boston Harbor on July 22, 1861. He later served in Co. C, 38th Massachusetts Volunteers, and following promotion to sergeant was wounded in the ankle at Winchester, Virginia, on September 19, 1864, and in the side at Cedar Creek on October 19, 1864. *Dr. Michael J. Cunningham collection*.

The matching plain gray trousers worn by Private Bickford are fully lined in brown cotton, and have black metal buttons at the fly and waist band, and an adjustment buckle in the rear. *Dr. Michael J. Cunningham collection*.

Resident at South Salem, 20-year-old Charles C. Perkins was a civil engineer when he enlisted in the Chadwick Light Infantry, Co. K, 1st Massachusetts Infantry, on May 24, 1861. He wears another example of the semi-chasseur-style gray uniform with red facing on collar front, and red trim around coat edges, shoulder straps and cuffs. Note the belt loops providing support at each side of his waist belt. His cap has a red top and band. Including a rifle musket cartridge box suspended from a shoulder belt made from bridle leather, his accoutrements may be some of those issued to his regiment when they received "Springfield muskets" on June 12, 1861. *U.S. Army Heritage and Education Center.*

John F. Baxter was a 28-year-old upholsterer resident in Roxbury, Suffolk County, Massachusetts, when he enlisted in the Chadwick Light Infantry (Co. K), 1st Massachusetts Infantry on April 17, 1861. Promoted to the rank of corporal, he was wounded in the left thigh at Bull Run on July 21, 1861, being part of his regiment that held a hill on the extreme left flank of the Union army from July 19 through 21. On January 5, 1862, he received a disability discharge due to his wound. His coat shows to good effect the red facings at the front of his collar, plus red trim on cuffs, and seam stripe on his trousers. *Carte de visite with pencil inscription—author's collection.*

On May 13, the *Boston Daily Advertiser* advised that the Committee on Military Supplies had "new uniforms for about sixteen companies."[54] Two days later, the Washington Light Guard (Co. K), 6th MVM received their "city uniform," which was "grey, slightly trimmed with red cord—Garibaldi jacket."[55] Most of the uniforms worn by the 1st Massachusetts Volunteers, the first regiment from the state to enlist for three years' service, were also completed as part of these contracts. According to Col. Robert Cowdin, original regimental commander, the city outfitted seven of his companies, while the Roxbury City Guards (Co. D) continued to be clothed by their home communities.[56]

In order to begin outfitting the three-month volunteers elsewhere in the sState, plus some of the three-year regiments being raised, including the 7th, 10th, 11th, 13th, 14th, and 15th Massachusetts, Lt. Col. John H. Reed, the state quartermaster-general, concluded a contract on May 8, 1861, with Haughton, Sawyer & Co., at 26 and 28 Pearl Street, Boston, to supply "3,000 suits of light wool [flannel] uniforms, of a gray color," which appear to have been based on the pattern produced for the Boston troops by Whitten, Hopkins & Co.[57] A major supplier of "Army Equipments," Haughton, Sawyer, & Co. was managed by merchants James Haughton, Samuel E. Sawyer, J. W. Woods, W. A. Richards, and J. J. Perkins. This firm also had stores at Astor House, in New York City; Continental House, in Philadelphia; Briggs House, in Chicago; and Neil House, at Columbus, Ohio.[58] By May 18, 1861, it was reported to have "completed a contract with the State of Massachusetts, for 6,000 all wool blue mixed garments, neatly trimmed, and suitable for a warm climate."[59] By September, it had also "obtained extensive contracts with the United States government, and from eight or ten of the Northern and Western states," and was also suspected of being "engaged in the business of furnishing army equipments and materials for the use of the rebels."[60]

By May 21, 1861, 1,400 suits of uniforms produced by Haughton, Sawyer & Co. were being transported aboard the steam transport *Pembroke* for distribution to the 3rd and 4th MVM at Fortress Monroe.[61] As a consequence, Capt. Luther Stephenson, Co. I, 4th MVM recorded, "Our trouble regarding our uniform was finally relieved by the receipt from Massachusetts of blouses, trousers, and caps, made from gray flannel and well suited for service in the summer months."[62] Already wearing this uniform on board the *Pembroke* was several companies being attached to the two militia regiments as three-year volunteers. That of the Plymouth Rock Guards, designated Co. E, 3rd MVM, consisted of "a full suit of reddish gray clothes, the coat reaching to the hips, and the whole—coat, trousers, and cap—trimmed with red braid." Each man in the Greenough Guards, Co. K, 4th MVM had "a full suit of gray clothes, the jacket being trimmed with red braid." Joining the 4th MVM as Co. M, the dress of the Wightman Rifles was similarly described as "a gray chasseur tunic trimmed with red, gray trowsers, and three-cornered gray felt hats trimmed with red." This company also received from the state "red blankets, cartridge-boxes, and the somewhat historic gray overcoats."[63] Following arrival at Fortress Monroe having been attached to the staff of post commander Gen. Benjamin Butler, Theodore Winthrop described the whole of the 3rd MVM as being "neatly uniformed in gray, with cocked felt hats."[64]

According to the *Boston Daily Advertiser*, the 8th MVM received "a neat uniform, consisting of a jacket of 'Garibaldi' grey, grey pants and red fez caps."[65] The regimental history of the 6th MVM described this state clothing as "a sort of Zouave suit, single-breasted, with full trowsers, and Fez caps with dark tassels for fatigue, and gray hats turned up at the side, with red trimmings, for 'dress.' Some of the boys thought there was a march of two or three hours inside their trowsers' legs. The officers wore the Massachusetts State uniform— dark blue frocks, light blue trowsers, with broad white stripes on the sides."[66] Some companies continued to receive clothing based on the state pattern from their local communities. Following the arrival of the 7th MVM in Washington, DC, the *National Republican* reported:

> The uniform of the Fall River companies [Companies A and B] of the regiment are of grey woollen cloth, commonly called Garibaldi material, from the red, white and blue spots in its texture. It consists of a jacket of more than ordinary length, bound at the wrists, collar and shoulder-straps with red cord. The pants are of material with similar trimmings at the seams. The uniforms of the other companies are of regulation grey, furnished by the State. The hats are of drab felt, circular in shape, and each uniform was fitted to the wearer.[67]

According to photographic evidence, most of the coats made for these uniforms were fastened by eight large buttons, with coat edges, cuffs, collar, and shoulder straps trimmed with red cord. Variation in collar and cuff trim may have been due to a difference between uniforms produced by the state and city of Boston, and those which continued to be produced by local communities. Some collars were edged with red cord, while others were embellished with a solid red patch at front. Some cuffs were trimmed with cord parallel with the edge of the cuff, with a single rectangular patch of the same color cloth as the coat, also edged with cord and decorated with three small buttons. Others, such as that furnished to the Chadwick Light Infantry, Co. K, 1st MVM had pointed cuffs, and trousers had ½-inch wide seam stripes.

As their new service uniforms were received, the companies of the 6th MVM sent their old dress clothing home. A report in the *Lowell Daily Citizen & News* stated that the uniforms of the Mechanic Phalanx (Co. C) looked "rather the worse for wear, the pantaloons especially, most of which are entirely ruined." The "grey frock-coats and pants" of the Watson Light Guard (Co. H) arrived back at Lowell two days later.[68] A week later, the *Daily Citizen & News*, of the same city, stated that this regiment had received on May 19, 1861, its "new government uniform" consisting of "a grey jacket and pants trimmed with red cord, and a Kossuth hat …"[69] This uniform was further described in a letter in the *Courier* of the same city that stated, "The Sixth wear loose uniforms, a gray sack coat and 'pepper-and-salt' pantaloons, and the Edmands hat."[70]

Supplied by Haughton, Sawyer & Co., the Edmands hat was reported in the *Salem Register* of May 2, 1861, as "a style of head dress...combining several suggestions of practical men who have seen service in warm latitudes, [and] has been prepared and offered to our State authorities by General B.[enjamin] F. Edmands. It is in appearance a combination of the old continental, the army and the Kossuth hats, and is designed to afford the best means of protecting the head from the sun's rays and consequently sunstroke. Messrs. Haughton, Sawyer & Co. have contracted to furnish hats of this style to our State authorities."[71] Designed by Benjamin F. Edmands, commander of the MVM during the 1850s and member of the Boston Committee on Military Supplies, it was made of gray felt and was looped up on three sides, although photographic evidence shows examples looped up on four sides, which may indicate that the supplier contracted the work out to different hatters who had differing interpretations of the design. These hats were also embellished with strips of vertical, red-tape trim sewn around each button hole through which the brim was looped up and fastened to the crown.

Based on both written and photographic evidence, the Edmands hat was issued to the 3rd and 4th MVM, plus the 10th Massachusetts Volunteers, or "Western Regiment," and 11th Massachusetts Volunteers, or "Boston Volunteers." It was also purchased via the Ohio branch of Haughton, Sawyer & Co. during July 1861, for issue to the 34th and 54th Ohio, or Piatt Zouaves. The Edmands hat was not popular with some Massachusetts troops as, when his regiment received them during the last week in June 1861, Lt. Joseph K. Newell, commanding Co. I, 10th Massachusetts recorded in his diary, "hats, 'what hats!' of unmentionable dirty, light drab color, that were discarded as soon as caps could be obtained."[72]

All three of these members of the 3rd MVM wear the semi-chasseur uniform consisting of seven-button coat with narrow, red trim around the collar and plain gray trousers, plus full-dress hat approved by Maj. General Benjamin F. Edmands, MVM and made by Haughton, Sawyer, & Co., of Boston. At left, 22-year-old Alvin Vaughn was a straw worker living at Carver, Massachusetts, when he enlisted in the Samoset Guards, Co. H, on April 16, 1861. On completion of his three-months' service, he reenlisted in Co. I, 9th Vermont Infantry on July 9, 1862 and was promoted to first sergeant. He was again promoted to second lieutenant on January 6, 1863, followed by first lieutenant on May 2, 1865. Of the same age, the man at right is Robert Parris who also enlisted in Co. H on the same date, being a sailor resident at Middleboro, Massachusetts. On completion of his three-months' service, he reenlisted in Co. D, 18th Massachusetts Infantry, on August 24, 1862, and was mustered-out on September 2, 1864. The man at center is unidentified. *Circa 1900 copy print of an earlier image—Michael J. McAfee collection.*

During a visit to the "Photograph and Ambrotype Gallery" of Benson C. Hazelton on Washington Street, Boston, during the cold New England spring of 1861, this unidentified volunteer of the 4th MVM wore an "Edmands"-pattern hat and gray state-issue, single-breasted infantry overcoat. *Sixth-plate ambrotype—author's collection.*

First published in the Boston press on May 4, 1861, this advertisement promotes "The New Hat" for "service in warm climates," as produced under the supervision of Maj. General Benjamin F. Edmands, MVM, which was referred to elsewhere as the "Edmands" hat or "the famous Military Hat." *Author's collection.*

This Massachusetts volunteer wears an Edmands hat. He is double armed with an M1849 Pocket Colt tucked inside his coat and sheathed M1850 foot officers' sword. The narrow width of fringe on his epaulets indicates he is wearing those prescribed only for corporals, privates, and musicians in the US Army. *Carte de visite by "J.W. Black, 173 Washington, Street, Boston"—author's collection.*

William W. Smith was a 22-year-old "boot maker" when he was mustered-in as a private in the Taunton Light Infantry (Co. G), 4th MVM, on April 22, 1861. He wears the company letter "G" on the strip of trim at front of his Edmands hat. Smith re-enlisted for nine-months' service in September, 1862, as a sergeant in Co. K, 4th MVM. *Ninth-plate ambrotype. Liljenquist collection, LC-DIG-ppmsca-3145.*

Listed in an 1858 directory as a "paper carrier" who boarded at Tremont Street in Lowell, Massachusetts, Andrew J. Herrick was 27 years old when he enlisted in the National Greys, Co. A, 6th MVM on April 15, 1861. He was mustered-out at Boston on August 2, 1861, but reenlisted on September 27, 1862, being mustered-out again at Suffolk, Virginia, on November 30, 1862. He wears a rare example of the undress red fez cap with blue tassel, and semi-chasseur-style gray coat, issued by the state to his regiment on May 19, 1861. *U.S. Army Heritage and Education Center.*

A resident of Quincy, in Norfolk County, Massachusetts, Hiram Barber Prior enlisted in the Hancock Light Infantry (Co. H), 4th MVM, and served for three months in 1861. He later enlisted in Co. B, 60th Regiment, Massachusetts Infantry, for 100 days' service in 1864. He wears the Edmands hat with state-issue overcoat. *Ninth-plate ambrotype—author's collection.*

This unidentified Massachusetts militiaman wears a variation of the Edmands hat which was looped up on only two or, most probably, three sides and had a narrower brim and slightly taller crown. *Ninth-plate ambrotype—Daniel J. Binder collection.*

A red fez was also issued for fatigue wear. Upon return to Boston at the end of their three-month period of service, the 8th MVM was reported to be wearing red fez caps.[73] Fatigue caps of both 1839 and 1858-Patterns were also worn, particularly by the 1st and 7th MVM, the latter being either gray with red band and top, or quartered with red cord trim. Observing a company leaving the State House in Boston on April 16, 1861, Robert Dollard noted that their caps had "a little broader top with flimsy cloth between that and the band so the top could be set to suit the disposition of the wearer, according to his inclination as an ordinary mortal, a dude, dandy, a slugger, etc."[74]

Much of the state clothing received did not match up to expectations. By June 6, 1861, the uniforms of the 1st MVM had much deteriorated, and the unit was promised "a new uniform and new overcoats."[75] After considerable delay without receiving replacement clothing, it left for Virginia on June 15, on which occasion Col. Cowdin ordered his men to wear their overcoats because their knapsacks were "so narrow and small that the coats could not be properly packed, and that some of the uniforms, though worn only about six weeks, were so ragged that they were not decent to march through the streets in."[76] Two days later, Cowdin faced criticism from reporters who did not understand the plight of his regiment when he again ordered it to wear overcoats on the march to the White House in the mid-day heat on arrival in Washington DC.[77]

Sent by Governor Andrew to examine the condition of the Massachusetts troops at Fortress Monroe and Fort McHenry at the beginning of June 1861, government officials reported:

> We beg leave to state that this uniform was much needed by our troops, and has placed them in a very presentable condition. The style in our opinion cannot be improved, but we regret to say that it is already proved that some of the flannel of which it is made is too weak to be serviceable. Though Col. [David W.] Wardrop [commanding the 3rd MVM] is exceedingly careful that all fatigue and guard duty shall be performed in old clothes, a large number of the jackets have already given way from the mere strain of the straps of the knapsacks.[78]

Footwear was also cause for complaint. On June 26, 1861, the *Boston Daily Advertiser* reported that thirty men of the 8th MVM were barefoot at the Relay House. Their shoes were described as being "too low to give any support to the ankle or to be easily kept in shape; the leather is of wretched quality, and a week of rainy weather is enough to finish a pair of the shoes." This footwear may have been some of that produced at the Massachusetts State Prison in Charlestown where about 140 inmates made approximately $26,000 worth of shoes, canteens, and other items for the state by the end of 1861.[79]

In a letter dated July 13, 1861, a correspondent of the *Daily Citizen & News*, of Lowell, wrote of the 6th MVM, "The uniform of the regiment is nearly worn out, and looks rather seedy, but it will be worn home to show our people how shabbily the three months' volunteers have been treated by the state of Massachusetts."[80] Upon return to Lowell at the end of their three-month period of service, the poorly made state uniforms worn by this regiment were described as "suits of Garibaldi gray," which made them look more like "rebel zouaves" than "the good Union soldiers they were."[81]

The wearing of gray inevitably caused confusion and drew friendly fire on Massachusetts volunteers at Bull Run on July 21, 1861. Regimental chaplain of the 1st Massachusetts, Warren H. Cudworth, recalled that "the rebels wore uniforms so nearly like ours in color, that, a few hundred yards apart, it was impossible to tell who were friends, and who foes." He also stated that "the gray uniforms of the Massachusetts men misled certain Michigan regiments…"[82] Serving in the 1st Brigade of Col. S.P. Heintzelman's 3rd Division, Sgt. Gustavus D. Hutchinson, Co. D, 11th Massachusetts (Boston Volunteers), recorded in his regimental history, "We were dressed in our new gray uniforms, which had been sent us by the State committee...The delusive color cost us dearly, for...one of our own regiments opened fire upon us, mistaking us for Confederates, and several valuable lives were sacrificed."[83] In a letter published in the *Boston Herald* on July 30, 1861, an anonymous corporal in Co. A, 11th Massachusetts, wrote, "a Minnesota regiment and the New York Zouaves, mistaking us for rebels on account of our uniform being the same as the Virginia militia, fired into us three times. Our company lost a great number on this charge."[84] Following service with the same brigade at Bull Run wearing the federal-issue blue uniforms mentioned earlier, the 5th MVM returned home on July 29, 1861, in a great variety of headgear of both "material and pattern." Accompanying them was a regimental mascot in the form of "a big, brindled bull-dog, marked by cutting off his hair, 5th Regt. MVM.'"[85]

The regiments organized for three-years' service via General Orders No. 16 and 20 issued in response to the presidential call on May 3, 1861, were clothed in a variety of uniforms. The gray state uniform supplied to the 1st Massachusetts has already been considered. Although efforts were made to have gray uniforms adopted by the 2nd Massachusetts, Col. George H. Gordon was determined that his regiment should wear blue. As a result, Whiting, Galloupe & Bliss, of Boston, were contracted to produce for "Gordon's Regulars" the "uniform of the regular army, cut to fit the form." Headgear consisted of the new army hat, or Pattern-1858 dress hat, made by S. O. Aborn, "of favorable hat notoriety," which was described in the *Boston Herald* of July 8, 1861, as the "black Kossuth, turned up on the left side, with black plumes and blue bands."[86] Of their arrival in New York aboard the steamer *Commodore* on July 9, 1861, the *Herald* reported, "They wore the black felt hat, turned up at the side. Their coats are made of serviceable blue cloth and their pants of blue flannel."[87]

Recruited during May 1861, primarily among the Irish-American citizens of Boston, the 9th Massachusetts (1st Irish Regiment) received their first uniforms on the 23rd of that month consisting of "blue mixed pants, blue shirts, knit woolen jackets, [&] gray caps."[88] State grey uniforms "complete in every respect" were received from the City of Boston on June 20 and distributed the next day, plus "haversacks, bed ticks, canteens, tin pots, camp kettles, knives, forks, spoons, lace-boots, &c."[89] During the same month, this regiment was presented with a banner bearing "an Irish harp, with strings of red and white upon a background of blue... surmounted by thirty-four stars, and surrounded by a wreath of shamrock, with two wolf-dogs, emblematic of Ireland."[90]

Produced by the firm of Isaac Fenno & Co., at 80 Federal Street, Boston, the first uniform of the 12th Massachusetts (Webster Regiment) was of "blue gray Cadet mixed cassimere, substantially sewn, the pants seamed with scarlet, and the frocks having a row of Massachusetts arms buttons up the breast and relieved on the collar with a scarlet facing."[91] This was replaced by "a blue uniform, like that of the 2nd Regiment" during July, 1861, and when they paraded for a flag presentation on the 18th of that month, they wore "the regulation army uniform, with forage caps."[92] When reviewed by Brig. Gen. Samuel Andrews, commanding the Fort Warren garrison five days later, the 12th Massachusetts was described as wearing "white 'Havelocks,' and had their overcoats neatly folded on top of their knapsacks, the bright red lining being outward, which contrasted oddly with their tanned faces and blue coats."[93]

The nucleus of the 4th Battalion of Rifles, MVM was the Boston City Guard, which "cut loose" from the 1st MVM to become a rifle company during the winter of 1860/61. Expanded into four companies following the surrender of Fort Sumter, the 4th Battalion was joined by six more companies to form the 13th Massachusetts Volunteers, which departed for the South on July 30, 1861. At a meeting held on April 15, 1861, the officers forming the initial rifle battalion adopted "a substantial gray uniform, suitable for work days"[94] made by Macullar, Williams and Parker, of Boston.[95] Similar in style to that worn by the British Rifle Volunteer movement of that time, it consisted of an English-style cap with

Both of these unidentified militiamen wear the uniform of the 4th Battalion of Riflemen, MVM, which appears to have been patterned after that worn by British Rifle Volunteer units. The man at left wears the cap with stiffened crown and red top with gray band, which was surmounted by a round red worsted pompon. The insignia attached at front consisted of a brass stamped wreath enclosing the numeral "4." The gray chasseur-pattern coat worn by both men has a nine-button front, is trimmed red around collar and cuffs, and has red "Russian" shoulder knots. Although painted over, the belt plate at left appears to have been a "US" oval, while that at right is a two-piece militia officers' "eagle" plate. As many Massachusetts volunteers were gifted revolvers during the heady first few weeks of war, the holstered weapon carried by the man at right may be his own, rather than a photographer's prop. The Pattern-1855 knapsack, with rolled red blanket on top, is being worn correctly by the man at left, with the breast straps attached to his waist belt. *Sixth-plate ruby ambrotype—collection of Martin Schoenfeld; copy print of carte de visite in Michael J. McAfee collection.*

stiffened crown, and coat with short skirts and shoulder knots. The latter garment was described in the history of the 13th Massachusetts as "a tight-fitting [jacket], with a short skirt. The shoulder-knots and trimmings were red, and the uniform gray. The cap was gray trimmed with scarlet and surmounted with a pompon. It made a handsome, serviceable uniform, and gave a very effective appearance to the battalion."[96] Officers of this unit wore dark-blue frock coats and gilt trimmed gray caps topped with plumes. As riflemen, the 4th Battalion was originally armed with "Windsor" M1841 rifles.

On May 24, 1861, the 13th Massachusetts received their state gray uniforms, which were replaced on July 26 by "the United States uniform." The latter was more fully described in the *Boston Herald* as consisting of "blue pantaloons and coat of the regulation pattern, and the men also have a fatigue dress, consisting of a blue blouse."[97] Prior to leaving the state on the 29th of that month, this regiment received 960 Enfield rifle muskets in place of their M1841 rifles.[98] According to the *Herald*, the men of this regiment "all wore their blue overcoats as they marched up State Street" on the day of their departure for the front.[99]

Responding to the executive call for a further 500,000 three-year volunteers issued toward the end of July 1861, the 1st Battalion Riflemen provided the initial base for recruiting volunteers for the 19th Massachusetts. This regiment was supplemented by those men of the 8th MVM who desired to reenlist. John G.B. Adams enlisted in Co. A of the 1st Battalion, known as "Poore's Savages," after battalion commander Maj. Ben Perley Poore, and recalled, "The uniform was dark green, trimmed with light green, and as I donned it for the first time it was hard to tell which was the greener, the soldier or the uniform." Armed with "Windsor" rifles with saber bayonets, their drill as Adams remembered was "running around the old Town Hall in single file, giving an Indian war-whoop and firing into the corner of the hall as we ran."[100]

A zouave style of dress was chosen in mid-June 1861 by the 2nd Battalion Riflemen, also known as the Boston Light Infantry, who had evolved from the old 1st Regiment of Light Infantry, or "Tiger First." Organized in the Boston area, they voted in June 1861 "to adopt the full Zouave costume, even to the turban," which would be made with "a red body and trimmed with blue. Jacket and trowsers of dark blue, gaiters of white."[101] Clearly adopted by the beginning of July, and worn on parade on the 16th of that month, this uniform was reported by the *Boston Evening Transcript* as consisting of "a Turkish turban, blue jacket, faced with orange trimmings, and having gilt buttons, which were set off by a red shirt and trousers of blue, with white leggings."[102] The jacket worn by this unit was edged at front with small brass ball buttons, and was extensively trimmed with tightly twisted orange yarn. The red vest was also trimmed with braid and a single row of slightly smaller ball buttons. On August 7, 1862, the 2nd Battalion would be expanded into regimental size to fill the quota of Massachusetts under the call issued three days earlier for nine-month troops, and became the 43rd MVM, also known as the "Tiger Regiment."

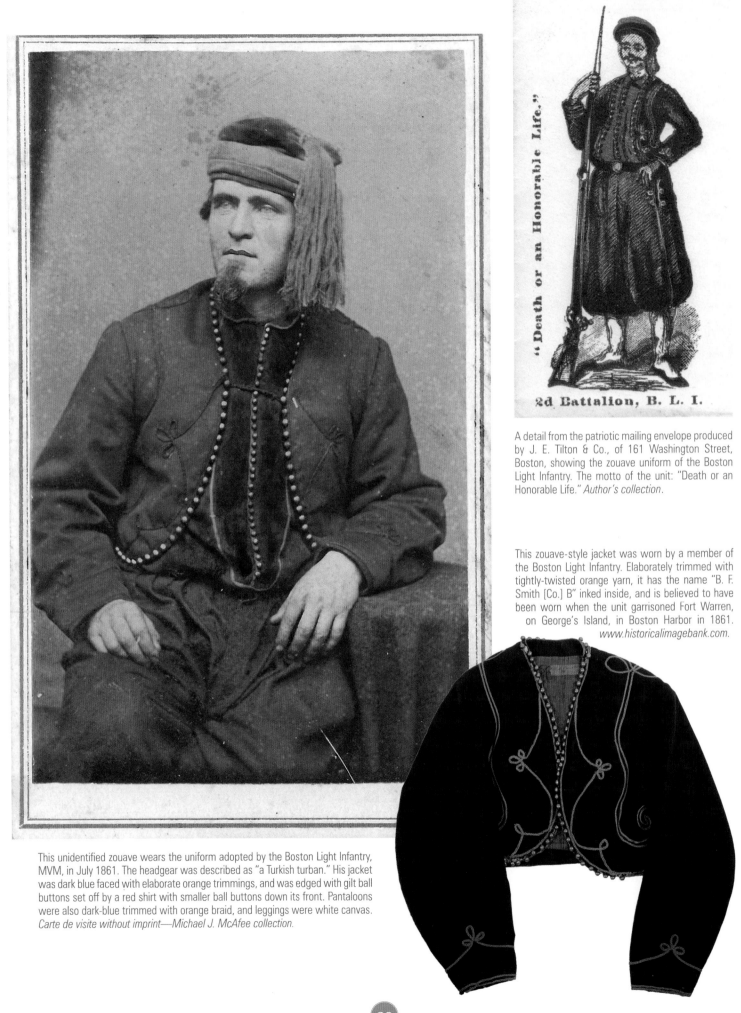

"Death or an Honorable Life."

2d Battalion, B. L. I.

A detail from the patriotic mailing envelope produced by J. E. Tilton & Co., of 161 Washington Street, Boston, showing the zouave uniform of the Boston Light Infantry. The motto of the unit: "Death or an Honorable Life." *Author's collection*.

This zouave-style jacket was worn by a member of the Boston Light Infantry. Elaborately trimmed with tightly-twisted orange yarn, it has the name "B. F. Smith [Co.] B" inked inside, and is believed to have been worn when the unit garrisoned Fort Warren, on George's Island, in Boston Harbor in 1861. *www.historicalimagebank.com*.

This unidentified zouave wears the uniform adopted by the Boston Light Infantry, MVM, in July 1861. The headgear was described as "a Turkish turban." His jacket was dark blue faced with elaborate orange trimmings, and was edged with gilt ball buttons set off by a red shirt with smaller ball buttons down its front. Pantaloons were also dark-blue trimmed with orange braid, and leggings were white canvas. *Carte de visite without imprint—Michael J. McAfee collection*.

Chasseur-pattern pantaloons worn by the New England Guard were sky-blue cloth trimmed with elaborate yellow braid around the side pockets and upper side seam. Note the pleating under the waist band at back and front, strap for adjusting the waist band at rear, buttons for suspenders, and ankle ties to aid tucking them into the leather gaiters. An American patent buckle in the back of this garment and lack of French markings indicates it was of US manufacture. *Dr. Michael R. Cunningham collection.*

George L. Tripp, Co. A, New England Guard, was photographed at the gallery of E. L. Allen at 13 Winter Street, Boston, wearing the chasseur uniform adopted by his unit by August 1861. This consisted of a dark-blue coat trimmed with yellow tape, yellow shoulder knots, sky blue pantaloons trimmed with yellow, russet leather gaiters, and a white cap trimmed with yellow. Reserved for dress occasions, this uniform was not worn when the New England Guard Battalion joined the ranks of the 24th Massachusetts in December 1861. *Carte de visite by Allen/13 Winter St.—Daniel Miller collection.*

One of the best drilled militia companies in Massachusetts, the New England Guard, was formed in 1812 and, by March 1861, constituted Co. A, 4th Battalion Infantry, MVM. A second company was organized at that time. On April 24, the 4th Battalion volunteered to garrison the largely unmanned Fort Independence in Boston Harbor, which it did without pay. During the period from September to December 1861, this battalion was expanded and volunteered for three-years' service as the 24th Massachusetts, or New England Guards Regiment, and in 1862 some of its members served for nine months as the 44th Massachusetts, or 2nd New England Guards. Prior to the Civil War, the uniform of the New England Guard consisted of a blue tail-coat and pants trimmed with yellow, and headgear was a blue dress cap with yellow pompon and gilt eagle plate. When the battalion occupied Fort Independence, it was issued with the state overcoat, gray shirts, and forage caps.[103]

Another detail from a patriotic envelope produced by J. E. Tilton & Co., this illustrates the chasseur uniform adopted by the New England Guard by August 1861. Note the yellow trim on the pantaloons. *Author's collection.*

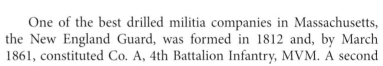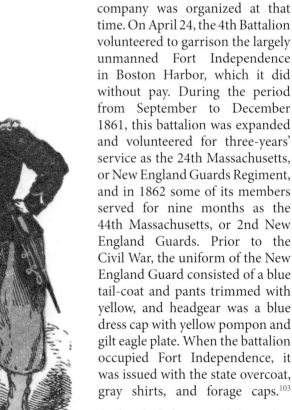

By August, a chasseur uniform of probable American manufacture had been adopted by the unit, which consisted of a blue coat trimmed with yellow, yellow shoulder knots, sky blue pantaloons with yellow trim, white forage cap with yellow piping, and russet leather gaiters.[104] When organized into the 24th Massachusetts, members of this unit were issued "a substantial uniform," which included "shoes, coats, pants, hats," all of which were probably of federal pattern.[105]

Commanded by Capt. Ansel D. Wass, an ex-member of the United States Zouave Cadets, the Tiger Fire Zouaves were mainly recruited among the firemen of Boston and voted to join the 19th Massachusetts as Co. K on August 9, 1861. Initially provided with the state uniform issued to the rest of their regiment, this company adopted "a complete Zouave uniform," received after their arrival in Washington, DC, which was described as being "without a particle of red about it, the jacket being dark and the pants and shirts of light blue." Possibly influenced by that worn by the Boston Light Infantry, their jacket was also embellished with small brass ball buttons, and edged and trimmed with light blue, including very unusual cuff braid. Headgear originally appears to have been a dark-blue fez cap. The rest of the uniform included a tight-fitting dark-colored vest, waist sash and yellow leather leggings.[106] Organized in December 1861, the Boston Fire Zouaves (Co. I), 30th Massachusetts (Eastern Bay State Regiment) adopted the same zouave-style uniform as the Tiger Fire Zouaves.

A Home Guard company formed in Boston during June/July 1861 named the Boston Cabot Zouave Cadets in honor of the local Cabot family, adopted the same style of uniform as "the Chicago Zouaves."[107] A company organized in Pittsfield, Massachusetts, by Charles M. Whelden known as the Independent Zouaves proposed to adopt a uniform consisting of "the regular Zouave-pattern crimson cap with blue tassel, dark blue jacket, light blue pants, and russet gaiters."[108] This outfit may not have been acquired by the whole unit as, on August 7, 1861, it turned out to welcome the return of the Allen Guard, 8th MVM, in "a handsome uniform, extemporized for the occasion, consisting of black pantaloons, white shirts, and Zouave caps. The captain wore the full Zouave uniform."[109] Helping recruit the 31st Massachusetts during the fall of 1861, Whelden became acting lieutenant colonel of that regiment.

Formed partially from the 10th MVM, the companies of the 10th Massachusetts Volunteers mainly wore "grey uniforms with felt hats."[110] The Great Barrington Company (Co. A) and Barton Roughs (Co. E), of Hampden Park, wore gray trimmed with black. Enlisted at North Adams, the Johnson Grays (Co. B) had jacket and pants of cadet gray, the cloth for which cost $700 while "making and trimming" cost $707, plus caps at $75.95.[111] The Pollock Guard (Co. D), of Pittsfield, wore a "crimson badge," or rosette, until they received their first uniform of cadet gray cloth produced at the Pontocrac Mill and made by local merchant tailors Tagert & Wilson.[112] The whole regiment received state-issue clothing on August 4, 1861. A letter written the next day from a visitor to their camp at Washington, DC, stated that they had "just received their new uniform,

Born in Ireland about 1836, George W. Gordon wears the uniform of the Boston Tiger Fire Zouaves, Co. K, 19th Massachusetts Infantry. His jacket is trimmed with light blue and edged with brass ball buttons, and has very distinctive cuff trim. Pantaloons were light blue, and headgear consists of an unusual stiff-crowned kepi with round worsted pompon attached. Gordon was variously listed as a carpenter and painter when he enlisted on August 13, 1861. Surviving the war, he was mustered-out on August 28, 1864. *Carte de visite without imprint—Michael J. McAfee collection.*

The unidentified N.C.O. of Co. G, 19th Massachusetts, wears an unusual combination of corporal's chevrons and five-pointed star. Also note the elaborate cuff braid. *Carte de visite by J.W. Black, Boston —Michael J. McAfee collection.*

Organized in December 1861, the Boston Fire Zouaves (Co. I), 30th Massachusetts, a.k.a. the "Eastern Bay State Regiment," adopted the same zouave-style uniform as the Tiger Fire Zouaves, which consisted of a dark-blue jacket edged with ball buttons and trimmed with light blue, and light blue pantaloons. Headgear in this image consists of a fez. Lying flat on the back of his head, this was probably red. Also wearing a dark-blue vest, Martin A. Munroe served as a private in Co. I, 30th Massachusetts. *US Army Heritage and Education Center.*

Aged 24, Herbert E. Larrabee, of South Danvers in Essex County, Massachusetts, worked as a "Morocco Dresser" before he enlisted as first sergeant in the Foster Guard, Co. B, 17th Massachusetts Volunteers on July 22, 1861. He was mustered-out on April 5, 1863 at New Berne, North Carolina. Three years his junior, his brother Henry Luther Larrabee, who was a shoemaker, enlisted on the same date and was mustered-out on August 3, 1864. Photographed before their regiment received its fatigue state clothing, both men wear the uniform of gray, trimmed with red acquired from a Boston tailor during April, 1861. *Sixth-plate ambrotype courtesy of the Liljenquist Family collection—Library of Congress LC-DIG-ppmsca-27277.*

consisting of grey pants with narrow black stripes down the sides, and a blouse made of dark blue material, such as are worn in the regular army."[113] According to regimental historian Alfred S. Roe, "the former [gray] attire was thought to resemble too closely that of the enemy."[114]

The Methuen Light Infantry, Co. B, 14th Massachusetts, was the only company of that regiment "fortunate" enough to receive a fatigue uniform upon organization at Fort Warren. In early June 1861, David Nevins, proprietor of the Pemberton Mills of Lawrence, Massachusetts, invited Captain Bradley to visit his mill to "get cloth for fatigue uniforms for his entire company. The gift was gratefully accepted and Captain Bradley soon afterward had the uniforms of durable pepper-and-salt fitted and made for his men."[115] Both Companies F (Scott Grays, of Lawrence) and K (City Guards, of Lowell) of this regiment were provided with "the regulation shoddy" by the state government, which suggests they also wore gray. The Putnam Guards (Co. I) of the same regiment, wore jackets and trousers of light blue, with gray caps, while officers wore "Rebel gray." This regiment was issued with uniforms of "national blue" a few days prior to departure of Washington on August 7, 1861.[116]

Enlisting as a private in the Barre Volunteers, Co. K, 21st Massachusetts, during June 1861, James M. Stone recalled that the only item of uniform he had until his regiment received US regulation issue was "a cap of the Barre Militia Company," which was "navy blue...trimmed with red cord." Stone further qualified that it was "a French type of cap...afterwards known as the McClellan cap throughout the army."[117] A report in the *Barre Gazette* dated July 19, 1861, stated that the full uniform received by this company consisted of "dark blue pants and short jacket, with scarlet piping in the seams. The cap is also blue, of the Zouave pattern." The ladies of the community also provided them with "a Havelock, two handkerchiefs, towel and pocket-housewife containing needles, thread, plus buttons, scissors and a comb."[118]

The 13th through 31st Massachusetts were issued federal-style uniforms consisting of dark coats and blouses, and either gray or light-blue pants. Both the 14th and 15th Massachusetts were supplied with new uniforms prior to departure for the South at the beginning of August 1861, the state clothing being worn until that time having been condemned.[119] According to photographic evidence, that issued to the latter regiment consisted of Pattern-1858 hats with looped horn insignia at front, and regulation frock coats with brass shoulder scales.[120] The 17th regiment received "800 fatigue uniforms" while still encamped at Lynnfield on July 29, 1861,[121] which consisted of "dark blue jackets, grey pants and overcoats, and army caps" upon arrival at New York City.[122] Stationed at Baltimore from late August, a man in the

When he enlisted in Co. F, 18th Massachusetts Infantry, on June 1, 1861, Edward F. Richards was a clerk resident at Dedham, Massachusetts. He was mustered-in on August 21 and was promoted to the rank of quartermaster sergeant on March 13, 1862, being mustered-out on September 2, 1864. He wears the full-dress chasseur uniform imported from France by the federal quartermaster's department in November/December 1861. This consisted of the Model 1860 leather shako with dark green fountain plume, dark-blue-trimmed light yellow jacket with cast pewter buttons, green and yellow worsted epaulets, light blue pantaloons, black leather leggings and light brown leather gaiters. As some men in the 18th Massachusetts, including Private Richards, were photographed wearing shakos minus the elaborate plate normally attached to its front, it is possible the 18th Massachusetts were not immediately issued with this item, or that some of its personnel did not receive them at all. *US Army Heritage and Education Center.*

Private Richards was also photographed wearing an example of the fatigue cap, or a *bonnet de police*, which was dark blue with light yellow trim and tassel. *US Army Heritage and Education Center.*

Also living at Dedham when he enlisted in Co. H, 18th Massachusetts, First Sgt. Erastus Everson wears the French fatigue jacket, or *habit-veste*, and French-manufactured rifleman's belt. Note the belt loop seen on his jacket under his left arm. Everson was wounded at Second Bull Run and again at Fredericksburg. Discharged as a first lieutenant on December 10, 1863, he finished the war in the Veteran Reserve Corps. *Carte de visite without imprint—Michael J. McAfee collection.*

This Model 1860 full-dress leather shako of the type issued to the 18th Massachusetts has the rarely seen dark green worsted pompom attached, which was issued for field service. It also has attached the metal rosette and elaborate plate with spread eagle and coat of arms surmounting a wreath of oak and olive branches with hunting horn inset. *Dr. Michael R. Cunningham collection.*

Part of the 10,000 uniforms imported from France, this French light infantry of the line, or *chasseurs á pied de la ligne*, jacket is based on that worn by the French army, and was issued to Cpl. James D. Weeks, Co. C, 18th Massachusetts Volunteers, who was an 18-year-old nail maker from Marion, Massachusetts when he enlisted on September 17, 1861. It was trimmed with light yellow piping with a broad silver inverted chevron on each cuff indicating rank. Epaulets were green worsted trimmed with yellow. Note the side vents, single belt loop at the waist and yellow embroidered looped hunting horn on the tail in the rear view. The cuffs were also slightly different from that worn by the French army by having a cuff with a yellow-edged button flap. Buttons were cast pewter with "CORDIER FRERES/ PARIS" back mark and bore an eagle and shield above which was an arc of thirteen stars. *Dr. Michael R. Cunningham collection.*

17th Massachusetts wrote that his regiment was "in want of warm clothing, which, however, will soon be furnished them by the general government."[123]

En route for the capital on August 26, the 18th Massachusetts passed through Providence, Rhode Island, on which occasion the *Daily Post* of that city commented, "The uniform of the men is quite similar to that of Rhode Island troops, consisting of felt hats, dark blue blouse and mixed blue pants."[124] During December 1861, this regiment was clothed in French uniforms produced by the Paris military outfitter Alexis Godillot, sole manufacturer for the French Army, and imported by the Federal Quartermaster's Department.[125] A report in the *New York Times* stated, "Early in the spring, M. Godillot had sent to Washington a copy of his large book of uniforms and military outfits, and the order was made by Gen. [Montgomery C.] Meigs, of the Quartermaster's Department."[126] Eager to find additional sources of clothing for his already overstretched department, Meigs placed an order on August 9 for 10,000 complete suits, plus accoutrements and equipage, which were based on the 1860-Pattern *chasseurs á pied de la ligne*, or light infantry, dress and fatigue uniforms, with the intention of eventually clothing the entire Union army in this manner. Upon arrival, these uniforms were issued as a first step to the five best drilled regiments, as chosen by Maj. Gen. George McClellan, during a review of the division of Gen. Fitz-John Porter, Army of the Potomac, at Bailey's Cross Roads, Virginia, on November 9, 1861.[127] The regiments selected were the 18th Massachusetts, 62nd and 83rd Pennsylvania, plus the 49th and 72nd New York.

At a Grand Review of McDowell's Division on December 20, 1861, the 18th Massachusetts paraded in their new uniforms, which were described as consisting of "natty caps...and small cock-tail fountain plumes; short skirted coatees, with white buttons and yellow trimmings; baggy trousers tucked into gaiters; hairy knapsacks &c."[128] Received as part of the undress were "1,000 fatigue coats," which were actually dark-blue woolen jackets, or *habit-veste*, fastened by a single row of nine pewter buttons. With tight sleeves closed at the wrist by two small buttons, they had a belt loop support on the left at the waist, as did their dress jacket.[129] Fatigue head gear consisted of a *bonnet de police*, or dark-blue pointed and tasseled cap with light yellow piping and embroidered hunting horn at front. These European uniforms proved generally too small for the average-sized American soldier, and were left with the Quartermaster's Department at Georgetown, Virginia, when McClellan finally began offensive operations on March 10, 1862.

The 19th Massachusetts left Boston on August 28 wearing "the regular army uniform of blue blouses, gray pantaloons and blue forage cap."[130] Shortly after arrival in Washington, DC, this regiment received "dress coats, with brass shoulder scales and leather neck stocks." One volunteer remarked that when not in line or on guard duty "the spare moments of the men were spent in cleaning the brasses."[131] A recruitment notice placed in the *Pittsfield Sun* on August 1, 1861, stated that the 20th Massachusetts would wear "the US Uniform."[132] Encamped at Lynnfield, the 22nd Massachusetts (Senator Wilson's Regiment) were uniformed and armed on September 25, 1861, and left for the seat of the war wearing "light blue overcoats" and "army hats." One company of sharpshooters wore "a suit of grey, with grey overcoats," and carried "Kentucky rifles," while the remainder of the regiment was armed with Enfield rifle muskets.[133] During the same month, the 27th Massachusetts was issued with "a navy-blue coat and 'blouse,' light-blue pants and overcoat, with a black felt hat."[134]

On September 30, 1861, the state advertised for proposals to furnish "three thousand military uniform Overcoats, Frock Coats, Blouses, Pantaloons, Fatigue Caps, and three thousand pairs of Shoes, of the kind, style and quality required by the United States Government; to be delivered one thousand per week."[135] This contract would have been sufficient to clothe the 28th through 30th Massachusetts, and was probably mostly completed by Whitten, Hopkins & Co., who supplied 5,150 "Infantry Coats" and 15,736 pairs of "Infantry" trousers; and Pierce Bros. & Co., who produced 5,210 coats and 6,831 pairs of trousers.[136]

Formed during August 1861 with members of the Boston Light Artillery as its cadre, the 1st Battery, Massachusetts Light Artillery, was supplied with a fatigue uniform consisting of "a blue blouse, [and] gray pants."[137] "Havelock hats" of the type patented by Jonathan F. Whipple and produced by his Seamless Clothing Manufacturing Company of New York City, were worn by several Massachusetts units that took part in Gen. Benjamin Butler's New Orleans expedition, including the 4th Battery, Massachusetts Light Artillery, commanded by Capt. Charles H. Manning, and Read's Mounted Rifle Rangers.[138] Made of a seamless piece of light-blue felt, this headgear had a brim or "cape" running around the back and sides for the protection of the back of the head and neck, while a leather visor covered the front and kept the hat in shape. Recruited by Capt. S. Tyler Read, the Rifle Rangers received their "Havelock hats" with brass letters "MRR" at front, plus overcoats, on November 28, 1861.[139] The *Boston Evening Journal* of December 31, 1861, reported, "They carry heavy sabres and short rifles [or Sharps carbines], and are to be provided with revolvers beside. The uniform, without being showy, is a very superior and imposing feature of the equipments, and reflects great credit upon Pierce Bros. & Co., of this city, by whom it was manufactured. The overcoats are of dark blue cloth, the collars being trimmed with green cord. The jackets are trimmed green, and the shoulders mounted with brass scales."[140] Organized into two "divisions" or companies, the Mounted Rifle Rangers were initially attached to the 30th Massachusetts Infantry, but were merged into the 3rd Massachusetts Cavalry on January 2, 1862, and served with Gen. Benjamin Butler in Louisiana.[141]

During December 1861, Thomas G. Colt of the Pollock Guard (Co. D), 10th Massachusetts, wrote home, "You have no idea what a change six months in the United States service has wrought in the condition of the regiment. The dirty grey uniform that we wore on Hampden Park has been changed to the regulation blue blouse, pants and cap. New frock coats are being made up for us in Massachusetts, when they arrive the regiment will look finely."[142] The frock coats referred to were possibly some of those being made by D. H. Brigham & Co., of Springfield, Massachusetts, who had received a contract to produce 10,000 "army uniform coats" during the previous month. Merchant tailor James M. Tagert, of Pittsfield, had been contracted to make "artillery jackets and uniform coats" at the same time.[143]

This unidentified Massachusetts volunteer wears the uniform of the Mounted Rifle Rangers, a unit recruited in the Boston area for "outpost duty" during September and November, 1861, being armed with "the rifle and sabre." He wears the light-colored Havelock hat with brass letters "MRR" at front, as produced by the Seamless Clothing Manufacturing Company of New York City, plus dark-blue mounted service overcoat with green trim around the collar, supplied by Pierce Bros. & Co., of Boston. The Mounted Rifle Rangers received their headgear and overcoats on November 28, 1861. *Ninth-plate ambrotype—author's collection.*

Having a lengthy coastline that was felt might be threatened by Confederate gunboats or privateers, the volunteers of Massachusetts produced a naval force, albeit company-sized. First proposed on April 16, 1861, by Robert B. Forbes, a prominent Boston ship merchant who had made his fortune with the opium and China trade, the Coast Guard was recruited among the Boston Marine Society plus those who had "the ability and taste for an occasional cruise for the defence of the coast."[144] Commanded by Forbes, who gave himself the rank of commodore, the Coast Guard acquired a navy blue uniform on June 12, which consisted of "plain jackets and pants, with blue cloth cap and a band, with the name of the company thereon in gilt letters." Additionally, this was described as "navy blue pants, coat and cap, with the 'Coast Guard' button."[145] They were armed with "Sharpe's breech-loading rifled carbines [sic] and sabres," plus "four Dahlgren howitzers," which they were reported to have dragged along with their "carbines slung upon their backs."[146] As such, the Coast Guard was "equally well adapted to artillery warfare on land or sea." For the latter service, they had four launches "severally named as follows: No. 1, Morris; No. 2, Hull; No. 3, Decatur; No. 4, Perry." By June 29, the unit consisted of eighty men, not including officers, many of whom had seen service in the merchant marine.[147] Earlier, on June 16, they were presented with a flag described as a "handsome banner, bearing upon one side an eagle with the words 'Coast Guard'" and upon the other the state arms with the motto "Non sine Causa."[148]

By June 13, 1861, Forbes had offered the services of the Coast Guard to both the navy and war departments advising that he could not afford to continue financing the unit. As both Secretary of the Navy Gideon Welles and Secretary of War Simon Cameron refused his offer, he disbanded the Coast Guard on July 12, despite a successful voyage south to Nantucket Island, advising his men that he "should now take leave of them for awhile, till such time as government shall need them." Many of the Coast Guard probably enlisted in the US Navy.[149]

Worn by 29-year-old George W. Taylor, of South Danvers, Massachusetts, this "Havelock"-style hat is based on that originally designed in June 1861 by Chicago hatter James M. Loomis, and patented in New York by J.F. Whipple in July 1861. Made of blue-gray felt, it is an unusual combination of cap and brimmed hat, with the brim cut away at the front and a leather visor added in its place. The felt brim is edged with narrow, black silk tape and it has a leather band and chin strap at the base of the crown. It has the metal numeral "4" attached to the front of the crown, below which "MASS. BATTERY" has been inked in block letters. On its two-inch high sweatband is a gold embossed trademark in the form of an eagle on shield with the lettering "Seamless Clothing Mfg. Co." arced above and "Patd. July 16, 1861" in a scroll below. Working as a "shoe maker," Taylor enlisted as second lieutenant in the 4th Massachusetts Independent Battery on November 27, 1861. He received promotion to first lieutenant on September 17, 1862, and was a captain by the war's end. *C. Paul Loane collection.*

MASSACHUSETTS
Order of Battle, 1861

Massachusetts Volunteer Militia (MVM) (Three-months' Service)

1st Battalion Riflemen (Poore's Battalion)	4th Regiment	6th Regiment
2nd Battalion Riflemen (later expanded into the 43rd MVM or Tiger Regiment)	4th Battalion Infantry (expanded into 24th Volunteer Infantry)	8th Regiment
3rd Regiment	4th Battalion Riflemen (expanded into 13th Volunteer Infantry)	Boston Light Artillery (Cook's Battery; 1st Battery Light Artillery)
3rd Battalion Riflemen (Deven's Battalion)	5th Regiment	

Volunteer Infantry

1st Infantry	13th Infantry (see 4th Battalion Riflemen)	23rd Infantry
1st Infantry Battalion (later expanded into 32nd Infantry)	14th Infantry (converted into Heavy Artillery)	24th Infantry (New England Guards Regiment)
1st Company Sharpshooters (Andrew Sharpshooters)	15th Infantry	25th Infantry (Worcester County Regiment)
2nd Infantry	16th Infantry (Middlesex County Regiment)	26th Infantry
2nd Company Sharpshooters	17th Infantry	27th Infantry
7th Infantry (Bristol County Regiment)	18th Infantry	28th Infantry (2nd Irish Regiment; Faugh a Ballagh Regiment)
9th Infantry (1st Irish Regiment)	19th Infantry (see 1st Battalion Riflemen)	29th Infantry
10th Infantry (Western Regiment)	20th Infantry	30th Infantry (Eastern Bay State Regiment)
11th Infantry (Boston Volunteers)	21st Infantry	31st Infantry (Western Bay State Regiment; later 6th Cavalry)
12th Infantry (Webster Regiment)	22nd Infantry (Senator Wilson's Regiment)	Massachusetts Battalion (expanded into 29th Massachusetts)

Volunteer Artillery

1st through 7th Independent Batteries of Light Artillery

Volunteer Cavalry

1st Cavalry

Mounted Rifle Rangers (later merged into 3rd Cavalry)

Bearskin caps were a popular form full dress headgear in 1861—and particularly in Massachusetts. Several companies of the 8th MVM wore them when mustered-in during April of that year. The man at top was a member of the Lawrence Light Infantry who enlisted for three months' service as Co. I, 6th MVM. Not identified to a specific company, the volunteer at bottom with typical Massachusetts combination of white shoulder belt and black waist belt proudly wears his bearskin cap for the photographer. *Sixth-plate ambrotype—Liljenquist collection, Library of Congress LC-DIG-ppmsca-38351/under-sized quarter-plate tintype—Author's collection.*

RHODE ISLAND

On April 15, 1861; the War Department informed William Sprague, the "Boy Governor" of Rhode Island, that the quota for his state in answer to the presidential call for 75,000 militiamen in defense of the Union would be one regiment of thirty-seven officers and 743 men. However, Sprague had already made an offer to Abraham Lincoln of "a force for the protection of the capital," so that contingency plans were already in place. Within two days, he was able to report to Secretary of War Simon Cameron that the regiment was organized on the original basis, adding, "We are using every exertion to be first in the field." Upon arrival at Providence, former commander of the state militia Ambrose Burnside, then resident in New York and treasurer of the Central Illinois Railroad Company, accepted command of the regiment. On April 18, Sprague telegraphed Cameron stating, "Our troops are leaving in detachments today. Will be pushed forward as rapidly as transportation can be obtained. One thousand men fully armed and equipped."[1] As a result, the first regiment left for Washington in two detachments totaling 1,096 men on the 20th and 24th, being transported by steamers from Sandy Hook, New Jersey. The first detachment consisting of 544 officers and men was accompanied by Col. Burnside and Governor Sprague, while the second detachment travelled under Lt. Col. Joseph S. Pitman and Maj. Joseph P. Balch.

Taken from the rooftop of a building on Steeple Street, Providence, this photograph by Gorham & Co. shows crowds lining the sidewalks on April 24, 1861, as the second detachment of the 1st Rhode Island Detached Militia forms up opposite the railroad station in Exchange Place prior to marching through the main streets of the city to Fox Point, from where it departed via steamer *Empire State* for Washington, DC, Gilmore's Cornet Band stand at the head of the column. *Rhode Island Historical Society—RhiX31692.*

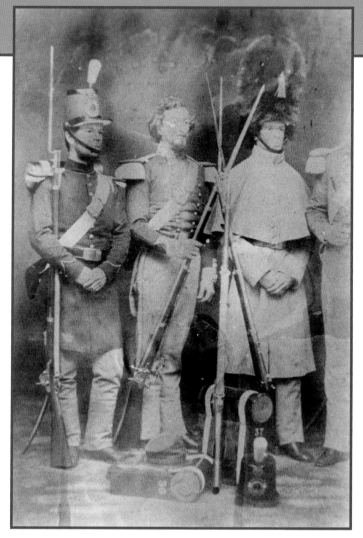

The First Light Infantry, of Providence, wore a bearskin hat and scarlet tail-coat with light-blue collar decorated with gold loops, plus light-blue cuffs and skirts, and buff facings. Pantaloons were also light blue with white seam stripes. Other dress included a Pattern-1858 dark-blue uniform coat and cap with numeral "1" set in a "sunburst" plate. Note the fatigue cap placed on the knapsacks. This unit provided companies C and D for the 1st Rhode Island Detached Militia in April 1861. According to a report in the *Providence Evening Press* on April 16, 1861, this corps would enlist in their "own fatigue dress, overcoats and knapsacks, with the gray, regulation pants furnished by the State." *Copy prints—Michael J. McAfee.*

As Rhode Island lacked a full militia regiment prior to the Civil War, the ten companies that formed the 1st Regiment, Detached Militia were drawn from various existing companies of volunteer, or active, militia, as it was known in that state. This included such colorfully clothed units as the First Light Infantry, Woonsocket Guards, and Newport Artillery.[2] Known as "regimental companies," these company-strength chartered corps consisted of colonels and full regimental staffs, and some company members were wealthy businessmen or "gentlemen of leisure" with ancient pedigrees. Although not normally impressed by such matters, Lincoln's private secretary John Hay commented, "When men like these leave their horses, their women and their wine, harden their hands, eat crackers for dinner, wear a shirt for a week and never black their shoes, all for a principle, it is hard to set any bounds to the possibilities of such an army."[3]

After service in the Mexican and Frontier wars, Indiana-born Ambrose E. Burnside (1824-81) resigned from the US Army in 1853 to manufacture firearms in Bristol, Rhode Island, where he developed the Burnside breech loading carbine. Although the Army purchased about 900 of his carbines, Burnside went bankrupt and turned over his patent rights to creditors in 1860. A major general of Rhode Island Militia from 1855 through 1857, he became treasurer of the Illinois Central Railroad in 1861, and was resident in New York when he accepted command of the 1st Rhode Island Detached Militia in April 1861. According to a report in the *Milwaukee Sentinel* dated April 25, when asked how long it would take him to make himself ready for command, he replied, "One minute." In response, the newspaper commented, "That is the right sort of a "minute man" to command a Rhode Island regiment." Burnside later commanded a brigade at First Bull Run and led a successful expedition against coastal installations in North Carolina. Reluctantly accepting command of the Army of the Potomac on November 7, 1862, he was removed from that post following his failure at Fredericksburg during December 1862 and the "Mud March" fiasco of January 20–22, 1863. He remained in the army in a subordinate position and, by 1864, commanded the IX Corps, Army of the Potomac. His support for the abortive mine operation of July 30 of that year led to his final resignation on April 15, 1865. Having chosen the pattern of uniform supplied to the 1st Rhode Island, his own pullover hunting shirt, or blouse, cost $3 to make and had a double-breasted placket front. His plain gray trousers cost $4.50. The blouse worn in this well-lit image has a short placket and patch pocket set high on the left breast. Note the absence of rank insignia. Made of fairly coarse cloth, it may well have been a "prototype" for the garment worn by the rest of the regiment. The brim of his hat has been pinned up with what appears to have been a Union cockade. *Carte de visite without backmark—Michael J. McAfee collection.*

Also lacking militia uniform regulations in 1861, the state required a regimental service dress for the 1st Rhode Island Detached Militia within a few days, and the responsibility for this task fell on Ambrose Burnside. Based on experience in his youth as a tailor's apprentice, and also patterned on the hunting shirt favored by the Continental Army during the Revolutionary War as service or field dress, Burnside suggested a blue wool garment, which would be both practical and simple to make. This consisted of a blouse with falling collar and placket front opening, which was double-breasted for field and staff officers and single-breasted for line officers and enlisted men. This was closed by three small brass state buttons, and also had a breast pocket closed by a single button of the same type. Cut full and gathered at the cuff, sleeves were also fastened by a single button.

This blouse and trousers were worn by Edward Newton Whittier at First Bull Run on July 21, 1861. Born in Maine in 1843, 17-year-old Whittier was a student residing in Providence, Rhode Island, when he enlisted as a sergeant in Co. C, 1st Rhode Island Detached Militia on April 17, 1861. He was detailed for hospital duty on June 28, and mustered-out on August 2. Reenlisting as a first sergeant in the 5th Maine Light Artillery Battery on December 21, 1861, he was promoted second lieutenant on September 23, 1862, first lieutenant on June 13, 1863, and brevet captain on October 19, 1864. He commanded the battery on Culp's Hill at Gettysburg in July 1863, and was awarded the Medal of Honor for gallantry at Fisher's Hill, Virginia, in 1864. Newton was mustered-out at Augusta, Maine, on July 6, 1865. He qualified as a doctor after the war and worked at the Harvard Medical School. He died at Boston, Massachusetts on June 14, 1902. Made by the ladies of Providence from cloth purchased in Boston, Massachusetts, his blouse was fastened by three small brass flower-pattern buttons on the placket, and has one button of the same type on the gathered cuffs. A pocket was originally attached to the left breast. The infantry-pattern gray trousers have "frog pockets" open at the side and fastened by black-painted metal buttons. The same type of button secures the fly and serves to attach suspenders. *www.historicalimagebank.com.*

The blouse worn by Burnside in this image, photographed on another occasion, has a longer placket front and shoulder straps indicating the rank of colonel. Once again he appears to have a Union cockade pinned to his hat. He holds an 1850 Staff and Field Officer's Sword, and his sword belt is fastened by an 1851-Pattern "eagle-wreath" plate. *Carte de visite by "E. Anthony, 501 Broadway, New York, from Photographic Negative in Brady's National Portrait Gallery"—author's collection.*

In order to produce this garment, 4,223 yards of blue flannel was purchased by the state on April 16, 1861, at a cost of $2,006.46. Cloth sufficient to make 1,000 blouses for the 1st Rhode Island was rushed to the clothing store of Henry A. Prescott in Providence and the local ladies were advised, "The work must be done by tonight."[4] According to a news report published four days later, work on blouses to be worn by the first detachment of the regiment was undertaken by "the ladies of the Mathewson and Chestnut Streets Methodists, the Westminster Congregational, First and Second Universalists, Beneficent Congregational and Grace Church congregations. The garments were taken to the several vestries, and the ladies assembled there to do the work."[5] Writing on April 19, one of those involved commented in a letter to her children in Albany, New York, "To describe the scenes of yesterday is impossible. Indeed we have no time for words, nor even for thought—only for action. We, the ladies of Providence, made a thousand blue flannel tunics for the Infantry yesterday."[6]

The shirts for the second detachment of the 1st Rhode Island were made under similar circumstances on April 23.[7] Meanwhile by April 18, the same style of uniform for two more regiments had been produced by the Boston firm of Macullar, Williams and Parker, who filled an order for "11,000 pairs of pants, 3,000 flannel shirts, and 15,000 pairs of drawers for the use of Rhode Island troops."[8]

Blouses worn by officers of the regiment varied in style, either because they were made by different tailors throughout the city, or their wives made them and added personal touches. That worn by Ambrose Burnside consisted of a plain pullover pattern with double-breasted placket front, while those made for some of the other officers had varying numbers of pleats each side of the breast and opened completely at the front. Trousers made for all ranks by the Boston firm were of gray wool with a homespun weave.

Procured from the "hat manufactory" of Charles W. Bowen and Benjamin F. Pabodie, which was at 11 Arcade on 72 Broadway, Providence, full-dress headgear for enlisted men consisted of a black felt hat that resembled the Pattern -1858 US Army hat, but had a taller crown and curled brim. Referred to at the time as a "Kossuth hat," its brim was pinned up on the left side with a brass eagle insignia. Silver company letters were also pinned to the crown at the front.[9] On April 18,

Photographed in Providence (possibly outside Railroad Halls) on return from their three-months' service on August 2, 1861, Burnside and staff wear a variety of different styles of hunting shirt. Seated at center, Burnside, plus Maj. Joseph P. Balch seated second from left, and the officer stood second from right, wear the plainer version. Standing at far right, Capt. William Lloyd Bowers, Commissary officer, plus the officer seated at right, wear the pleated style with broad-falling collar. Standing to the right of the tree, Lt. Isaac P. Rodman, Aide-de-Camp, wears the single-breasted blouse designated for company-grade officers. Seen standing at left, Sgt. Maj. John F. Shaw wears a blouse with open front. *Library of Congress LC-USZC4-6316.*

Joseph Pope Balch (1822-72) was a druggist in Providence, Rhode Island, when he was appointed major of the 1st Rhode Island Detached Militia in April 1861. Previous experience within the Marine Corps of Artillery, and as commander of the Second Brigade, Rhode Island Militia, put him in good stead, and he acquitted himself well when he took command of the 1st Rhode Island following the promotion of Burnside to brigade commander. At First Bull Run he was recognized for "coolness, steadiness, and courage under fire," and was promoted by brevet to brigadier general of volunteers. When the regiment was disbanded, Balch returned to the militia and commanded the Second Militia brigade until the close of the war. Possibly photographed at the beginning of his three-months' service, Balch wears an extremely long hunting shirt, and also appears to have a Union cockade pinned to his dress hat brim. A holstered Colt Army or Navy revolver is attached to his waist belt. *Carte de visite—Michael J. McAfee collection.*

This image is tentatively identified as Surgeon Francis L. Wheaton, Field & Staff, 1st Rhode Island Detached Militia. Wheaton was mustered-out with the rank of major, and reenlisted as surgeon with the 2nd Rhode Island Volunteers. He wears a field and staff officers'-style, pullover hunting shirt with double-breasted placket, forage cap with 1858-Pattern gold bullion horn insignia and silver numeral "1" inset. His sword belt also supports a cap pouch to accommodate a revolver. Note his white-patent footwear with dark leather toe cap and quarter piece. *Carte de visite— Michael J. McAfee collection.*

Cyrus G. Dyer was a 29-year-old agent for the woollen mill at Belleville in North Kingston, Washington County, Rhode Island, when he enlisted as a first lieutenant and quartermaster in the field and staff of the 1st Rhode Island Detached Militia on April 17, 1861. On June 25, he resigned and was appointed captain of Co. A, 2nd Rhode Island Infantry. During October 1862, he was promoted major in the 12th Rhode Island, and in February 1864 was given command of Co. A, 26th US Colored Troops. He was mustered-out on August 28, 1865. Dyer wears an elaborate line officer version of the hunting shirt with broad-falling collar and six pleats either side of a single row of a ten-button single-breasted front. His full-dress headgear consists of a fur felt hat with black ostrich feather plume, which is pinned up at right with what is probably an 1858-Pattern "eagle" plate. *National Archives 528374.*

Author of the regimental history of the 1st Rhode Island Detached Militia, plus numerous other works, Augustus V. Woodbury was born in Beverly, Massachusetts, in 1825. He prepared for the sophomore class of Harvard University, at Phillips' Exeter Academy, New Hampshire, and entered the Divinity School, Harvard University in 1846, from which he graduated in 1849. He was ordained into the Unitarian Ministry in 1849. Pastor of the Second Congregational Church in Lowell, Massachusetts, from 1853 to 1857, he took up his position within the Westminster Congregational Society, Providence, Rhode Island, in 1857 and remained there until his death in 1892. Appointed chaplain of the 1st Rhode Island Detached Militia in April, 1861, he served as an aide on the staff of Burnside and took an active part in the action at Bull Run. He was appointed Chaplain-in-Chief of the Grand Army of the Republic in 1873 and 1874. Woodbury wears a company-grade hunting shirt and holds a plain chasseur-pattern forage cap. *Carte de visite with pencil inscription on reverse, "Chaplain Augustus V. Woodbury, 1st RI Regiment"—Anne S. K. Brown Collection, Brown University, Rhode Island.*

James H. Chappell wears a pullover version of the line officer hunting shirt with placket fastened by four small ball buttons, and a fifth button at the neck. This is embellished with a pocket on the right lower breast, plus an inside pocket higher on the left breast. An example of the small enamelled pin worn by several officers and bearing the inscription "Gov. Sprague & The R.I. Boys" is attached to the latter. He holds an M1850 Foot Officers' sword. Chappell was a twenty-four-year-old watchmaker resident in Newport, Rhode Island, when he enlisted as second lieutenant in the Newport Artillery (Co. F), 1st Rhode Island Detached Militia, on April 17, 1861. He was mustered-out on August 1, 1861. *National Archives—111-B-3992.*

Charles Bowen informed the *Providence Daily Journal* that "the girls employed in trimming them would not complete the job" until five o'clock the next morning. Dress hats for officers were made of fur felt, with the brim pinned up with either brass eagle or leather cockade, and often sported black feather plumes. For fatigue wear, enlisted men wore blue chasseur-pattern forage caps with metal company letter attached at front. Officers wore what later became known as the McDowell-style cap with tall crown and 1858-Pattern "looped" horn insignia at front.

Issuance of the first batch of uniforms on April 19, 1861, was described by the *Providence Daily Post*:

A busy scene was enacting at Mr. Prescott's store on Weybosset Street, throughout the day. It was there that the uniforms and clothing were given out, and detachments from each company were marched over there, when to each man was delivered the blue outside shirt, grey pants, red blanket, and under-garments. They were then marched to Bowen & Pabodie's, in the Arcade, when each obtained a black felt hat, with the brim fastened up on one side and the American eagle mounted thereon. The blankets have each a hole in the center for the head, and are worn in day time in place of coats.[10]

The undergarments supplied to each man consisted of "two cotton checked shirts, one undershirt, two pairs of socks, two pairs of white drawers."[11]

The press provided numerous other descriptions of the uniform received by the 1st Rhode Island. On April 17, the *Providence Journal* stated that it consisted of "Gray pantaloons, blue tunic, and a black hat with cockade and feather."[12] The *Newport Mercury* of April 27, 1861, reported more fully, "The uniform of the Regiment consisted of the regulation hat, a loose blue blouse, and gray pantaloons. A plain leather belt around the waist sustains the cartridge box, and the bayonet. The officers are distinguished by a small gold strap on the shoulders; they wear a sash and a long sabre, and a revolver supported by a plain belt." Observing the regiment en route to Washington, the Annapolis correspondent of the *New York Times* wrote:

This war is destined to create an entire revolution in uniforms. What looks very pretty on parade is very absurd when men have to cut their way through. The Rhode Islanders, under Sprague, are perfect in this respect. They wear a simple blue flannel shirt, with soft hat and plume, and a red blanket. It is picturesque in the extreme, and eminently easy for a fight.[13]

When the regiment passed through Baltimore on June 10, 1861, the *Sun* reported, "All the soldiers, without a single exception, wore the white linen Havelock [over their fatigue caps], a much recommended protection against the sun."[14] At the capital, the Washington correspondent of the *Utica Herald* reported, "Col. Burnside's Rhode Island regiment elicits universal admiration. Its simple uniform of gray pants, dark blue hunting shirts, Kossuth hats, and white cross belts, seems better adapted for service than the more elaborate dress of the New York regiments."[15]

Moses B. Jenkins was a wealthy resident and landowner of Providence, Rhode Island, when he enlisted in the Mechanic Rifles No. 2 (Co. H), 1st Rhode Island Detached Militia on April 17, 1861. According to a report in the *New York Tribune* dated April 22, 1861, he destroyed his ticket for "a passage to Europe that he might remain to fight in defence of the flag of his country." He was mustered-out on August 2, 1861. His white-cotton haversack is stencilled with "MB JENKINS/RI REGT." *Carte de visite— Michael J. McAfee collection.*

Upon arrival in Washington, DC, on April 24, 1861, Pvt. Frederic M. Sackett, Co. D, 1st Rhode Island Detached Militia, wrote home, "If I can get leave from quarters on Monday I am going to see if I can find a place where they take card visites [*sic*]—If so I am going to put on all my traps and have my picture taken as near as possible to the way I looked when I reached this city. Of course, the dirt and fatigue will not be there, but still it will give an idea of our condition." This unidentified enlisted man of Co. D, 1st Rhode Island is in "marching order." Based on the inscription beneath the photograph, he appears as Sackett describes, as he would have done en route to Washington, DC. The metal letter "D" is pinned to the crown of his hat. His pullover hunting shirt has a falling-collar and large patch pocket on the left breast. His tin-drum canteen is suspended from a cord and he is armed with a US M1855 rifle musket with fixed bayonet, and has a small pocket-model revolver attached to his belt, which is fastened with a plain rectangular brass plate. Rolled and slung on his back, his red blanket is supported by a leather sling. *Carte de visite—Michael J. McAfee collection.*

Photographed at the Washington, DC, studio of Matthew Brady, William S. Smith, Co. C, 1st Rhode Island Detached Militia, wears a state-issue forage cap with metal letter "C" at front, and pullover blouse closed at the neck with three small metal buttons down the placket, and a patch pocket low on the right breast, closed by a single button. This also has a falling collar, gathered cuffs, and skirts slit at the side. Tucked in his belt is one of the small revolvers presented to the regiment on April 30, 1861. Smith reenlisted as a first lieutenant in Co. D, 10th Rhode Island Infantry on May 26, 1862 and was promoted a captain on June 9, 1862. *Carte de visite by Brady/ Washington—Michael J. McAfee collection.*

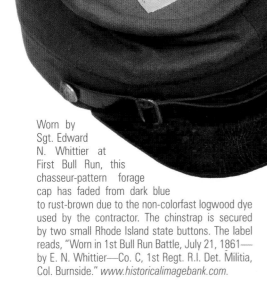

Worn by Sgt. Edward N. Whittier at First Bull Run, this chasseur-pattern forage cap has faded from dark blue to rust-brown due to the non-colorfast logwood dye used by the contractor. The chinstrap is secured by two small Rhode Island state buttons. The label reads, "Worn in 1st Bull Run Battle, July 21, 1861— by E. N. Whittier—Co. C, 1st Regt. R.I. Det. Militia, Col. Burnside." *www.historicalimagebank.com.*

In use since the mid-seventeenth century, the Rhode Island device used on buttons and breast plates consisted of an anchor with the motto "HOPE" in a scroll set within a rococo frame. This two-part convex example with "Scovill" back mark was the hat or sleeve size button. *The Civil War Relicman.*

Accompanying them to the federal capital, Governor Sprague wore "the same fatigue dress" as his troops. On May 11, 1861, a *Utica Herald* correspondent stated that he had just returned from "a dress parade of Col. Burnside's regiment in front of the Patent Building," and that they were "now marching down Pennsylvania Avenue—Gov. Sprague in his blue shirt and Kossuth hat at their head—to the music of the Providence band."[16] On an earlier date, the correspondent of the *Chicago Evening Journal* observed, "With the exception of the epaulette, yellow plume and sword, his dress is the same as the soldiers."[17] During the same period the *Philadelphia Press* reported, "Sometimes Governor Sprague appears, and then there is a commotion among the ladies, for the young Executive of Rhode Island is the pet of the petticoats here, with his long, yellow plume gracefully dancing over a neatly fitting uniform."[18]

Photographed at Greencastle Point, Rhode Island, in June 1861, three members of Co. F, 1st Rhode Island Detached Militia, proudly wear their red poncho blankets. Seated at left, Pvt. Charles E. Lawton holds a dress hat with brim pinned back with 1858-Pattern eagle. He later served in the Field & Staff, 5th Rhode Island Heavy Artillery, as a first lieutenant on enlistment and regimental quartermaster on mustering out. At center is Pvt. John S. Engs who mustered-out in June 1861 as sergeant major. Seated at right is Ensign James H. Chappell, whose dress hat bears an 1821-Pattern cap insignia. *Copy print—Michael J. McAfee.*

Instead of providing the regiment with overcoats, the state purchased 553 scarlet blankets with "black bar near the edge," at a cost of $5.50 per blanket, which totaled $3,041.50.[19] Carried diagonally on the soldier's back and suspended from a leather strap, these were slit at the center by order of Burnside, so that they could be worn as a cloak or poncho. The latter alteration was completed on April 19 by "the ladies of the city" who met at "the vestries of the 1st and 2nd Universalist, Mathewson Street Methodist and Congregationalist churches to prepare the blankets."[20] In a letter of the same date, "a lady in Providence" advised "Today we are to make a thousand blankets, with holes in the centre, to be worn instead of overcoats."[21] Regarding the wearing of this item, a correspondent of the *New York Evening Post* wrote that each man had "a light scarlet blanket, which they wear with inimitable grace, pinning it in the shape of a coat, with a skill unobtainable to ordinary mortals."[22]

As the first detachment of the 1st Rhode Island left New York after transfer to the steamer *Coatzacoalcos* for the last part of their voyage to the federal capital, they were described by a *Times* reporter as being "gathered upon the upper deck, and each with his red blanket on his shoulders."[23] This item was clearly not popular with some volunteers, as one man wrote home, "Our supply of one blanket to serve as overcoat and bed-quilt, places us at times very much in the position of the man with one shirt, which he wanted washed. I understand that the regiment is soon to be supplied with overcoats, which will allow us to keep our blankets exclusively for night service in the bunks."[24] On April 20, 1861, the *Providence Evening Press* added, "The blankets were all red, except 100 blue ones for the band and officers."[25]

The first indication that vivandieres were to be attached to the 1st Rhode Island occurred on April 20, 1861, when the *Providence Daily Journal* reported that "several ladies" had signified to one of the surgeons "their readiness to go to the aid of the Rhode Island Regiment should any hospital services be required."[26] As the second detachment of this regiment left Providence aboard the steamer *Bienville* on April 24, 1861, Kady Brownell "stood out prominent upon the upper deck, and received much attention from all."[27] On May 4, the *Newport Mercury* commented that several ladies, later confirmed as being Kady F. Brownell, Maria

F. Strahan, and Sarah Beasley, had indeed volunteered to "come and attend the sick and wounded. Two of them wear the uniform of the French Vivandieres, and they march in the rank of file closers of their company. They attract much attention."[28]

Describing the dress of one of these vivandieres on arrival of the regiment in Washington, DC, a correspondent of the *Chicago Evening Journal* stated, "She dresses in the regimental pants and shirt, over all having a loose petticoat of red flannel. Her head dress consists of a little blue cap slashed with gold lace."[29] As the 1st Rhode Island marched out of "Camp Sprague" en route for Harpers Ferry on June 3, 1861, it was accompanied by "the daughters of the regiment...dressed in their blue tunics and red skirts."[30] Earlier, when the 1st Rhode Island was sworn-in at the federal capital on May 2, "the three *filles du regiment*," were not permitted to swear allegiance to the Union. Later that evening, vivandiere Sarah Beasley married the first corporal of the Mechanic Rifles, 1st Company (Co. G), with regimental chaplain Augustus V. Woodbury conducting the service, on which occasion the *Providence Daily Evening Press* reported that she "appeared at the Avenue Hotel with her comrade Charles Tibbets, and took the nuptial oath of allegiance...wearing her regimentals—a jacket of cherry-colored satin, improper-to-mentions [or pantaloons] of blue silk, made in full Turkish style, and a hat with white plumes—[tipped] with red, blue and white colors of our Union."[31] On May 17, a correspondent of *The Press* of Philadelphia, observed, "The daughter (now the young bride) of the regiment is a heroine. Her history has yet to be made, but it will honor her sex. Her ivory-handled bowie-knife, under her belt, is near a heart to prompt and a hand to use it, should occasion require."[32]

When the 1st Rhode Island received orders to return home at the end of its three-month period of service on July 25, 1861, the well-worn "war suits" of the 1st Rhode Island Detached Militia were described as consisting of "tattered tunics, dilapidated hats, more than one garnished with bullet holes, muddy trowsers, and leather scows, by courtesy called shoes, slit here and there to ease the chafe ..."[33] When the regiment reached Providence three days later, the *Daily Post* reported, "At the head of Company G, marched Miss Martha [sic] Strahan, in the costume of a Vivandiere, carrying an American flag, of silk, and at the head of Company H, marched Miss Kitty [sic] Brownell, similarly attired, and also carrying a flag."[34] Many years later, Kady Brownell was described by her husband as having "a uniform very much like that worn by the men consisting of a blue blouse, a red skirt to the knees, and gray

KADY BROWNELL

Although supposedly born in a tent in a British army camp in Caffraria, South Africa, of a French mother and Scottish father, Kady C. Brownell was listed in the 1860 US census as being born in Scotland. According to the former version, her father was Col. George Southwell and she was named for her father's friend, Sir James Kady. As her frail mother died shortly after her birth, she was adopted by Duncan and Alice McKenzie, and migrated to America via New Orleans, following which she moved north to Providence, Rhode Island, where she was raised by family and friends. In the early 1860s, she worked in the mills of Providence where she met and fell in love with Robert S. Brownell. With the start of the Civil War, Robert enlisted in the Mechanic Rifles No. 2 (Co. H), 1st Rhode Island Detached Militia, and Kady was determined to follow him to war. Leaving for the front with the second detachment of the regiment, she became one of several vivandieres attached to the 1st Rhode Island. This hand-colored period photograph of an original albumen has the instructions for the colorist written in pencil on the reverse, and shows Kady wearing the blue tunic and red skirt over gray trousers worn by "the daughters of the regiment" in 1861. *Albumen print—author's collection.*

Resident in Providence, Rhode Island, 28-year-old Walter B. Manton was a bookkeeper when he enlisted in the Providence Artillery (Co. B), 1st Rhode Island Detached Militia as a private on April 17, 1861. On June 9, he was commissioned a lieutenant in the company of carbineers organized as a separate corps within the regiment. Armed with .54 caliber Burnside carbines, this company served as skirmishers at the head of the column in line of march. Manton was mustered-out on August 2, 1861. He reenlisted as a second lieutenant in Co. L, 3rd Rhode Island Heavy Artillery on February 11, 1862, and was finally mustered-out at Hilton Head, South Carolina, on October 25, 1862. Headgear consists of a privately purchased forage cap, later known as a McDowell-style cap, with 1834-Pattern hunting horn insignia attached. His pleated blouse apparently opened at the front and has shoulder straps commensurate with his rank attached. He holds an M1851 foot officer's sword with waist belt fastened by an 1851-Pattern officer's eagle-wreath plate. In "marching order," his carbine is slung over his shoulder with barrel down. His red blanket is also rolled and slung. Accoutrements consist of a spheroid canteen on white cloth strap and oil-cloth haversack. *Carte de visite*—Michael J. McAfee collection.

trousers under that. She wore a sword and had her hair cut short...half of the people thought she was a boy, and the rest wondered what on earth she was."[35]

The 1st Rhode Island received up-to-date weapons compared with other early war militia regiments. Seven companies were armed with US M1855 rifle muskets, while three companies received the US M1855 rifle. According to a report in the *Providence Journal*, some of these weapons were part of a "thousand muskets" that arrived from Springfield, Massachusetts, on April 23, 1861.[36] Most of the men were also provided with a revolver after arrival in Washington, DC. According to a letter from an unidentified "Volunteer" published in the *Daily Post*, "The revolvers presented by the citizens of Providence were this day distributed. With but few exceptions every man is now armed with one of them. Many carry them in holsters, but the favorite method is to attach a cord to the stock and wear them in the breast, ready for instant use."[37] However, an order issued on May 18, stated that all revolvers and Bowie knifes carried by enlisted men should be handed in, and "left in some safe place, properly labelled."[38]

Col. Burnside also arranged for the state to purchase eighty M1856 carbines of his own patent from the Bristol Fire Arms Company at a cost of $35 each, and these were issued to six men in each company who had proven to be the best marksmen. On June 9, 1861, these men were organized as a separate "Company of Carbineers," who marched at the head of the regiment and served as skirmishers.[39] After the 1st Rhode Island was mustered-out in August 1861, the Burnsides were issued to the "First New England Regiment of Cavalry" which contained two battalions of Rhode Island troopers. (See below.)

According to Pvt. Frederic M. Sackett, Co. D, en route to Washington, DC, each man had about "seventy pounds of baggage" on his back, plus "loaded musket, revolver, powder and shot."[40] Regarding accoutrements, the 1st Rhode Island was equipped with metal drum-style canteens, white cloth haversacks, and knapsacks of unknown pattern. The former were made by W. H. Fenner & Co., who "furnished 1,300 canteens" by April 20, 1861.[41] Waist belts were black leather with plain rectangular brass belt plates. In a letter dated June 12, 1861, Cpl. Louis W. Chase of the same company stated, "We had on our backs two large blankets, knapsacks filled with wearing apparel, canteen of water, knapsack filled with rations for two days, forty rounds of ammunition, besides a musket."[42]

When the "Carbineers" were organized in June 1861, the men of that company were supplied with distinctive star-pattern belt plates. Each man also wore a cloth patch in the shape of a carbine horizontally on both upper sleeves. At the beginning of June, the 1st Rhode Island received 1,000 sets of standard federal-pattern accoutrements from E. A. G. Roulstone, a military goods dealer in Boston. According to the diary of Pvt. William R. Arnold, cap boxes were distributed to Co. C on May 6, and "new haversacks" were issued on July 7, 1861.[43]

The 1st Rhode Island was eventually joined at the federal capital on May 7, 1861, by the Providence Marine Corps of Artillery, which had left the state for Washington on April 18 aboard the steamer *Empire State* bound for Jersey City, from which place it received orders from the War Department to proceed to Easton, Pennsylvania, to receive guns.[44] Originally chartered in 1801, the Marine Artillery was led by Capt. Charles H. Tompkins, who would be appointed to command the 1st Regiment Rhode Island Light Artillery on September 13, 1861. The Marine Artillery had been able to depart from Providence so promptly in April due to the exertions of Quartermaster George H. Smith, who had placed its caissons, battery wagons, and other materiel in complete order during the winter of 1860-61.[45] According to the *Providence Journal* of April 24, 1861, which cited the *Springfield Republican*, of Massachusetts, the six James rifled cannon received by the Marine Artillery were "made to the order of the State of Alabama" in October 1860, but were not delivered because "the State seceded."[46]

Also attached to the 1st Rhode Island was a two-man observation balloon detachment, consisting of aeronaut James Allen, of the Marine Artillery, and

These two enlisted men of the "Company of Carbineers," 1st Rhode Island Detached Militia, wear a cloth patch in the shape of a carbine horizontally on both their upper sleeves. The man at right also has a star-pattern plate fastening his waist belt, and both have their distinctive red blanket rolled and slung over their shoulders. They are armed with M1856 carbines patented by their commanding officer Ambrose Burnside and produced by his Bristol Fire Arms Company. They carry their .54 caliber rounds in what appear to have been 1839-Pattern cartridge boxes. *Collection of the late Herb Peck Jr.*

Both the 1st and 2nd Rhode Island regiments had elements of the Marine Artillery attached to them. The first company of Marine Artillery left Providence on April 18, 1861, and proceeded to Easton, Pennsylvania, where it remained for ten days during which its smooth bore guns were exchanged for 12-pounder James rifled cannon. This battery was mustered-into federal service on May 7 and was mustered-out on August 6, 1861, following which it was reorganized as Battery A, 1st Rhode Island Light Artillery. The second company became Battery B of the same regiment. As both units were issued state clothing, this unidentified artillery sergeant may have belonged to either unit. He wears a plain, pullover hunting shirt with dress hat, and carries an M1840 Light Artillery saber in an iron scabbard. *Carte de visite—Michael J. McAfee collection.*

William H. Helm, of Co. C of the regiment. Although they were put out of action before the Rhode Islanders fought at Bull Run, the two gas-filled, oiled-linen balloons accompanying these men were the first example of a military balloon being used by American troops on active service.[47]

Described as wearing "a blue uniform" when it arrived in New Jersey,[48] the Marine Artillery also received the state's distinctive hunting shirt, black felt hat, and poncho-style blankets, its "uniforms and equipments" being supplied after it had left Rhode Island for Pennsylvania.[49] On April 23, the *Providence Evening Press* reported that, after arrival in Easton, it "went in a body to the house of Gov. [Andrew H.] Reeder, (of Kansas [Free-State] fame)...to receive their blankets, which the ladies of Easton had kindly volunteered to make into ponchos, by a pattern."[50] The Marine Artillery was also supplied with fatigue caps as, when they

Residing at Bristol, Rhode Island, William J. Bradford enlisted for three years as a corporal in the Warren and Bristol Company (Co. G), 2nd Rhode Island Volunteers, on June 5, 1861. He was promoted to sergeant major on July 24, 1862, and first lieutenant and adjutant on March 20, 1863. He was again promoted to full aide-de-camp to General Wheaton on November 15, 1863, and to acting adjutant on June 5, 1864. He was mustered-out on June 17, 1864. Placed on the chair, his dress hat is looped up with an 1821-Pattern cap insignia and has the numeral "2" pinned at front beneath the letter "G." The manner in which his 1858-Pattern fatigue cap is slung from the button securing his pocket is reminiscent of a militia style of wearing fatigue headgear "slung" from the coat tails. *Carte de visite—Michael J. McAfee collection.*

This unidentified enlisted man of the 2nd Rhode Island Infantry also wears a well-worn example of the plain enlisted man's hunting shirt with large pocket set low on right breast. Photographed after his regiment had received federal-issue equipment, his cartridge box is suspended on a federal-pattern sling with an "eagle" breast plate. He holds a US M1855 rifle musket with sling and bayonet. *Carte de visite—Michael J. McAfee collection.*

passed through Baltimore during the first week in June, the *Sun* reported, "The men wore the linen Havelock, and though the day was hot, didn't suffer materially."[51]

Organized in response to Lincoln's call for three-year enlistments issued on May 3, 1861, the 2nd Rhode Island Volunteer Infantry was commanded by Col. John S. Slocum, who had been major of the 1st Rhode Island Detached Militia. Slocum would be wounded in the head and ankle at Bull Run and die two days later in captivity. The state's first three-year unit, the 2nd Rhode Island was formed at "Camp Burnside" on the Dexter Parade and Fair Grounds, in Providence. The ladies of the city commenced making blouses for this regiment "at several of the churches" on May 13 and, with "twelve sewing machines put in requisition," the work was completed within two days.[52] However, the regiment did not begin to receive them until the end of the month.[53] Prior to the departure for "the seat of war," the Bristol County Volunteers (Co. G), 2nd Rhode Island, were reported to be wearing "the Rhode Island Regimental uniform, blue tunics, gray pants and army felt hats" on June 11, 1861.[54] According to Cpl. Elisha Hunt Rhodes, who enlisted in the First Light Infantry, which provided part of Co. D, their clothing consisted of "the so-called 'Rhode Island blouse,' grey pants, and hats looped up at the side.[55] On June 6, the *Providence Daily Post* reported that a "sufficient number of Havelocks" had been furnished "by the ladies for the entire regiment."[56] Nine days later, the same newspaper advised, "The men now wear their linen Havelocks while drilling. In addition to these all are supplied with water proof ones for wet weather."[57]

The 2nd Rhode Island was initially issued converted muskets. Elisha Hunt Rhodes recalled, "Three ball cartridges were issued to each man in the railroad cars, and as we had the old style of flint-lock gun, altered to percussion, we found each cartridge to contain three buck shot in addition to the ball. Most of the men carried revolvers, although strict orders had been issued against the practice. In the search, which was made by officials for concealed weapons, I managed (as most of the boys did) to save mine from capture."[58] With the expiration of its three-month period of service, the 1st Rhode Island exchanged arms with the 2nd Rhode Island on July 25, 1861. As reported by a member of the former regiment in the *Providence Daily Journal*, "The Second regiment was drawn

This youthful volunteer of the 2nd Rhode Island Infantry wears the plain enlisted man's pullover hunting shirt, fastened with three small brass buttons on its placket front. His plain blue cap of "the Rhode Island Militia pattern" rests on the table by his side, and an oval 1839-Pattern "US" plate fastens his belt. *Ninth-plate ambrotype produced by "Geo. C. White, Ambrotype and Photograph Rooms—659 Washington Street, Boston—author's collection.*

According to the diary of Pvt. William R. Arnold, both the 1st and 2nd Rhode Island were photographed in camp on July 14, 1861—two days before McDowell's army began its march toward Manassas Junction. Possibly taken on that occasion, this image shows a group of the 2nd Rhode Island Infantry with three enlisted men in light marching order. Two wear blanket rolls and all three hold M1816 or M1822 conversion muskets at "order arms." Accoutrements include oil-cloth haversacks and various canteens. The man at right has what appears to be a small filter canteen suspended at his front, while the man at left carries both cloth-covered "bullseye" canteen and small tin drum version. The volunteer at center, plus several others in the group, has the numeral "2" pinned to the front of his cap. *National Archives—111-B-5324*.

Also probably photographed on July 14, 1861, these enlisted men of either the 1st or 2nd Rhode Island wear a variety of headgear. The man at left wears a Pattern-1858 forage cap, while the man seated at center has a civilian-brimmed hat. The man at right has a Pattern-1821 army or militia "eagle" insignia attached to the front of a fez or camp cap. The young soldier lying on the ground was probably a musician. *National Archives—111-B-5344.*

up in the grove before the tents, and by the uncertain light of a lantern we exchanged arms with them, company by company, giving them our superior Minie muskets, receiving in return their somewhat antiquated smooth-bores, which they used with such deadly execution on the field."[59]

Although the state clothed the 2nd Rhode Island, its equipment was furnished by the federal government. Following its departure from Providence on June 19, 1861, the *Newport Mercury* reported, "each soldier carried on his back a knapsack containing his 'kit,' which weighed from twenty to twenty-five pounds. The muskets each weighed thirteen pounds. Besides these men carried haversacks, canteens and cups, making altogether no easy burden for so warm a day."[60] Following action at First Bull Run, in which it sustained ninety-eight killed, wounded and missing, including Col. Slocum among the former, the 2nd Rhode Island was issued "new pants, and those who needed supplied with new blouses" on August 28, 1861.[61]

During the fall of 1861, the 2nd Rhode Island received new uniforms patterned on US army regulations. On October 27, Elisha Hunt Rhodes recorded in his diary, "New dress coats were issued today, but as all the companies did not receive them we did not wear them at dress parade. I still like the Rhode Island blouse the best, as it is loose and more comfortable."[62] Although of regulation pattern, the frock coats received lacked piping on collar and cuffs.

Upon organization at Camp Ames during August 12–16, 1861, the 3rd Rhode Island, commanded by Col. Nathaniel W. Brown, and initially containing several all-Irish companies, including the Jackson Guards, Emmett Guards, and Montgomery Guards, was also issued with blue blouse, gray pants, and blue cap of the Rhode Island Militia pattern. Following its departure from Providence on September 7, 1861, this regiment was ordered via New York to Fortress Monroe where, during

October, it laid aside its state clothing, except for fatigue duty, and "drew blue pants and coats, and donned the genuine regulation fatigue caps common to most of the troops." Their arms were "the old style Springfield rifles," or US M1842 smoothbore muskets.[63] This regiment was reorganized as the 3rd Rhode Island Heavy Artillery at Hilton Head, South Carolina, on December 19, 1861.

Organized at Camp Greene, on the Pawtuxet River, during September 1861, the 4th Rhode Island was reported on September 14, 1861, to be wearing "the blue tunic [or hunting shirt] at present, as a fatigue dress, and blue pants," although it was to be "fully uniformed in accordance with US Army Regulations."[64] On October 16, 1861, 1,000 overcoats were forwarded from Providence to Washington, DC, for this unit.[65]

Recruitment for the five-company "Burnside Rifle Battalion," which was expanded into the 5th Rhode Island Infantry and mustered-in on December 27, 1862, began in Providence during November, 1861.[66] Armed with short Enfield rifles with sword bayonets, this battalion was issued blue hunting shirts and blue caps, and was re-organized into the 5th Rhode Island Heavy Artillery in July 1863.[67]

A second volunteer company of the Marine Artillery, commanded by Capt. William H. Reynolds, was mustered-in for three years on June 6, 1861. Attached to the 2nd Rhode Island Infantry, this unit was later in the year redesignated Battery A, 1st Regiment Rhode Island Light Artillery. Between August 1861 and January 1862 seven more batteries of light artillery were organized to form this regiment, all of which are believed to have received state clothing. When Battery B was mustered-in on August 13, the men were issued Rhode Island uniforms that Sgt. John H. Rhodes described as consisting of:

> pantaloons with a piece on the inside of the leg down to the knee. They were called reinforced pants. An outside shirt or tunic, which came down to the knee, was called a blouse. A high felt hat with one side turned up, a brass eagle pinned on to hold it, with brass cross cannon in front completed the outfit. They were distributed regardless of size or fit which gave the boys the appearance of a gang of Chinaman rather than gallant defenders of their country.[68]

Especially reinforced in the seat for light artillery service, the trousers were originally an almost black logwood-dyed jean cloth, but subsequently faded to a light tan after prolonged exposure to sunlight.[69]

By November 1861, the 1st Rhode Island Light Artillery had received an additional uniform from the state. This included a short, nine-button jacket, piped in red, with Rhode Island buttons, which was based on the US Army uniform jacket prescribed for issue to all mounted men since 1854. Also issued were sky-blue trousers and dark-blue forage caps. Some men continued to wear their hunting shirts until they were completely worn out.[70]

Organized at Pawtucket from December 1861 through March 1862, and the original idea of Governor Sprague, the "First New England Regiment of Cavalry" contained two battalions of Rhode Islanders, and one of New Hampshire troopers. Commanded by Col. Robert B. Lawton, of Rhode Island, this unit was issued with "a uniform of the United States regulation pattern," and was armed with sabers, Colt revolvers, and the Burnside carbine, which was later replaced by the Sharps carbine.[71]

Among the Rhode Island Militia not organized into active service in 1861, the home guard of the Newport Artillery, the bulk of which volunteered for three-months' service as Co. F of the first regiment, was reported on May 18 to be having "new uniforms made—the former, tunic and pants such as is worn by the R. I. Regiment in Washington, and a blue Zouave cap." These uniforms were worn for the inauguration of Governor Sprague on May 26, 1861. The Old Guard of this unit adopted "gray coats, black pants and gray cap" at the same time.[72] On July 2, the Providence Horse Guards paraded for the first time in a new service uniform consisting of "blue frock coats with cavalry button, and blue pants, regulation hats with plumes, and cross sabres in front." The *Daily Post* added, "The coats and pants are trimmed with yellow cord and braid."[73] The Home Guard paraded at Pawtucket on May 31, 1861, wearing a "dark blue tunic, gray pants with side stripe, and gray forage cap."[74]

Following the suggestion that "a corps of Zouaves" be formed in Providence on April 22, 1861,[75] the Burnside Zouaves were organized on June 11, with Col. S. Smith Wells in command. On July 18, the *Providence Daily Post* advised that the uniforms of this corps were being made and were to consist of "blue jackets, trimmed with orange, red pants, white caps and drab gaiters." Eight days later, the Zouaves made their first excursion to Smith's Palace.[76] Parading to receive the 1st Rhode Island on its return to Providence on July 28, the Burnside Zouaves were reported in the *Daily Journal* as wearing "loose flowing scarlet trousers, yellow stripes down the side." The jacket was "of blue with yellow trimming," and the cap was "white, and made in the usual military style."[77] This uniform was further described in a later regimental history as "a blue jacket, trimmed with orange, full red pants, gathered at the ankle, with a drab gaiter, a blue mixed undershirt, faced with red, and a white foraging cap, trimmed with red."[78] This company eventually served for three months in 1862 as one of the newly formed "National Guard" units that made up the 10th Rhode Island and performed garrison duty receiving instruction in heavy artillery drill until its muster-out on August 25, 1862.

Although heavily tinted, this *carte de visite* of an enlisted man of the Burnside Zouaves, identified by the pencil inscription "Johnnie Stone," shows the double seam stripes on the pantaloons, which would have been yellow, plus high drab gaiters originally issued to this company. Headgear seems to have varied within this company, as this man wears a red fez with yellow tassel. *Carte de visite without back mark—Michael J. McAfee collection.*

Sgt. J. B. Gardner wears the "flowing red pants" and light blue trimmed orange/yellow jacket of the Burnside Zouaves as adopted in 1861. His undershirt is "blue mixed" cloth with a red plastron-style front. He holds a forage cap with white top and red band, and has an ornate militia-pattern NCO's sword and scabbard. *Carte de visite with pencil inscription—Michael J. McAfee collection.*

RHODE ISLAND
Order of Battle, 1861

Active Militia (Three-months' Service)	Volunteer Infantry	Volunteer Artillery
1st Regiment Detached Militia	2nd Infantry	1st Regiment Volunteer Light Artillery
Providence Marine Corps of Artillery	3rd Infantry (later converted into 3rd Heavy Artillery Regiment)	3rd Rhode Island Heavy Artillery
	4th Infantry	**Volunteer Cavalry**
	5th Battalion Infantry (Burnside Rifle Battalion)	1st Regiment Cavalry, two battalions (First New England Cavalry)
	6th Infantry (failed to organize)	

8th N. H. Regim

NEW HAMPSHIRE

Found in a trunk with other militia items from Keene, New Hampshire, this image shows an unidentified volunteer a few days after his enlistment in April/May 1861. Many volunteers were gifted revolvers by fund-raising groups, and this man is holding what appears to be a .22 caliber Smith & Wesson pocket revolver. Based on a pattern dating to 1828, his cap with cockade was popular with fire companies on the eve of Civil War, and may indicate he was also a volunteer fireman at the time of enlistment. *Ninth-plate ruby ambrotype—author's collection.*

The Granite State provided one infantry regiment of thirty-seven officers and 734 men in April 1861. Although a well-established volunteer militia existed in New Hampshire, Governor Ichabod Goodwin felt he did not have the right to require them to serve the federal government, so new companies of volunteers were recruited that rendezvoused at Camp Union, on the Fairground near Concord, and the organization of the 1st regiment progressed rapidly. According to a reporter for the *New Hampshire Statesman*, of that city, an examination was made by a surgeon "as to the quickness of sight and hearing of each soldier. Each one shows his hands, and uses the muscles of his limbs, that any defects may be noted. Attention is also paid to the capacity of his lungs."[1]

Clothing for the first volunteers of the 1st New Hampshire became an immediate necessity. As early as April 22, the ladies of Keene, New Hampshire, had provided the state authorities with "shirts, flannels, bandages, etc."[2] On May 2, the *New Hampshire Sentinel*, of the same township, reported that the first company of volunteers assembled at Concord were in "a destitute condition for underclothes,

These unidentified privates, who may have been brothers, wear the gray dress uniform provided for both the 1st or 2nd New Hampshire Volunteers by the state quartermaster in May 1861. The man at left seems to be seated in order to show his unusual "spike-tail" coat off to best advantage. Their chasseur-pattern caps had red bands, and the high standing collars and closed cuffs of their coats were trimmed with narrow red cord. Trousers were plain gray. *Sixth-plate ruby ambrotype—author's collection.*

Red trim and facing color on coat and cap is much in evidence in this full-length view of an enlisted man of either the 1st or 2nd New Hampshire. Also clearly seen is the "spike-tail" on his coat. As the two regiments were originally issued M1842 smoothbore percussion muskets, the unaltered M1816 flintlock musket he holds at "Parade-rest" must have been a photographer's prop. *Sixth-plate ambrotype— Daniel J. Binder collection.*

Posing for the photographer at "Order arms" with their M1842 smoothbore percussion muskets, these unidentified enlisted men of either the 1st or 2nd New Hampshire display to good effect the Cadet Grey uniforms made in Boston, Massachusetts, by clothiers Whiting, Galloupe, Bliss & Co., and Whitten, Hopkins & Co. Note the absence of trim on the cuffs of the man on the left, which may have been lost if he had to shorten the length of his sleeves. It may also indicate a lack of uniformity within clothing provided for these early war regiments. *Sixth-plate ambrotype—courtesy of Ron Swanson.*

not having carried a change, which they should have done. The ladies will send to Concord such articles as our soldiers will need...such as shirts, drawers, stockings, shoes, and pants, they will be forwarded to them immediately."[3]

Meanwhile, Joseph Carter Abbott, the state adjutant general, advertised contracts for uniforms and equipment. On April 26, 1861, the *Sentinel* advised that this would consist of a "Cadet gray coat and pants, gray overcoat, gray fatigue cap, two flannel shirts, one pair flannel drawers, one extra pair of socks, one pair of shoes and one large camp blanket. They will probably be armed with the plain percussion musket. The other equipments to be furnished them are cartridge-box, scabbard, cap box, an Indian Rubber knapsack, haversack and canteen, and utensils for cooking and eating."[4] The coat, pants, and overcoats of "grey military cloth" for both the 1st and 2nd New Hampshire Volunteers were made by Whiting, Galloupe, Bliss & Co., and Whitten, Hopkins & Co., of Boston, at a cost of $7 for the coat and pants combined, and $7.87 for the overcoats.[5] Both regiments began to receive their uniforms around the same time, although by mid-May some elements of the 1st Regiment were still not in receipt of theirs, which resulted in about 400 of them refusing to drill.[6] Following a visit to

George R. Tower was an 18-year-old farmer's son at Walpole when he enlisted for three-months' service in the Cheshire Light Guards, Co. A, 2nd New Hampshire, on April 25, 1861. Not mustered-in, he re-enlisted in the same unit for three-years' service on May 22, but was discharged for disability at Washington, DC, on July 16, 1861. The square-cut collar and lack of red cord trim on his nine-button coat, plus shoulder straps, is unusual, and may indicate it was "home-made," or possibly not made by the Boston suppliers. *Ninth-plate ambrotype—author's collection.*

This unidentified private of either the 1st or 2nd New Hampshire wears an example of the gray overcoat made in Boston, Massachusetts, by Whiting, Galloupe, Bliss & Co., and Whitten, Hopkins & Co. With its elbow-length cape and single-breasted five-button front, this garment was based on the pattern of 1851 infantry overcoat. *Carte de visite without back mark—Michael J. McAfee collection.*

Buttons worn by New Hampshire militia units depicted the state seal showing the frigate *Raleigh* being built for the Continental Navy at Portsmouth, around which is the designation "New Hampshire" and "Vol. Militia." According to the back mark, this two-part coat button was produced by the Scovill Manufacturing Company, of Waterbury, Connecticut. *The Civil War Relicman.*

Concord, New Hampshire, a correspondent of the *Boston Evening Transcript* reported that the men of the 1st New Hampshire were "uniformed in cadet grey—dress coat, pants and fatigue cap, with dark grey overcoat."[7] On May 10, Martin A. Haynes, who enlisted in Co. I, 2nd New Hampshire, wrote:

> The regiment is now uniformed—the queerest-looking uniform in the world. You have probable [*sic*] seen some like them in the streets of Manchester, on the First Regiment boys. The suit is gray throughout, with light trimming of red cord. The coat is a "swallow-tail," with brass buttons bearing the New Hampshire coat-of-arms; a French army cap to top off with.[8]

In his history of the 2nd New Hampshire, Haynes further described this uniform as "gray, the jaunty forage caps and "spiketail" dress coats banded with red cord."[9] According to an anonymous member of the 1st Regiment, the remainder of his unit had received their uniforms by May 17, on which date he wrote, "We got our uniforms today. The cut of the coat is 'swallow-tail.' Caps, small, gray, military, with a red stripe around them."[10]

Although pre-existing tailed coats were worn into Civil War service by a few older militia companies in the North, those of the 1st and 2nd New Hampshire represent two of only three examples of coats specially fabricated for a whole Union regiment at the behest of a state quartermaster (the third regiment being the 1st Vermont Volunteers). Unusual and old-fashioned, these dress coats had plain tails without turn backs or pocket flaps, but were trimmed around the high-standing collar, and the closed cuffs, with narrow red cord, and had a single row of six, and in some cases nine, yellow metal buttons bearing the state coat of arms consisting of the frigate *Raleigh* on the stocks, next to a rising sun, with "NEW HAMPSHIRE" above, and "VOL. MILITIA" below.

The remainder of the uniform worn by the 1st and 2nd New Hampshire was made in-state, as well as in Boston, Massachusetts. One thousand gray chasseur-pattern caps with red bands were supplied by George A. Barnes, a merchant based at Manchester, New Hampshire, who acquired them from S. Klouse & Co., of Boston.[11] Although photographic evidence indicates that many men wore buttons bearing the state coat of arms on their cap fronts, an intoxicated man accused of being "a scallawag in the regiment" was stripped of his uniform, including "the letters on his cap," on June 14, 1861.[12]

Their shirts, drawers, and socks were purchased from Whiting, Galloupe, Bliss & Co. (the firm that made their coats and pants), and B. F. & D. Holden, of Concord, New Hampshire. According to receipts dated May 4, 1861, the former were made from blue flannel.[13] Described as being of gray wool when the regiment reached Washington, DC, blankets were provided by Pierce Brothers & Flanders of Boston. Shoes were supplied by George M. Herring of Farmington, and Charles C. Mooney of Alton, New Hampshire; George L. Thayer & Co. of Boston; and by the workshops at the New Hampshire State Prison.[14]

Regarding accoutrements and equipage, the musket slings, cartridge boxes, percussion cap pouches, scabbards and belts, received by the 1st New Hampshire were made by James R. Hill of Concord, New Hampshire. The "India rubber" knapsacks, "rubberized" haversacks, and canteens were obtained from Haughton, Sawyer & Co., of Boston, and Horace H. Day, of 91 Liberty Street, New York.[15]

Both the 1st and 2nd New Hampshire regiments were also issued with blue-flannel fatigue blouses, or 1857-Pattern four-button sack coats. Regarding the 1st Regiment, Col. Mason W. Tappan inserted an appeal in the *Statesman* dated May 18, 1861, stating:

> one thousand flannel blouses are absolutely indispensable for the comfort and safety of the soldiers. These articles are light, and, in a warm climate, will take the place of the thick uniforms with which the regiment is now provided. They will cost about three thousand dollars, and we confidently appeal to the people of New-Hampshire to furnish this sum at once...All donations should be forwarded without delay to the Colonel, as the Regiment will leave the State in a few days, and the blouses must be had the present week.[16]

On arrival in Washington to join the ranks of Co. F, 1st New Hampshire in late May 1861, Pvt. Thomas L. Livermore received his uniform,which consisted of "a blue blouse, gray trousers, and gray cap with a red band."[17]

Having sent their gray dress coats "forward to Washington" possibly after having had them re-sewn (see below), the 2nd New Hampshire was reported to be wearing "blue stuff loose jackets, with a brass plate in the centre, bearing the New Hampshire arms," when they marched through Boston on their way to the capital.[18] The *National Republican* reported them uniformed in "gray caps and pants and blue jackets" on arrival at the federal capital.[19] The officers of both regiments were required to provide their "own uniforms and other equipments."[20]

As their regiment marched through Boston, Massachusetts, on their way to Washington on June 20, 1861, the officers of the 2nd New Hampshire were described as wearing "blue cloth frock coats, and the Colonel and his staff wore regulation cavalry hats, Kossuth style, with black plume."[21] Company officers wore red French-style forage caps, or kepis, with gold rank lace, with the regimental number within an infantry bugle horn at the front. The 1st New Hampshire was accompanied by a group of about "20 female and laundresses" dressed in "dark clothing" consisting of "gray travelling dresses and straw flats."[22]

The two regiments were armed with M1842 smoothbore percussion muskets. On April 23, the state adjutant general complained to Secretary of War Cameron about these weapons, and asked the federal government to furnish 2,000 of the "latest pattern of the rifled [*sic*] muskets." A week later Cameron was obliged to reply, declining the request, and the 1st New Hampshire had to make do.[23] However, a limited number of better weapons were purchased for the 2nd New Hampshire. The regimental historian noted, "Nine companies were armed with smoothbore muskets, caliber 69, carrying 'buck and ball'—a most efficient weapon for close work. The 'Goodwin Rifles' (Co. B) were armed with Sharps rifles—breechloaders—which had been provided by the subscriptions of citizens of Concord....The muskets were exchanged, soon after the first Bull Run battle, for Springfield rifled [*sic*] muskets."[24] As the other flank company of the regiment, the Cheshire Light Guards (Co. A) were provided with Enfield rifle muskets. According to a report in the *New York Tribune* after the arrival of the 1st New Hampshire in New York City, nearly every man in this unit had been "presented with revolvers by their friends on their departure."[25]

The 1st New Hampshire left for Washington on May 26, 1861, accompanied by "a band of music," and "about eighty horses, sixteen baggage wagons, and one hospital wagon, containing tents, provisions, and hospital stores and instruments."[26] The regimental band was Baldwin's Cornet Band of Manchester, formed in the summer of 1860 from a more informal group of music students who had employed Edwin T. Baldwin as instructor. Baldwin's band had served its apprenticeship in the employment of the local Republican committee, furnishing music for parades and political meetings during the presidential campaign. Most of its members were also excellent singers and doubled as vocalists to provide entertainment for the regiment.

On May 27, the 1st New Hampshire was the first regiment to pass through Baltimore on its way to Washington since the attack by the mob on the 6th Massachusetts. In a display of bravado, the band led the way down Baltimore's Pratt Street proudly playing "Yankee Doodle" with Fife Maj. Francis "Saxie" Pike clearing the way with his baton. The crowd was somewhat annoyed, but the band was backed by a thousand loaded muskets.[27] According to Thomas L. Livermore, who enlisted in Co. F of the regiment, Pike wore "brilliant light-blue trousers well striped, a double-breasted blue broadcloth coat with broad 'fishbones' of gold slashed from button to button in front, a black skin shako towering, with its peacock's feather, two feet or more above the six of the wearer."[28]

Assigned to Gen. Robert Patterson's Army of the Shenandoah, the 1st New Hampshire had its baptism of fire at Conrad's Ferry in June, and after a march to Maryland and back to Virginia, returned home, being mustered-out at the expiration of its three-month term on August 9, 1861. A three-year regiment, the 2nd New Hampshire served in the Washington defences from June 20 through July 16, and formed part of Burnside's Brigade, Hunter's Division, Army of Northeastern Virginia, during First Bull Run, following which it "marched from the field in good order."[29]

The uniforms and shoes made for the 1st New Hampshire were worn out after over two months of campaigning and marching in Maryland, and Virginia as part of the Army of the Shenandoah under Gen. Robert Patterson. Recalling the period of encampment at Martinsburg, Virginia, July 8-15, 1861, regimental historian Stephen Abbott wrote:

> The clothes of the men, which were poor at best, had become much worn, and they were almost shoeless. What new pants they had were distributed, but not a pair of shoes could be found. Necessity, the mother of invention, came to the rescue. Lieut. George W. Colbath [Co. A], of Dover, at this writing warden of the State prison at Concord, was detailed to head a force. In a very brief space of time, leather, thread, awls, and hammers were collected; pegs were made with pocket knives; benches were extemporized, shoes were mended, and the men's feet were made comfortable for a time. Many were the shifts to which they resorted to cover their nakedness. In one case, three of the boys found a strip of cloth on which was painted: "Pies and Cakes," which was converted into three patches for

Bearing the company letter "F" on the front of his dark brown "Havelock hat" made by Purinton & Ham, of Dover, New Hampshire, this unidentified volunteer of the 3rd New Hampshire was probably recruited at Nashua, New Hampshire, as was most of his company. His accoutrements include a gutta percha canteen, and white-canvas haversack stenciled with "NH" and "F 44." The latter indicated his company and "rack number," or muster roll number. *Sixth-plate ambrotype—Jeremy Rowe, vintagephoto.com.*

This unidentified corporal of the 3rd New Hampshire wears the "cape," or rear visor, of his hat flipped up. Tucked in his waist belt is either another photograph of himself, or of a comrade from the same regiment who also wears a "Havelock cap." He holds a small pin-fire revolver and Bowie knife. *Sixth-plate ambrotype— Monte Akers.*

their pantaloons. Another made a similar use of a discarded covering of a ham, and appeared on dress parade labelled: "Sugar-Cured Hams for Family Use."[30]

Concerning the same problem with worn-out footwear, Col. Tappan wrote Governor Brown on July 13, 1861, that his regiment had "improved the same problem with worn-out footwear, Col. Mason W. Tappan wrote Governor Brown on July 13, 1861, that his regiment had "improved the time in resting and mending our shoes. Nearly 150 of the men were next to shoeless. It has been difficult to procure any, but I have managed to get here some sole leather and shoemaker's tools, and now...the click of the hammer driving pegs would make you imagine yourself in a Yankee shoemaker's shop instead of a military camp. I have set all the shoemakers in the regiment mending up the old shoes, otherwise one third of the regiment would be barefoot."[31] On return of the 1st New Hampshire to Concord after the expiration of their three-months' service, a local newspaper reported, "The appearance of the regiment is miserable in the extreme. There are scarcely fifty whole pairs of pants...Many are destitute of shoes, and others have their pants worn away up as far as the knee, leaving the leg exposed."[32]

Uniform clothing supplied to the 2nd New Hampshire fared little better. In fact, there were problems even before the regiment left its home state. Appointed to replace Col. Thomas P. Pierce, who resigned his commission on June 4, 1861, Col. Gilman Marston ordered "the uniforms of the whole regiment to be sewed over again."[33] Writing from Camp Sullivan, Washington, DC, on July 7, 1861, John W. Odlin, who served as a musician in Co. B (Goodwin Guards), stated, "The clothes furnished us were miserable, and we present a very interesting array of rags when on dress parade. Looks however will amount to nothing after we pass into Virginia, and so long as the garments hold together we shall be comfortable."[34] By July 20, the uniforms supplied to this regiment were clearly falling apart as, on that date, New Hampshire militia officer Brig. Gen. George Stark advised that its men had been "neglected until their rags prevented their appearance on parade." Since the issue of their original uniforms, this regiment had, he claimed, "not been clothed by the state, except to the extent of a few shoes, and shirts, and, since the extreme hot weather came on, only a general outfit of heavy cape overcoats."[35] The deterioration of its gray dress uniforms by the beginning of July 1861 is a probable indication that the 2nd New Hampshire wore their blue flannel fatigue blouses during the battle of First Bull Run. By September 13, this regiment had been re-uniformed in "the dress of the regular army."[36]

The 3rd New Hampshire was organized at Concord and mustered-in for three years on August 23, 1861. By that time, the state authorities had decided that this regiment, and those that followed, were to be uniformed in New Hampshire cloth, and that "swallow-tail" coats were out of fashion. According to one local press report, the 3rd Regiment was to be dressed in "the uniform prescribed for the regular army" and would be of "blue cloth—frock, pants and coat—with a black felt hat, the rim looped up on one side." However, a letter dated August 27, and published in the regimental history, states that the uniforms received were "grey, and not blue as has been supposed."[37] To be of "a better shade than that of the other regiments," the frock coats and pants worn by the 3rd New Hampshire were of gray doeskin cloth made by the Harris Mill at Harrisville, Cheshire County, and supplied by Lincoln & Shaw of Concord at a total cost of $9,505.[38] Listed as "dealers in clothing" on the "Exchange Block" in the *Concord City Directory* of 1860-61, the firm of John G. Lincoln and Wentworth G. Shaw not only provided the uniforms for the 3rd New Hampshire, but went on to supply the same for the 4th, 5th, and 6th New Hampshire regiments.[39] Those received by the 3rd regiment were "fitted" at the State House, Concord, by Lincoln and Shaw, with the assistance of Nathaniel W. Cumner, who owned a clothing store at Manchester, New Hampshire.[40]

Based on photographic evidence, the frock coats were patterned on the 1854 US Army frock coat with nine-button front, two-button cuff, and rear skirts with two buttons at waist level. Collar and cuffs were plain, although the latter were

The enlisted man of the 3rd New Hampshire in this image holds an M1842 smoothbore musket that must have been a photographer's prop, as his regiment was armed with Enfield rifles. He has a Colt Pocket revolver and Bowie knife with ivory grip tucked in his waist belt. *Sixth-plate tintype—Liljenquist collection. Library of Congress LC-DIG-ppmsca-32055.*

Published in the regimental history, this line drawing shows the style of "Havelock hat" worn by the 3rd, 4th, and 5th New Hampshire volunteers. The front visor was of leather as for a regular forage cap, while the rear brim or "cape" was of the same material as the body of the hat. The crown of the New Hampshire version of this headgear was made of six triangular pieces of cloth sewn together, as opposed to the seamless felt type worn by troops of other states. *The Third New Hampshire and All About It, 1893.*

Identified as a member of Co. D, 3rd New Hampshire by the company letter pinned at the front of his "Havelock hat," this volunteer has a M1849 Pocket Colt revolver tucked in his waist belt. *Sixth-plate ambrotype—Liljenquist collection. Library of Congress LC-DIG-ppmsca-33435.*

Depicting a morning detail armed with picks and spades going to work on the fortifications at Hilton Head, North Carolina, toward the end of 1861, this *Frank Leslie's Illustrated* engraving published on January 25, 1862, shows the 4th New Hampshire wearing "Havelock hats" and overcoats. *Author's collection.*

This enlisted man of the 3rd New Hampshire wears an overcoat made by Abraham Thorpe, of Weare, New Hampshire. He was photographed by Darwin A. Simons, whose daguerreian rooms were at 27 and 28 Smyth's Block, Manchester, New Hampshire. *Ninth-plate ruby ambrotype—author's collection.*

"pointed" as opposed to the "round" cuffs of the tail-coats worn by the first two regiments. Pants were also plain for all enlisted ranks.

Pants were also plain for all enlisted ranks.

Regarding the remainder of the uniform supplied to the 3rd New Hampshire, the overcoats were produced by Abram, or Abraham, Thorpe of Weare, for $7,021.[41] Blue flannel fatigue blouses were procured from Samuel A. & Benjamin F. Haley's Tailoring Establishment of Newmarket, for $3,208; and caps from Purinton & Ham, of Dover, for $1,158.[42] Headgear produced by the latter firm was patterned after that worn by units within other states. Later known as the "Havelock hat," the version worn by New Hampshire troops was, according to the *Statesman*, designed by [Charles F.] Brooks, who was a member of the Military Committee of the Governor's Council.[43] It is possible that Brooks saw an example of the headgear patented by New York hatter Jonathan F. Whipple on July 16, 1861, and produced by the Seamless Clothing Manufacturing Company, which was in turn based on what James M. Loomis had developed in Chicago during June 1861, and copied the idea himself adding seams to the New Hampshire version.[44]

With reference to this headgear, the *Farmer's Cabinet*, of Amherst stated, "Instead of the kepi, the men have a soft-crowned hat of dark brown mixed stuff, with a stiff visor and cape, which seems at once comfortable, and conducive to health, for the rain is shed off behind, instead of being suffered to run down the man's back, in a storm."[45] The *Patriot* of Concord commented, "The cap is black, water proof, and turns down before and behind, so as to keep off both sun and water."[46] When the 3rd New Hampshire passed through Wilmington, Delaware, on September 15, 1861, they were described as wearing "caps of gray-mixed cloth of a peculiar pattern, with vizor in front and rear—a good protection for the back of the neck."[47] Brass company letters were acquired for these caps at a cost of $62.[48] Purinton & Ham went on to provide this style of headgear for the 4th and 5th Regiments. Shoes for the entire 3rd New Hampshire were made at the state prison. Each man was also supplied with "a Poncho rubber blanket with an opening in the centre so that it can be used for a cloak in rainy weather."[49]

Having taken part in the Port Royal expedition under Gen. Thomas W. Sherman during November 1861, the clothing of many of the 3rd New Hampshire was becoming threadbare. According to the regimental historian Daniel Eldredge, the "hard service soon after landing at Hilton Head soon put those grey uniforms into a condition where we'd got to have new uniforms." On November 20, he wrote, "'...to complete the equipment of the regiment requires 936 pairs pants, 936 pairs socks...179 forage caps...' That showed that at that early date our Concord (grey) pants had worn out or that it was extremely desirable that we change to blue." On December 16, he recorded, "Gen. McClellan, Commanding the Army, ordered a change in the uniform. Trousers to be sky-blue mixture for officers and men, the officers to have dark-blue welts, and non-coms, to have dark-blue chevrons." The latter detail indicates that, although their worn out gray trousers were replaced by those of sky-blue, their gray frock coats continued to be worn. Finally, on January 9, 1862, the 3rd New Hampshire assembled for dress parade in their "new (blue) uniforms."[50]

No longer required at the end of the three-month term of service, the leather accoutrements used by the 1st New Hampshire were issued to the 3rd regiment, although according to a report in the *Sentinel*, published in Keene, New Hampshire, any deficiency was made up from "the new lots being rapidly manufactured."[51] Knapsacks acquired were the waterproof duck version of the patent knapsack designed by Joseph Short of Salem, Massachusetts. On September 20, 1861, Governor Nathaniel S. Berry stated, "We have adopted the same Knapsack for our 5th, 6th and 8th Regiments...and can most cheerfully recommend it to the attention of all who are fitting troops for the army."[52] As the rubberized Haversacks carried by the first two regiments were found to "impart a taste of rubber to their contents," those issued to the 3rd New Hampshire were of white canvas. Each man was also issued a "rubber poncho blanket," through which "a man may put his head and use the garment for a rainy day cloak in addition to its usefulness when placed on the ground beneath a tent, to keep dampness from the couch of the soldier."[53] Regarding long arms, the 3rd New Hampshire was issued 1,030 Enfield rifles at a cost of $30,149.[54]

Organized at Manchester, New Hampshire, during August/September 1861, the 4th New Hampshire was the first regiment from this state to receive a blue uniform based on that worn by the regular army. This consisted of "one pair of pants, one dress coat, one blouse, one light gray overcoat, one woollen and one rubber blanket, together with caps, shoes, stockings, woollen shirts and drawers."[55] The dark-blue dress coat and sky-

This recruiting notice requesting volunteers to "FALL IN!" was published in the *New Hampshire Statesman* in Concord, New Hampshire, on August 17, 1861. Edward E. Sturtevant later served as a major in the 5th New Hampshire. *Author's collection.*

David R. Royce, alias Roys, was an 18-year-old farm laborer resident at Claremont, in Sullivan County, when he also joined the ranks of Co. G, 5th New Hampshire on September 6, 1861. Becoming the company bugler, he was wounded at Sharpsburg, Maryland. Reenlisting on January 1, 1864, he was mustered-out at Alexandria, Virginia, on June 28, 1865. Photographed shortly after enlistment in 1861, he poses proudly in an ill-fitting "Havelock cap" and dark-blue frock coat with light-blue-trimmed shoulder straps. *Albumen print—Monte Akers.*

Samuel Brown Little wears the uniform coat and pants made for his regiment by Lincoln & Shaw, of Concord, New Hampshire. Note his collar and cuffs are plain. Resting on the photographer's prop is his "Havelock cap" produced by Purinton & Ham, of Dover. Attached to its front is the brass company letter "G" above a small militia-pattern infantry "looped" Horn with regimental number inset. The long arm carried by his regiment, an M1842 musket stands at his right. Little was born at Newburyport, Massachusetts, in 1828. Resident at Claremont, in Sullivan County, New Hampshire, in 1861, he was a house painter when he enlisted on September 27, and was mustered-in on October 12, 1861, as first sergeant, Co. G, 5th New Hampshire Volunteers. Appointed second lieutenant on August 1, 1862, he was wounded at Antietam, Maryland, on September 17, 1862. Wounded again at Fredericksburg, Virginia, on December 13, 1862, Little died of his wounds at Falmouth, Virginia, thirteen days later. *Carte de visite without back mark— Michael J. McAfee collection.*

This youthful volunteer of the 5th New Hampshire displays on his "Havelock cap" a small Militia infantry die-struck, imitation embroidery horn of non-regulation pattern with numeral "5" inset. His Lincoln & Shaw-produced frock coat is indicated by its wide shoulder straps with trim all around, and plain collar and cuffs. As his regiment was armed with Pattern-1853 Enfield rifle muskets, the weapon he holds must have been a photographer's prop. *Sixth-plate tintype—Liljenquist collection. Library of Congress LC-DIG-ppmsca-31304.*

Most of the officers' uniforms for the first few New Hampshire regiments were made by merchant tailors James D. Kelley and Andrew J. Edmunds, who advertised their business in Merrill & Son's *Concord City Directory for 1860-61. Author's collection.*

blue pants were produced by Lincoln & Shaw from cloth made at the mill of B. F. & D. Holden in West Parish, Concord. The blue blouses worn by the 4th New Hampshire were made by S. A. & B. F. Haley's of Newmarket. Once again of the "Havelock"-pattern, caps were supplied by Purinton & Ham. Overcoats were made by Adams B. Cook of Weare; gray flannel shirts and drawers by Joseph W. Thorpe of Hillsborough; poncho blankets by Warde, Humphrey & Co. of Concord; socks by John Pepper of Holderness, and shoes, once again by the workshop in the state prison.[56]

Regarding equipage, knapsacks were of the waterproof duck version designed by Joseph Short of Salem, Massachusetts; while James R. Hill supplied the belts, cartridge boxes, and cap pouches. This regiment was also armed with Enfield rifle muskets.[57]

The 5th New Hampshire was to be "a Light Infantry Regiment, armed, uniformed and equipped precisely like the Regular Army."[58] Despite a poor experience with Boston-made uniforms for the first two regiments, the state authorities still went out-of-state and contracted with a firm in Portland, Maine, to make the uniforms for the 5th Regiment. Received on October 3, 1861, these were found to be of "an inferior quality and shabby make." As a result, uniforms of not much better quality made by Lincoln & Shaw, and intended for the 6th regiment, were issued to the 5th New Hampshire.[59] Enlisting as a first sergeant in this unit on October 12, 1861, Thomas L. Livermore recalled, "Our company was given the letter 'K,' and a uniform consisting of brogans, light-blue trousers and overcoat with cape, and dark-blue blouse and frock coat…." He described the "Havelock hat" as "a helmet-like structure of…waterproof cloth, with visor before and behind, the top resembling a squash, and the whole lined and padded, I think. This was the New Hampshire cap, and although it would do in a row to keep blows from the head and was good to protect the neck from rain, yet in summer it was a sweltering concern."[60]

The frock coats received by this regiment, plus the 4th, 6th and 8th New Hampshire, were made of "shoddy" flannel. Unlike the Pattern-1854 frock coat worn by the regular US army, they were devoid of trim around collar and cuffs, but had sky-blue edging all around shoulder straps, which were an additional feature. The surviving example worn by John Currier, Co. F, 6th New Hampshire, has a poorly cut collar that does not "slope up and backward at an angle of 30 degrees," as prescribed for a Pattern-1851 coat. Although the cuffs are closed, they had two small buttons for decoration, and cuff seams were straight rather than pointed. Based on the officers' version of the Pattern-1861 coat, the pockets in the folds of the rear skirts had small buttons at top and bottom. Each pocket also had an unusual curved flap to which the lower button was sewn.

Made by merchant tailors Lincoln & Shaw, of Concord, this frock coat was worn by 53-year-old John Currier of Langdon, in Sullivan County, New Hampshire, who was a farmer when he enlisted as a fifer in Co. F, 6th New Hampshire on October 14, 1861. Made from "shoddy" flannel, it is poorly cut and plain, except for sky-blue cord around the shoulder straps, which are hidden under brass shoulder scales. The buttons on coat front, shoulder straps and cuffs are of General Staff pattern with "Scovill Manufacturing" back mark. The narrow sleeves are enclosed at the cuff, and have two small buttons for decoration only. The body lining is brown, polished cotton and that in the skirts and collar is dark green, possibly faded from black, polished cotton. Currier was promoted to principal musician on November 30, 1861, and was mustered-out on November 24, 1862. He died on August 27, 1883.

The pockets in the folds of the rear skirts originally had small buttons at top and bottom, which is normally only found in the officers' version of the Pattern-1861 coat. Note that each pocket also has an unusual curved flap to which the lower button was sewn. *www.historicalimagebank.com.*

With a shoulder scale removed, this detail shows the sky-blue trimmed shoulder strap on the Currier frock coat. *www.historicalimagebank.com.*

The "equipments" for the 5th New Hampshire, i.e., belts, cartridges boxes, and cap pouches, were made by Solon S. Wilkinson of Keene, New Hampshire, who was reported to have "employed from twenty to twenty-five hands in the work, and the whole amount of his contracts is between eleven and twelve thousand dollars."[61] On October 28, 1861, "1010 Butcher Knives, [&] 1060 Sheaths" were issued to this regiment via James B. Gove, Keeper of Military Stores for the state of New Hampshire.[62] According to two surviving examples, these were eleven inches in total length and of clip point Bowie knife-pattern, with dark red leather sheaths and German silver mounts.

Regarding long arms, the 5th New Hampshire received Enfield rifle muskets purchased via George W. Drew & Co., at the Eagle Hotel Block in Concord. Reported to have "the largest and choicest stock" of military goods in New Hampshire, Drew also furnished swords and epaulets for all officers of the 3rd New Hampshire, as well as "most of the Fourth, all of the Fifth." He would go on to provide the same service to officers in the 6th, 7th, and 8th regiments.[63] Uniforms for most of the officers were made by Kelley & Edmunds, next door to Drew's premises. According to the *Patriot* on September 11, 1861, this firm was giving their customers "perfect 'fits,' and their superior cutters have to work early mornings and late nights to keep up with the demand. The cloth is mostly of New Hampshire manufacture."[64]

The 6th New Hampshire was organized at Keene and mustered-in on November 27, 1861. Despite forfeiting the dark-blue frock coats and sky-blue pants intended for it, this regiment quickly received replacement clothing of the same color and pattern from the prolific Lincoln & Shaw. Possibly based on the unpopularity of the Havelock hats issued to the previous three regiments, Purinton & Ham supplied the 6th Regiment with a more orthodox fatigue cap with a curved, stiff leather visor extending from its sides and rear. This form of headgear was also worn by the 8th New Hampshire (see below).

Blue flannel blouses worn by the 6th New Hampshire were made by B. F. Haley & Co. of Newmarket. Overcoats were produced by A. B. Cook of Weare; shoes from the prison workshops in Concord; and "gun equipments and harness" by Solon S. Wilkinson of Keene, New Hampshire.[65] On December 12, 1861, a letter published in the *New Hampshire Sentinel* reported that all was not well with some of this clothing, stating, "The uniforms give good satisfaction, except the dress coats and blouses, which are rather thin and poorly made."[66] Once again, "shoddy" uniforms were being issued to New Hampshire volunteers. A surviving frock coat worn by John Currier, a musician in Co. F

Carried by Second Sgt. Everett S. Fitch, Co. C, 5th New Hampshire, this knife is one of those issued to the regiment on October 28, 1861. Although referred to as a "Butcher Knife," it was of Bowie knife pattern. Original ownership of this sidearm is indicated by the inscription stamped into the brass crossguard, which reads "EVT S. FITCH 5 N.H. VOL." *Dave Nelson collection.*

Photographed at the Daguerrian Gallery of French & Sawyer at Keene, New Hampshire, this unidentified enlisted man of the 6th New Hampshire Infantry wears a modified version of the Havelock cap produced by Purinton & Ham. Possibly based on the unpopularity of the Havelock hats issued to the previous three regiments, this version was patterned after a more orthodox fatigue cap, but has a stiffened leather visor curved around its rear and sides. *Ninth-plate tintype – author's collection.*

Probably photographed at Manchester, New Hampshire, these two young volunteers of Co. H, 7th New Hampshire appear to have been twins and are identified as Albert F. and Alfred F. Hills, of Hollis, New Hampshire. They wear the uniform supplied to their regiment by the central government, which was largely based on US Army regulations. Held aloft by both men, their Pattern-1858 dress or "Hardee" hats have black ostrich feathers fastened to the right side, while the brim is looped up on the left via a brass "eagle" device. The regulation brass infantry horn, with numeral "7" set within the loop, and company letter "H" above, are secured to the front of the crown. Their Pattern-1851 frock coats are trimmed with sky-blue around collar and cuffs. They hold P1853 Enfield rifle muskets. *Sixth-plate ambrotypes—author's collection.*

of the regiment, was made from a flannel-type material usually found in blouses or sack coats and, like those worn by the 4th, 5th, and 8th New Hampshire, is devoid of ornamentation other than light blue cord edging to the shoulder straps. While it was anticipated that the 6th New Hampshire would be armed with New Model 1859 Sharps breech loading rifles, this regiment received Austrian M1854 rifle muskets. According to the regimental historian, "They were very light and pretty, with a bayonet as sharp as a needle."[67]

Although raised within New Hampshire and credited to that state, the 7th New Hampshire was organized upon the request of Adjutant Gen. Joseph C. Abbott by direction of the War Department at Washington, DC, under date of September 2, 1861. Having served as state adjutant general from 1855 through 1861, Abbott wished to defend the Union cause in the field, and was commissioned a lieutenant colonel of the 7th regiment with West Point graduate and regular army officer Haldimand S. Putnam as colonel. Organized at Manchester and mustered-in on December 13, 1861, the 7th New Hampshire subsequently received its clothing, arms, and equipment from the central government. According to a report in the *New Hampshire Statesman*, the uniforms were "precisely like those of the regular army," and were sent direct from Washington, DC.[68] The regimental historian Henry Little described them as consisting of "'keg hats' of black felt, trimmed with feathers and brasses, dark blue dress coats, dark blue trousers, light blue overcoats, dark blue blouses, and dark blue fatigue caps, the trimmings and chevrons of light blue, except the dark blue on the overcoats." The arms issued were "Enfield rifled muskets, brass mountings, calibre 57—with bayonet—and of English manufacture." Little added that these weapons were "very little lighter than the United States Springfield pattern, had all the steel parts blue-bronzed, and were really a beautiful arm and presented a natty appearance."[69]

Pvt. Joseph Foster, Co. H, 8th New Hampshire, wears the modified version of the Havelock cap issued to his regiment. He holds a US M1816 musket probably altered to percussion. To compensate for the effect of the reversed image, he has his bayonet propped on the end of the barrel to make it appear to be on the correct side of the musket. Foster died of disease at Camp Kearney in Louisiana October 29, 1862. *Sixth-plate ambrotype—Daniel J. Binder collection.*

Twenty-one-year-old James H. Marshall was a clerk resident at Manchester, in Hillsborough County, when he originally enlisted in Co. F, 1st New Hampshire on May 3, 1861. Mustered-out at Concord on August 9, 1861, he reenlisted in Co. B, 8th New Hampshire at Nashua on December 20, 1861, and was promoted to sergeant. He holds an example of the second type of Havelock cap supplied to his regiment by Purinton & Ham. He wears the frock coat of "inferior quality" made for the 8th regiment by S. A. & B. F. Haley, of Newmarket, New Hampshire, and has a Model 1840 NCO's sword attached to his belt, which is fastened by a decorative militia-pattern belt plate. *US Army Heritage and Education Center.*

Also organized at Manchester and mustered-in on December 23, 1861, the 8th New Hampshire was the last regiment to be uniformed and equipped by the Granite State. Once again some of the clothing received by this regiment was of inferior quality. Made by S. A. & B. F. Haley of Newmarket, the blue flannel frock coats and blouses received on January 16, 1862, were described by an unknown volunteer as being "not so good but will hold vermin." The same man added that the pants made by the same firm, and caps produced by Purinton & Ham, were "very good."[70] The latter were Havelock caps of the same pattern as issued to the 6th New Hampshire, being an orthodox fatigue cap with a curved, leather visor attached to its back and sides. Based on photographic evidence, it seems the coats made by S. A. & B. F. Haley were of the same pattern as those supplied by Lincoln & Shaw, with light blue-trimmed shoulder straps being devoid of any other form of decoration. Regarding other clothing received by this regiment, overcoats, shirts, and drawers were made by J. W. Thorpe and David F. Brown of Hillsborough Bridge, and socks by the Holderness Woollen Mill. "Gun equipments" were supplied by James R. Hill of Concord, knapsacks by Joseph Short, and haversacks by Lincoln & Shaw.[71] The inferior quality coats had been replaced by February 1862, as on the 12th of that month a member of this regiment known only as "Sam" wrote, "We got all our new clothes and they are as smooth as cat fur."[72]

The 8th New Hampshire was armed with Austrian rifled muskets of which R. Howarth Jr. of Co. B complained, "…a very poor article. Its weight sagged down many of the tender youth who had before only occasionally swung the axe at the home woodpile." The volunteer known only as "Sam," disagreed stating, "It is first rate, so to shoot long distance."[73]

NEW HAMPSHIRE
Order of Battle, 1861

Volunteer Infantry

1st Infantry Regiment (three-months' service)	4th Infantry Regiment	7th Infantry Regiment
2nd Infantry Regiment	5th Infantry Regiment (Fighting Fifth)	8th Infantry Regiment
3rd Infantry Regiment	6th Infantry Regiment	

Volunteer Cavalry	Volunteer Artillery
One battalion in First New England Cavalry	1st Light Battery

8th N. H. Regiment.

Both of these unidentified New Hampshire volunteers wear their first issue uniforms. The corporal of either the 4th, 5th, or 6th New Hampshire Infantry at top has the rear visor of his brown Purinton & Ham Havelock hat turned up. The trim on the shoulder straps of his frock coat supplied by Lincoln & Shaw is clearly shown. The man at left is proudly posed in the gray tail-coat with red trim around collar, as worn by the 1st and 2nd New Hampshire Infantry. *Ninth-plate tintype—author's collection/sixth-plate ambrotype.* — Daniel J. Binder collection.

POST NUBILA P

HARTFORD CITY

Organized, Jan. 8

CONNECTICUT

CONNECTICUT

Tentatively identified as the Brewster Rifles, or Rifle Company C, 3rd Connecticut, these volunteers were photographed at Camp Douglas, near Washington, DC, armed with M1842 muskets. In conjunction with the 2nd Maine, the 3rd Connecticut charged a Confederate battery near the Stone Bridge on July 21, 1861, sustaining four killed, thirteen wounded, and eighteen missing. According to the report of brigade commander General E.D. Keyes, members of this regiment later "brought off in the retreat two of our abandoned guns, one caisson, and several baggage wagons, and behaved with great coolness in the retreat." *Library of Congress LC-USZC4-7989.*

When Governor William A. Buckingham received the first call for three-months' volunteers from Connecticut on April 15, 1861, he did not feel he had the legal authority to order out one of the eight existing regiments of what was known in that state as "active militia." Instead, he requested a new regiment of volunteers, followed a few days later by two more. These regiments were made up of a combination of existing active militia companies, which volunteered intact, plus others newly formed. Two additional infantry regiments for three years' service designated the 4th and 5th Connecticut were raised before the first major clash of arms in the east at Bull Run on July 21, 1861. The latter regiment was originally intended to be organized by Col. Samuel Colt as the "First Connecticut Revolving Rifles," but this plan had to be abandoned, and a new regiment was formed in its place. Connecticut subsequently produced eight more regiments of three-years' volunteers during 1861, plus one regiment and one squadron of cavalry, the last being assigned to the 2nd New York Cavalry.

Some of the companies within the first two regiments wore their dark-blue militia uniforms based on 1856 state regulations, which in turn were patterned on US Army regulations of 1854, while others were uniformed by their local communities.[1] The latter may also have conformed in part to the 1854 regulations.

Parading in New Britain, about nine miles southwest of Hartford, Connecticut, on May 11, 1861, this company of Connecticut volunteers, which is possibly Co. G, 1st Connecticut, wears a distinctive pattern of sack coat with cloth shoulder straps. These may have been some of the blouses supplied by the state quartermaster general before the end of April, 1861. *Connecticut Historical Society 1999.66.1.*

In Hartford, the company rapidly being recruited by Capt. Ira Wright, which became Infantry Co. B, 1st Connecticut, was clothed in uniforms made by Charles G. Day, a clothier located at 54 and 56 Asylum Street, Hartford. This firm also provided uniforms for Infantry Co. F, enlisted in Meriden, Connecticut.[2] Other Hartford tailors, including Henry Schulze, at 384 Main Street, and Fisher & Co., at 64 State Street, cut uniform coats and trousers without charge, and the ladies of the community undertook the sewing. According to the *Hartford Daily Courant* of April 22, 1861, "A great many ladies served God and served their country, in making uniforms for its gallant defenders."[3] Similar efforts were made throughout the state. The ladies of New Haven were recorded as having supplied "all deficiencies in uniforms, and worked by scores so diligently, that, within ten days, they had finished and distributed more than five hundred full sets. They also provided a large number of caps, shoes, and socks." The ladies of Brooklyn, Woodstock, and Pomfret produced "three hundred and fifty shirts, eighty pairs of pants, and eighty coats" in six days during the same period.[4]

By the end of April, the state military authorities had begun to supply uniforms to its volunteers. State Quartermaster Gen. Maj. J. M. Hathaway contracted with firms in Hartford, Manchester, and New Haven, Connecticut, and in Monson, Massachusetts, to produce "coats, pantaloons, and blouses

This volunteer from Hartford, Connecticut, wears an example of the gray five-button coat with standing collar and chest pocket acquired by some Connecticut companies during the first few weeks of the war. His chasseur-pattern cap appears to be a darker color and was probably dark blue. *Ninth-plate ambrotype—author's collection.*

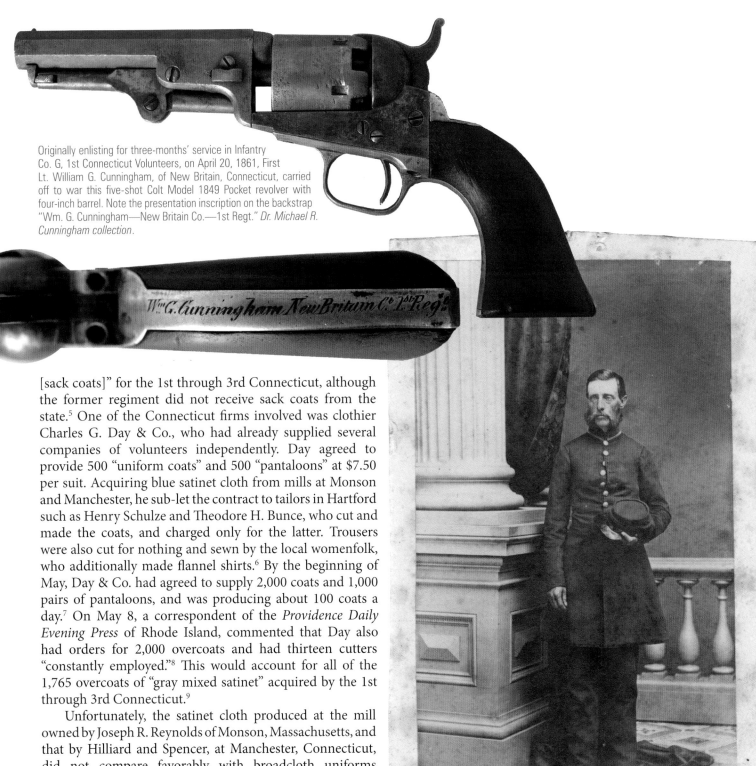

Originally enlisting for three-months' service in Infantry Co. G, 1st Connecticut Volunteers, on April 20, 1861, First Lt. William G. Cunningham, of New Britain, Connecticut, carried off to war this five-shot Colt Model 1849 Pocket revolver with four-inch barrel. Note the presentation inscription on the backstrap "Wm. G. Cunningham—New Britain Co.—1st Regt." *Dr. Michael R. Cunningham collection.*

[sack coats]" for the 1st through 3rd Connecticut, although the former regiment did not receive sack coats from the state.[5] One of the Connecticut firms involved was clothier Charles G. Day & Co., who had already supplied several companies of volunteers independently. Day agreed to provide 500 "uniform coats" and 500 "pantaloons" at $7.50 per suit. Acquiring blue satinet cloth from mills at Monson and Manchester, he sub-let the contract to tailors in Hartford such as Henry Schulze and Theodore H. Bunce, who cut and made the coats, and charged only for the latter. Trousers were also cut for nothing and sewn by the local womenfolk, who additionally made flannel shirts.[6] By the beginning of May, Day & Co. had agreed to supply 2,000 coats and 1,000 pairs of pantaloons, and was producing about 100 coats a day.[7] On May 8, a correspondent of the *Providence Daily Evening Press* of Rhode Island, commented that Day also had orders for 2,000 overcoats and had thirteen cutters "constantly employed."[8] This would account for all of the 1,765 overcoats of "gray mixed satinet" acquired by the 1st through 3rd Connecticut.[9]

Unfortunately, the satinet cloth produced at the mill owned by Joseph R. Reynolds of Monson, Massachusetts, and that by Hilliard and Spencer, at Manchester, Connecticut, did not compare favorably with broadcloth uniforms being produced in New Haven. A report in the *Hartford Daily Courant* for May 20, 1861, stated that "seams ripped and buttons came off."[10] Complaints from Capt. Wright, 1st Connecticut, and others, led to an investigation being conducted by a state legislative committee at the beginning of May 1861. This body established that both gray and blue satinet had been acquired for trousers, and that the latter, made of "Reynolds satinet" had proved inferior. The trousers made up voluntarily by "the ladies of Hartford" for Day & Co. were of the inferior blue cloth produced by Hilliard and Spencer.[11] Findings of the investigation indicated that the cost of blue broadcloth was prohibitive, and that suppliers had resorted to blue satinet, which did not stand up to camp and campaign wear. In addition, one of the women who volunteered to make the pantaloons stated on May 22, 1861, that she had heard comment among the

Photographed at the studio of G.W. Davis, at 245 Main Street in Hartford, this unidentified Connecticut volunteer wears an example of the dark-blue uniform being produced in that city during April and May 1861. His frock coat has a double strand of trim around the collar, his pants appear to be plain, and he holds a chasseur-pattern cap. *Carte de Visite by "G.W. Davis, Photograph, Ambrotype & Daguerreotype Rooms, No. 245 Main Street, Hartford, CT"—author's collection.*

seamstresses that what they were making could not possibly "last the soldiers until they reach Washington."[12]

It was not until May 31 that the 1st Connecticut received replacement trousers, which were probably some of the 4,412 "Uniform Pants" eventually supplied by the state.[13] A letter with that date published in the *Connecticut Press* stated, "today, for the first time, they have a chance to get pantaloons. But the price must be deducted from their wages. Six weeks wear and tear, day and night, at all kinds of labor, made sad havoc with that satinet."[14] In the 2nd Connecticut, uniforms received by the Clinton Guards who enlisted as Rifle Co. D were rejected and replaced by sack coats acquired by their regimental commander Col. Alfred H. Terry (see below), which were probably some of the 3,873 "Blouses" supplied by the state.[15] According to the *New Haven Register*, "Yesterday came down from Hartford the uniforms for Capt. [James W.] Gore's company [Clinton Guard]— but it was difficult to tell pantaloons from jackets, or the color, or material, of which they were composed. One of the soldiers, who was trying a coat the sleeves of which were at least six inches too long, while it would not come within as many inches of buttoning about the waist, remarked that 'the uniforms for this company must have been mowed out with a stub scythe.' They were all condemned, and a blouse uniform adopted."[16] On May 18, 1861, the correspondent of the *Providence Daily Evening Press* reported, "Capt. Gore's company refused to receive their pants, some of which were made of different colored cloth, and left New Haven in all sorts of clothes, some of them in overalls."[17]

An ex-member of the staff of the *Hartford Weekly Times* who enlisted in the 2nd Connecticut added:

> The character of the uniforms sent to Capt. Gore's company I need not mention, nor the chagrin and disappointment of our men, who were compelled to be made an exhibition to the whole regiment and hundreds of spectators. Col. Terry deeply sympathized with them, and made an encouraging speech to them, which did much to restore good humor. He provided us with blue flannel blouses which are now worn by our officers and men. He went to New Haven to obtain pants but was unsuccessful. In consequence our men wear pants of every hue.[18]

Problems were also experienced with footwear. According to a letter from Capt. Joseph R. Hawley, commanding the Hartford Rifle Company (Rifle Co. A), 1st Connecticut, published in the *Columbian Weekly Register* on June 8, 1861, "Shoes were not ready when they first went to New Haven, and as fast as needed, new ones were bought by the men with their own money, or with funds given or advanced by officers." He concluded by stating, "I ought to say that since the occasion referred to at New Haven, the men have had no opportunity to draw for shoes."[19]

The uniforms worn by Connecticut troops arriving at the nation's capital were reported briefly in the Washington press. Commanded by Col. (later Gen.) Daniel Tyler, the 1st Connecticut Volunteers were described on arrival on May 11, 1861, as wearing "blue frock coats, grey pants and fatigue caps." The 2nd Connecticut,

The New Haven Grays were photographed in front of the Lyon Building in Chapel Street, New Haven, just prior to their departure for three-months' service as Co. C, 2nd Connecticut Volunteers, in April 1861. Most wear gray overcoats, that of three officers being double-breasted with longer capes. Their forage caps are gray with a black band and probably have the letter "A" attached at front, which was the company designation of this unit within the 2nd Connecticut Active Militia. The enlisted man at extreme left wears the full-dress tail-coat of his unit, which had black facings on collar and cuffs, and was double-breasted with buttons arranged in twos. The enlisted man at extreme right wears a three-button sack coat under his overcoat, which was probably worn by the Grays for fatigue wear. *Todd Album, Anne S. K. Brown Military Collection, Brown University.*

which reached Washington two days later, wore "dark blue frock coats, pants, and fatigue caps," and all were provided with "the almost indispensable Havelocks." The one exception regarding uniform appears to have been the New Haven Grays, Co. C, 2nd Connecticut, which was clothed in "gray, with black [trouser seam] stripes."[20] Commanded by Capt. E. Walter Osborne, the New Haven Grays, which was also Co. A, 2nd Connecticut Active Militia, wore for prewar full dress a distinctive gray tail-coat and trousers with black facings, white epaulets, and a taller version of the 1851-Pattern black felt dress cap with the initials "NHG" beneath the stamped brass state coat of arms, surmounted by a white pompom. Their gray fatigue clothing faced with black was probably worn throughout their entire three months' service as, upon their return to New Haven, the *Columbian Weekly Register* reported, "The Grays, whose friends turned out *en masse*, wore the company uniform in which they left us."[21] With the exception of knapsacks, the Grays also provided their own "equipments."[22] Many members of the New Haven Grays reenlisted in 1862, forming a company in the 27th Connecticut Infantry.

The 3rd Connecticut, under Col. John Arnold, were described as wearing uniforms of "various styles, some having the state uniform like the First and Second, and others [the flank companies] a dark blue, trimmed with green on a wide green stripe."[23] Rooted in the 1856 state regulations, uniforms with green facings for flank or rifle companies was a Connecticut militia style. Hence, the 1st Connecticut had two rifle companies, and the 2nd and 3rd Connecticut had six. The 3rd Connecticut also received "the army regulation overcoat, a large heavy blanket, and an India rubber mantel, to be used either for a covering or as a protection from wet ground." Unusually, Infantry Co. D, commanded by Capt.

This enlisted man of the New Haven Grays wears the uniform adopted by his company in 1858, which includes a full-dress tail-coat with black facings on collar and cuffs, with double row of buttons arranged in twos. Pants are also gray with black seam stripes. His undress headgear consists of a gray cap with black trim and band. The full-dress cap worn by this company was a taller version of the M1851 black-felt dress hat having the initials "NHG" beneath the stamped brass state coat of arms surmounted by a white pompon. His rectangular waist belt plate bears the designation "NEW HAVEN GRAYS," and his buttons are probably of the 1860-period Connecticut state seal pattern rather than unit specific. His empty bayonet scabbard appears to be a Massachusetts alteration of a Pattern-1853 Enfield scabbard changed to accept the socket bayonet for the M1855 rifle musket. His cartridge box is non-regulation and probably specific to the New Haven Grays. *Sixth-plate ambrotype—Daniel J. Binder collection.*

In this detail from the larger image, the volunteers of the 3rd Connecticut wear their dark-blue state clothing, which was probably trimmed with green facings. The cap worn by the first lieutenant at left has light-colored trim around the band and the letter "C" at front. The coats worn by the enlisted men are trimmed around the cuffs, and have a small state button attached either side of the low-standing collar. Bridle straps adorn their shoulders. Trousers of both officer and men have narrow seam stripes. Headgear for all consists of a chasseur-pattern forage cap. *Library of Congress LC-USZC4-7989.*

The company letter "E" on the cap, plus a Hartford back mark, indicates that this Connecticut volunteer enlisted in the Hartford Invincibles, Rifle Co. E, 3rd Connecticut Infantry. He has turned his trimmed coat collar down in order to assume a more civilian appearance. *Carte de visite by "N.A. & R.A. Moore/ Photographers/Corner East of/The Allyn House"—author's collection.*

Frederick Frye, left for New Haven wearing overcoats made "by the ladies" of Bridgeport.[24]

According to a report in the *New London Daily Chronicle*, the 3rd Connecticut also received "blouses [or sack coats] of blue flannel" on May 20, 1861,[25] some of which may have been produced for the state by Winchester & Davis of New Haven. On April 26, the *Norwich Morning Bulletin* reported that this firm had "about two hundred ladies, in addition to the regular employees...making mattresses, shirts and blouses for the volunteers."[26] On May 21, the same journal stated that the 3rd Connecticut had been "presented with blue flannel blouses," which were "more convenient and comfortable than the regulation uniform."[27] Based on photographic evidence, some of these garments were of a distinctive style with five buttons, shoulder straps, and/or standing collars.

The fact that Connecticut was the home of four major arms manufacturing concerns to some extent facilitated the arming of its volunteer regiments in 1861. Located at Hartford was the Colt Fire Arms Company, owned by the illustrious Samuel Colt, who was also an officer in the Active Militia (see below). Near the same community was the Sharps Rifle Manufacturing Company, which, by the end of the year, had supplied a total of 1,362 New Model Sharps rifles to Connecticut troops. At New Haven was the New Haven Arms Company and the factory owned by Eli Whitney Jr. that worked under contract with Colt. In addition, there were at least seven other smaller arms manufacturing concerns in the state, including the Savage Revolving Fire Arms Company at Middletown and the Joslyn Fire Arms Company at Stonington. As a result, the two flank companies of the 1st Connecticut received 144 Sharps rifles with saber bayonet, while the remainder of the regiment was armed with 581 M1855 Springfield rifle muskets. Many of the latter had been recalled by the state from militia companies such as the Norwich Light Guard and the Union Guards, of Danielsonville.[28] With six rifle companies, the 2nd Connecticut received 576 Sharps rifles that the state originally intended selling to the Egyptian government, plus 144 M1855 rifle muskets. The former were subsequently reissued to the 8th and 11th Connecticut.[29]

Although it also possessed six rifle companies, the 3rd Connecticut was disappointed to receive 720 M1842 smoothbore muskets. When these arms were issued to Rifle Companies A and B at the state arsenal in Hartford on May 17, both units refused to accept them and were placed under guard and their officers arrested. Released shortly afterwards, both companies were assured they would receive rifles "as soon as they could be procured."[30] Of the occasion, a volunteer recalled that they "brought out a lot of old Springfield smooth-bore muskets for us, the same as they had already given to some of the other companies of our regiment. We just informed them that we were not going to carry them guns—we preferred Sharp's rifles [*sic*]. We were a rifle company; hadn't we got green stripes sewed on our pants?"[31]

By June 25, 1861, much of the clothing supplied to the 1st Connecticut was the worse for wear. On that date, Capt. John C. Comstock of the Hartford Light Guard (Co. A), wrote from the encampment near Falls Church, Virginia, stating, "We are yet suffering for lack of shoes and pantaloons. Why they are not supplied is a mystery I cannot solve. Many of the men are absolutely shoeless, and have not trowsers enough to cover their legs. The weather is warm and clear, and thus far the fellows have got along without material inconvenience, except from the intolerable dust, which pervades everything here. But if a rain sets in the want of shoes and trowsers will be seriously felt."[32] Earlier on June 2, the Clinton Guard (Co. D), 2nd Connecticut, had received a new uniform that was "infinitely superior" to that first received.[33] Seemingly, the poor-quality satinet trousers issued to the whole regiment had been replaced by July 8 as, on that date, a member of the same company wrote from Camp Mansfield, near Falls Village, advising, "We have lately been re-fitted with new pants, shoes, canteens and haversacks."[34]

Organized into the 1st Brigade, 1st Division, Army of North Eastern Virginia, under Col. E. D. Keyes, the 1st, 2nd, and 3rd Connecticut (plus 2nd Maine) distinguished themselves at Bull Run on July 21, 1861. Rather than retreat in disorder, the bulk of the brigade maintained discipline and, following their withdrawal from the battlefield, remained at their encampment near Falls Church the next day, until all remaining government property possible to save had been transported back across the Potomac. On return to Hartford at the end of their three-months' service, on July 28, 1861, the 1st Connecticut were described in the *Hartford Daily Courant* as "an interesting and strange sight in their war-worn and dusty garments, with every variety of head-dress imaginable, many of them wearing Zouave and other caps taken from the enemy."[35] *The Columbian Weekly Register* added, "Their 'uniforms' were generally pretty nearly 'played out,' and few came home in the suit which they wore away. Their arms and equipage were left at Washington in the hands of the Government. They brought home several captured horses, ten or a dozen runaway slaves, and any quantity of 'relics' in the shape of cavalry sabres, pistols, knives, &c." That this regiment received some clothing from the central government before the end of its three-month service is indicated via a report in the same journal, which stated that the men "who were still obliged to wear the State contract clothing, continued to be shabby."[36]

As a result of the shortage of good-quality blue cloth, the 4th Connecticut was uniformed in "gray throughout." On June 8, 1861, the *Connecticut Press* advised that the regiment had "got into its new gray uniform," which consisted of "gray jackets, pantaloons and felt hat, and gray felt overcoats." Also provided were 1,024 "light blouses."[37] A correspondent of the *Hartford Weekly Times* reported that the jacket was substituted for the coat and looked "much neater, is easier to wear and work in."[38] Pvt. Elisha Benjamin Andrews, Co. C, 4th Connecticut, recalled this uniform as being of:

> the thickest sort of gray woollen, made, one would have thought, especially for midwinter wear in Greenland. There were heavy gray felt hats to match. We had no blouses. The coats were short, without skirts; the pants of so generous girth that if any hero, beating perchance a hasty retreat, should have the misfortune to lose his knapsack, he might not be destitute of a good place to bestow his blanket. Some of the trousers were three inches too long; some nearly as much too short. The average coat, too, had a considerable surplus of circumference. Vests there were none; for which lack, coarse, heavy, gray flannel shirts, with the redundant longitude of the trousers, were expected to make amends.[39]

This unidentified Connecticut militiaman wears an infantry-pattern overcoat with red facings on collar and cuffs. Trouser seam stripes are also red, which may indicate that he belonged to an artillery company. *Kris VanDenBossche.*

Buttons worn by Connecticut volunteers bore the state seal consisting of three grape vines beneath which is the Latin inscription, "He who transplanted continues to sustain." This convex coat-size example has the back mark "EXTRA QUALITY" indicating it was probably made by the Waterbury Button Co., of Connecticut. *The Civil War Relicman.*

As he enlisted in the City Guard, of Hartford, Connecticut, organized as one of the flank companies (Co. A), 4th Connecticut Volunteers, 27-year-old Walter D. Ives is armed with a Sharps rifle. He wears the fatigue uniform adopted by the City Guard following its formation on January 8, 1861. This was described by a correspondent of the *Providence Evening Press* on May 3 as "resembling somewhat that of the French Chasseurs," and consisted of "blue shirts and red pants, after the zouave style," which gave them "a very dashing appearance." The next day, a report in the *Connecticut Press* of Hartford confirmed that this unit wore "red pantaloons, blue zouave jackets, fatigue caps, knapsacks and blankets." Ives carries a rigid, militia-style knapsack with gray blanket roll on top. A resident of Hartford, he enlisted on May 22, 1861, and had been promoted to first lieutenant by December 27, 1861. He was mustered-out on March 24, 1862. *Re-touched carte de visite—Michael J. McAfee collection.*

On arrival in Jersey City, New Jersey, this regiment was described as "thoroughly equipped and uniformed; their dress is that of a national guard, gray fatigue, with a light gray Kossuth cap. The officers are also equipped in the regular army officers' uniform, with the Connecticut State buttons."[40] When the 4th Connecticut reached Camp McClure, near Chambersburg, Pennsylvania, on June 12, 1861, a member of the 1st Wisconsin reported, "They are better clothed than any regiment I have seen, having a grey suit, pantaloons and roundabout, grey overcoat and felt hat."[41]

The 1,007 overcoats supplied to the 4th Connecticut were described as being "a beautiful grey color, known as Cadet mixed." Made of "the finest American wool" known as Norwalk Felt cloth and produced by the Union Manufacturing Company; they were cut and sewn by Charles G. Day & Co. of Hartford. This regiment and the 5th Connecticut received blankets made of Norwalk Felt.[42] Although the regimental history states that the reorganized 4th Connecticut finally drew new federal uniforms on October 30, 1861, a report in the *Hartford Daily Courant* advised that it had been "newly clothed" by September 21, 1861.[43] According to the *Hartford Daily Courant*, the state forwarded "a supply of new pants" to the regiment on October 7, 1861.[44] The flank companies of the 4th Connecticut were armed with 192 New Model Sharps rifles with sword bayonet, while the remainder of the regiment received 768 M1842 smoothbore muskets.[45] This regiment was reorganized into the 1st Connecticut Heavy Artillery on January 2, 1862.

With his armory and factory located by the Connecticut River near Hartford, millionaire inventor and firearms manufacturer Samuel Colt had offered to Governor Buckingham on April 19, 1861, "one thousand most recently improved Revolving Breach [*sic*] Rifles, Carbines, Holster or Belt Pistols of United States calibre, whichever may be preferred, for arming one Regiment of Connecticut volunteers." Also included were the services of the officers of the Colt Guard, a volunteer militia company formed amongst the employees of his factory, to "drill and teach" in the use of whichever weapon was accepted.[46] Formed in 1858, the Colt Armory Guard wore "a neat and plain uniform of black, with a light glazed forage cap in the French style," and were armed with "Colt's five-shooting rifle," or M1855 Colt revolving rifle.[47] In return, Colt required that the "First Connecticut Revolving Rifles" should be mustered-in as regulars in the federal army, and as each volunteer was enlisting in a "model regiment" he should be over five feet, seven inches in height.

With his offer accepted, Col. Colt was commissioned a colonel by the state of Connecticut on May 16, 1861, and proceeded to enlist the 1st Connecticut Revolving Rifles "for the war." Recruiting actually began six days earlier at an office owned by the Fire Arms Manufacturing Company in Hartford. Mustered-in as Co. F, the Smith Guard arrived on May 20 wearing "new dark blue US army suits and gray overcoats, supplied through the liberality of Rockville citizens and made up by the gratuitous labours of C. T. Ward and M. Koffman, tailors, and the ladies of that vicinity." Commanded by Capt. J. G. Beckwith, Co. E had taken up quarters three days earlier "brilliant in red shirts, looking for all the world like a company of visiting firemen."[48] Enlisting as Co. H, the Union Guards had been provided with "350 shirts, 80 pairs of pants and 80 coats in less than 6 days" by the ladies of Danielson, in Windham County. They arrived in Hartford wearing "a gray sack tunic, trimmed with red; a fatigue cap the same, and blue pants." The *County Transcipt* commented, "Each soldier is provided with four shirts and a new pair of boots in addition."[49]

However, due to a "disagreement concerning arms, the appointment of subalterns, and other important matters," such as the height of volunteers, Colt's commission was revoked on June 20, 1861, and his regiment, by then numbering nearly 700 men, was disbanded. Although more than half the men returned home, those remaining were organized into skeleton companies and designated the 5th Connecticut.[50] Commanded by Col. Orris S. Ferry, the 5th Connecticut was fully organized by July 18, 1861, and left for the front eleven days later having been issued with a regimental uniform consisting of light gray felt hats, plus "indigo blue coat and pants and army gray overcoats."[51] Made of "regular army cloth, the most durable in the world," the 1,000 coats and 1,058 pants were supplied by Day & Co. The 1,020 overcoats were made from cloth produced by the mill owned by Lounsbury, Bissell & Co. of Norwalk, which was cut and sewn by military goods suppliers Rogers & Raymond of 214 Broadway and 125 Fulton Street, New York.[52] The 5th Connecticut also appears to have received federal-style sack coats as, on July 13, the *Connecticut Press* observed that "blue blouses" were "plenty on the streets" of Hartford when this regiment was granted furlough prior to departure for the war.[53] According to the "Annual Report of the Adjutant General" this regiment was finally armed with "Mississippi rifles and United States Springfield Rifled [*sic*] Muskets."[54]

Regarding the remaining regiments formed during 1861, the 6th Connecticut received dress and fatigue uniforms based on state or US regulations, with gray overcoats. Flank companies at first had green facings. The 7th Connecticut left New Haven for Jersey City on September 18, 1861, dressed in "the regular uniform" plus gray overcoat, and armed with "Enfield Rifles."[55] The 8th Connecticut was uniformed in the same fashion initially, minus overcoats, which prompted a comment in the *Hartford Daily Courant* that a few "wide-awake capes" might be made available for "the use of the picket guard."[56] By October 7, "the soldiers of the 8th and 10th regiments" had received "hats, overcoats and shoes."[57]

Known as the "Irish Regiment" and formed using the Emmett Guard of New Haven as its nucleus, the 9th Connecticut was initially poorly clothed receiving "one suit of blue, of poor material," which constituted "their entire equipment." Stationed for two months at Camp English in New Haven, their pantaloons began to assume "various degrees of dilapidation."[58] On Thanksgiving Day, the 9th Connecticut left for Camp Chase near Lowell, Massachusetts, "numbering about six hundred men, ragged, unarmed, and dispirited." By November 12, 1861, all the "knapsacks, haversacks and other equipments" issued to this regiment were condemned as being "unfit for service."[59]

A member of the Mechanic Rifles, of Hartford, Connecticut, Henry T. Burpee enlisted in Rifle Co. A, 3rd Connecticut Infantry, on May 11, 1861. His uniform includes a chasseur-pattern cap and woolen frock coat with plain collar and cuffs. His unusually wide waist belt is fastened by a standard clipped corner militia belt plate. Burpee was mustered out on August 12, 1861, and re-enlisted in Co. A, 8th Connecticut on September 25, 1861. *Carte de visite—Michael J. McAfee collection.*

Originally organized in Hartford, Connecticut, in 1858, the Putnam Phalanx was named in honor of Revolutionary War General Israel Putnam. Composed of two companies, they wore a "Continental"-style uniform consisting of a black cocked hat with gilt trim and red over black feather plume, blue tail-coat with buff facings and gilt buttons and epaulets, a buff waistcoat and black breeches and stockings. For undress this unit wore a Mexican War-style cap with brass letters "PP." When Lincoln issued a call for 75,000 troops in April 1861, the Putnam Phalanx placed itself on a war footing and escorted volunteer units as they left the city heading south. Although it did not volunteer as an entire u,nit, many of its individuals enlisted for war service in Connecticut regiments. *Carte de visite—Michael J. McAfee collection.*

The 9th Connecticut finally received Enfield rifles once it had reached Ship Island, Mississippi, at the beginning of December 1861. With many of his command bare-footed by this time, Col. Thomas W. Cahill appropriated a supply of canvas shoes consigned to the post sutler and distributed them to his command.[60] In his history of the 9th Connecticut, Thomas H. Murray concluded, "Its uniforms, in some instances, showed the signs of wear and a sufficiency of other articles of apparel, that should have been supplied by the state or the National government, was in many cases wanting. Nevertheless, the Irish buoyancy of the regiment rose superior to these drawbacks."[61] Organized as a rifle regiment at Camp Lincoln, Hartford, during October and November 1861, the 11th Connecticut received a uniform with green facings, while several companies wore high, black leggings. The last Connecticut infantry regiment to be enlisted in 1861, the 13th Connecticut received "dark blue trousers in place of the regulation sky-blue" while encamped at New Haven.[62]

Formed at Camp Tyler near West Meriden, Connecticut, the artillery battery raised by this state received its uniforms by November 5, 1861.[63] Also at Camp Tyler, the 1st Battalion Connecticut Cavalry, commanded by Maj. Jordan M. Lyon, had received all its "equipments...except the pants," by November 12, 1861.[64] It is assumed that both units received clothing of US regulation pattern.

Although Connecticut zouave companies were practically nonexistent, several juvenile companies, such as Ellsworth's Zouaves, commanded by Capt. L. A. Dickinson, and the Deming Zouaves, led by Capt. George A. Belcher, were organized in Hartford by July 1861. On the 6th of that month, Capt. Dean's Zouaves, from the Asylum for the Deaf and Dumb, paraded through Main Street, following which the *Daily Courant* reported, "Not a word is spoken or a sound articulated, yet their evolutions are performed in the most orderly and regular manner. Music would, of course, be superfluous; the captain's orders are all given by signs and are obeyed with the most satisfactory alacrity and facility. The uniform is a red cap closely fitting the head and without a frontispiece, white shirt and red breeches, with white stockings." Their commander "learned the drill of the French Zouaves, in Paris, while travelling in Europe some years since."[65]

The Governor's Foot Guard traced its origins to the American Revolution, and was composed of two companies attired in distinctive uniforms. These two men wear the full dress of the First Company Foot Guards, of Hartford, Connecticut, which consisted of a scarlet tail-coat with black velvet facings trimmed with gold lace on collar, lapels and cuffs, buff waistcoat and breeches, and black gaiters to the knee. Private George H. Haskell, at right, has placed his full dress grenadier bearskin cap on the photographer's prop. The unidentified man at left has his scarlet fatigue cap on the table by his side. Some men from the second company of Foot Guards later formed Co. K, 6th Connecticut Infantry. *Carte de visite by R.S. DeLamater, 258 Main Street, Hartford—Michael J. McAfee collection/carte de visite by Davis, 245 Main Street, of Hartford, Conn.—Buck Zaidel collection.*

CONNECTICUT
Order of Battle, 1861

Volunteer Infantry

1st Regiment (three-months' service)	6th Regiment	10th Regiment
2nd Regiment (three-months' service)	7th Regiment	11th Regiment
3rd Regiment (three-months' service)	8th Regiment	12th Regiment (Charter Oak Regiment)
4th Regiment (redesignated 1st Heavy Artillery Regiment)	9th Regiment (Irish Regiment)	13th Regiment
5th Regiment (reorganized from elements of 1st Connecticut Revolving Rifles)		

Volunteer Cavalry	Volunteer Artillery
1st Battalion	One battery
One squadron assigned to 2nd New York Cavalry (Harris Light Cavalry)	

HARTFORD CITY GUARD,
Organized, Jan. 8th, 1861.

(top right) Originally organised in Middletown, Connecticut, in 1852, the Mansfield Guard enlisted as Rifle Co. A, 2nd Connecticut Infantry, in April 1861. The tail-coat worn by Corporal Charles Abner Pelton survives in the collection of the Middlesex County Historical Society at Middleton, Connecticut. Of navy blue wool, it was fastened by a single row of gilt "eagle" buttons, and had wide gold braid trim on collar and cuffs, plus gold braid bridle straps which helped secure full dress epaulets to the shoulders. The inscription on the oblate spheroid canteen indicates it was carried by Pelton at First Bull Run.

(left) This unidentified volunteer wears the full dress tail-coat and pants of the Mansfield Guard complete with epaulets. His undress fatigue cap rests on the chair by his side.

(bottom right) Believed to be a member of the 1st Company Horse Guards, of Hartford, Connecticut, this man poses in blue tail-coat trimmed with gold lace and sky blue pants. His grenadier-style bearskin cap is placed on the table. He is armed with a M1840 light artillery saber. *Middlesex County Historical Society/ carte de visite—Buck Zaidel collection/carte de visite by Daniel S. Camp, Hartford, Conn.—Buck Zaidel collection.*

Vermont.

FREEDOM AND U

For the Unio

VERMONT

VERMONT

Published in the *New York Illustrated News* on May 25, 1861, this engraving shows an officer and men of the 1st Vermont Volunteers, also known as the "Green Mountain Boys," wearing their dress uniform, which for enlisted men consisted of a gray tail-coat with black shoulder straps and gray pants with broad, black seam stripes. The officer appears to be wearing a dark-blue frock coat. Note the sprig of hemlock attached to their caps. *Author's collection*.

The "Green Mountain State" provided one regiment of infantry following the call for three-months' militia on April 15, 1861. As a result, Governor Erastus Fairbanks ordered the mobilization of the Active Militia but also made provision for the organization of three and, if necessary, seven regiments "for the war."[1] In order to raise the first regiment, the ten uniformed militia companies with the fullest ranks were ordered to rendezvous at Rutland, Vermont, where Camp Fairbanks was established on the fairgrounds south of the city. An 1836 graduate of West Point and a twenty-three-year veteran of the regular army, J. Wolcott Phelps was appointed to command the 1st Vermont Volunteers, also known as the "Green Mountain Boys."

Each of the chosen militia companies possessed prewar uniforms of various color and cut of cloth. For full dress, the Ransom Guards (Co. C), of St. Albans, wore "Cadet grey" with "Regulation caps," while the New England Guards (Co. F), of Northfield, wore "blue coats and bear-skin caps."[2] For probable fatigue or undress wear, the Burlington Light Guard (Co. H) had "a jacket and loose pantaloons of dark gray with black stripe, and gray military cap," which was described as being "not as showy as some, but every way excellent for service, and one which will retain its good looks after many a fancy's uniform has become shabby by wear."[3]

Discovered at Dummerston, Vermont, this tintype shows three members of the Green Mountain Guards, a uniformed volunteer militia company of Swanton, in the north western part of the state. Before enlistment as Company A, 1st Vermont Volunteers, this unit wore dark green trousers and slightly lighter green, seven-button coats. They hold M1855 rifle muskets which may have been part of the issuance of long arms to the newly forming regiment, and appear to have federal-issue accoutrements compatible with that weapon. *Marius Peladeau collection*.

This volunteer possibly belonged to the New England Guards (Co. F), 1st Vermont, which enlisted at Northfield, Vermont. He wears a fine-checked shirt, which may have been of civilian origin, and gray military trousers with one inch-wide seam stripes. It is unclear whether he is wearing a shop apron or medical sling, the latter indicating that he may have been wounded. Standing at his side with short hair, a young girl, who may have been his daughter, appears to have just recovered from an illness as the cutting of hair was believed would reduce a fever. *Carte de visite by "R.M. McIntosh, Northfield, Vt."—Marius Peladeau collection*.

Nonetheless, a regimental uniform was needed for the 1st Vermont and this was acquired in Boston by state Quartermaster Gen. George F. Davis, who also purchased "overcoats, blankets and general camp equipment," with 800 of the former being acquired from clothiers Isaac Fenno & Co.[4] In the meantime, the state proposed to supply each volunteer with "1 coat, 1 fatigue cap, 2 pairs woollen socks, 1 knapsack, 1 trowsers, 2 flannel shirts, 1 pair shoes, 1 haversack, 1 overcoat, 2 flannel drawers, 1 blanket, 1 canteen."[5] By April 29, the *St. Albans Messenger* was able to report of the 1st Vermont, "Their uniforms are being made with all possible haste, and will undoubtedly be ready by the time marching orders are received."[6] According to a report published in the *Vermont Journal* on June 15, 1861, the cloth for these uniforms was made at the mill owned by Prosper Merrill at Felchville, about eight miles west of Windsor, Vermont.[7]

Delivered on May 3, 1861, the uniform received by the 1st Vermont was illustrated in an engraving published in the *New York Illustrated News* on May 25, 1861, and consisted of a nine-button, gray tail-coat with black shoulder straps, gray pants with broad black seam stripes, and forage cap. Regarding the latter, on May 14 the *Vermont Chronicle* of Windsor stated, "All hands wear the Green Mountain sprig [of hemlock]" in remembrance of the Green Mountain Boys of the American Revolution. The *Watchman & State Journal* of May 24 added, "When the regiment arrived in the city [of Rutland], every soldier had a green sprig in his cap, and the people on the way, and at the Park, begged pieces to keep during the war. One informed me that he gave a piece from his sprig to several." According to the same report, two young ladies named "Miss Dorsey, of Cornwall, and a Miss Grace, of Middlebury," were found stowed away in the cars "resolved to go [with the regiment] as nurses." They were "voted in" with the pledge that any man who offered them "an insult" would be shot![8]

Some volunteers in the 1st Vermont wore a very distinctive cast brass "stag's head" plate attached to their cartridge box flaps and cap pouches, which was adapted from the crest of the coat-of-arms of Vermont borne on state militia buttons since the 1830s.[9] With regard to arms, the 1st Vermont received smoothbore percussion muskets from the Springfield arsenal plus 300 rifle muskets of "the latest pattern," which were procured by Col. Abijah Keith, a senior aide on the staff of Governor Fairbanks, during a trip to New York during the first week in May 1861. As the regiment passed through Troy, New York, these weapons were described as "new Minie rifles from the Springfield Armory, light, strong and true, with '1861' stamped on them."[10] Efforts also made to provide every man of this regiment with a revolver were abandoned by the governor following receipt of information that United States officers were discouraging "the arming of privates with revolvers, preferring to confine them to the gun and bayonet."[11]

Mustered-into federal service on May 8, the 1st Vermont departed the next day for New York City, where it arrived two days later. On May 11, the regiment embarked aboard the steamer *Alabama*, and arrived at Fortress Monroe, Virginia, on May 13. While passing through Troy, New York, the Vermonters were described as being dressed in "serviceably gray uniforms with glittering muskets and tightly strapped knapsacks."[12] A New York City reporter commented that they did "not attract attention by the showiness of their uniforms because a sober gray does not dazzle the eyes."[13] Numbering 779 men, the 1st Vermont was considered by Maj. Gen. Benjamin F. Butler to be one of the best regiments under his command on its arrival at Fortress Monroe. Occupying nearby Hampton ten days later, it was the first regiment in the service of the United States to take possession of the soil of Virginia. A member of a Massachusetts regiment camped nearby commented, "This evening they paraded, and in double ranks they extended across the parade-ground. Their gray uniforms gave them a handsome appearance, and our motley troops, some wearing uniforms and the larger part wearing shirts, did not enjoy the contrast."[14]

However, the gray clothing of the 1st Vermont quickly began to deteriorate. An officer of the regiment wrote from the regimental encampment on May 18, 1861, that the men were suffering from the "wearing out of their uniforms, particularly the pantaloons." He went on to suggest, "Fatigue duty is destructive to clothes, and a thousand pairs of common overalls (furnished by the town whence the company comes) would save a good deal...Some rolls of grey cloth, to patch with, would obviate the necessity of piecing out the legs of the trowsers at the expense of the seat, and vice versa, instances of which I observe in the regiment."[15]

In a letter to a friend in St. Albans, Vermont, dated May 29, Capt. Charles G. Chandler of the Ransom Guards (Co. C), wrote, "I have only time to say that my Company (in consequence of extra fatigue labor) is very sadly in want of a cheap uniform—two thirds of the pants are already given out, and in two weeks the men will be obliged to wear their shirts outside of their pants in order to preserve any uniform dress. I have only to add, that I think a "lindsey woolsey" grey jacket and trowsers would be the very thing for them."[16]

In response, Quartermaster Gen. Davis purchased "a supply of overalls" and "a supply of clothing to make good the wear and tear of the uniforms" which, according to the *Burlington Free Press* of June 7, 1861, were forwarded to the troops at Newport News.[17] Other items sent to the 1st Vermont included Havelocks by May 23 and more shoes by June 13.[18] Two sets of the former were made by "the ladies of Woodstock, Rutland, and other towns," one being of linen and the other of cotton. Of this item, the *Vermont Chronicle* reported, "It is made plain, with a high crown, and has a cape which falls over the neck and ears, and shades a large part of the face."[19] Having sustained only two killed and three wounded when five of its companies took part in the battle of Big Bethel on June 10, 1861, the 1st Vermont returned home on August 5 after the expiration of their three-month term of service.

As further volunteer companies were recruited for subsequent regiments, concern grew that an array of different uniforms would be adopted, and Adjutant and Inspector Gen. H. Henry Baxter issued an order on May 3, 1861, stating, "Volunteer companies are cautioned against incurring expense for uniforms, or for any other purpose until orders are given. A style of uniforms will be adopted for the state, and the uniforms will be furnished by the Adjutant General."[20] At the same time and possibly echoing the dissatisfaction with the uniform worn by the 1st Vermont, a report published during the first week of May 1861 in the *Rutland Daily Herald* stated that future regiments organized within the state would be "furnished with uniforms very similar to those worn by the Bradford Guard. It is gray pants, gray frock coats, with buff trimmings."[21]

Organized at Camp Underwood near Burlington and mustered-in for three years, the 2nd Vermont received uniforms during the second week of June 1861, which, according to the *Free Press*, consisted of "a frock coat and pantaloons of grey doeskin, with a dark blue cord." Overcoats were distributed five days later. All of these garments were reported to be of "an excellent material, of Vermont manufacture, with no indications of 'shoddy' (or rag wool), of strong texture, closely woven."[22] Described as being "a substantially sewed article," shoes were issued on June 20. With regard to equipage, this regiment received "knapsacks, belts, and cartridge boxes...of the best quality, and fully up to the US regulation standard." Distributed on June 21, canteens were "a substantial article of heavy tin, holding three pints apiece, and covered with cloth," which when wet kept "that within the canteen cool." Their haversacks were "of cloth, japanned on the outside, and with a lining which can be taken out and washed."[23] According to the *Vermont Watchman & State Journal* of Montpelier, the uniform received by the Capital Guards (Co. F), 2nd Vermont, on June 21 consisted of "a frock coat and pants—both made of very durable grey cloth—in the outside seams of the pants are sewed a blue stripe and the coats are trimmed with blue, and upon the shoulders are straps for the knapsacks, and altogether it is a fine uniform."[24]

This enlisted man was photographed at Springfield, Vermont, and may well have enlisted in Co. A, 3rd Vermont, which largely came from that township. Note the lower band on his gray chasseur pattern cap comes to a peak, which appears to have been a distinctive feature of early war Vermont headgear. *Carte de visite by "James D. Powers, Springfield, Vermont—collection of Marius Peladeau.*

Resident at Pomfret, in Windsor County, William C. Boynton enlisted on June 1, 1861, and was mustered-into Co. F, 3rd Vermont on July 16, 1861. He was eventually promoted a corporal and was mustered-out on July 24, 1864. He wears an example of the uniform issued to his regiment, made from cloth produced at the mill owned by Prosper Merrill & Co. of Felchville, Vermont. His plain, gray frock coat has nine Vermont "state seal" buttons. His shoulder straps were secured by smaller buttons of the same pattern. The lower band on his gray chasseur pattern also has the distinctive peak in its lower band. Of federal issue, his waist belt is fastened by an 1839-Pattern "US" oval plate. *U.S. Army Heritage and Education Center.*

Once again made at the Felchville mill owned by Prosper Merrill, the cloth used for the coats and trousers supplied to the 2nd and 3rd Vermont was known as "cadet mixed." The *Vermont Phoenix* of Brattleboro mentioned that "other mills in the state are engaged in manufacturing similar goods."[25] According to a history of Reading, Vermont, the Merrill mill was "even run on Sunday, to make this cloth under the contract with Governor Fairbanks."[26] Supplied to local tailors to make into uniforms, the cloth produced was clearly yet another example of "shoddy" despite earlier positive comment. That received by Pratt, Wright & Co., and Cune & Brackett, tailors of Brattleboro, to be made into uniforms for Co. C, 2nd Vermont, was inspected by a reporter for the *Vermont Phoenix*, who stated that it did not "seem suitable for the hard service it is sure to undergo. It appears to be nearly half cotton and is of a coarse, harsh texture. Somebody has evidently made a "big thing" out of the operation for suits of all wool cloth of excellent fabric are sold in the village...."[27]

According to other reports in the state press, Governor Fairbanks wanted to contract with Solomon Woodward of Woodstock, Vermont, to make all-wool uniforms for both the 2nd and 3rd Vermont, but Quartermaster Gen.

The cut of his uniform and headgear indicates that this unidentified private enlisted in Co. H of either the 2nd or 3rd Vermont in 1861. Magnification of the image also reveals that his buttons bear the state seal of Vermont. He holds an M1842 musket with socket bayonet fixed. His equipment includes a .69 caliber round ball cartridge box, 1845-Pattern cap pouch, and cloth-covered 1858-Pattern tin canteen. *Sixth-plate ambrotype courtesy of the Liljenquist Family collection—Library of Congress LC-DIG-ppmsca-31692.*

Davis insisted on the contract being given to Merrill & Co., despite the fact that Woodward had begun to produce the cloth. A reporter for the Woodstock *Vermont Standard* claimed that Davis was "instrumental in bringing about the arrangement, receiving for his influence a generous share of the spoils."[28] A week later this statement was refuted by the same journal, which stated that the Merrill cloth was produced "according to the terms of the contract" and that "shoddy" was not used in its manufacture.[29] Despite these assurances, the uniforms supplied by the end of June were once again reported to be of very poor quality. Caps for the 2nd Vermont were made by Paine, Allen, Pond & Co. of Rutland,[30] while 800 overcoats were produced in Rutland by "Mr. Chafee."[31]

Every man in the 2nd Vermont also wore "a sprig of evergreen in his cap and looked the type of sturdy Green Mountain Boy," when the regiment departed for the federal capital on June 24.[32] On its arrival in New York City en route for Washington, DC, the *Herald* reported that this regiment was "attired in a dark gray uniform, substantial and well cut, and, on the whole, present a very soldierly appearance."[33] At the same time a correspondent for the *New York Express* reported:

> The uniforms [of the 2nd Vermont] are of regulation gray, but there are few of them that fit the men. From the appearance of some of them, which hang sack like over the limbs of the wearer it would seem that the State tailor had thought that the Green Mountain military were veritably Falstaffs in corpulency. The material looks like grey fustian dyed in mud. They were furnished two weeks since, and, such is the counterfeit kersey of which they seem to be made, they are now completely faded and worn-looking. The men are naturally discontented with them, as they detract much from their appearance, and, on a close inspection, seem positively shabby.[34]

Regarding arms, the 2nd Vermont was issued with M1842 muskets of "the old fashioned smooth-bore pattern" with the exception of Co. A, which received the M1855 rifle musket. This caused great dissatisfaction as the regiment expected to be armed throughout with the latter weapon.[35] Accoutrements for the first three regiments of Vermont volunteers were produced in Boston, the 3rd Vermont receiving the "last installment" while still encamped at St. Johnsbury in Caledonia County, Vermont.[36] Canteens of India-rubber cloth issued to the 1st Vermont were unpopular. In a letter written from Newport News, Lt. Farnham stated, "Water carried in them three hours is unfit to drink. The men obviate this difficulty somewhat by carrying bottles of water in their haversacks. [Tin canteens have been ordered.]"[37]

The 2nd Vermont was brigaded with the 3rd, 4th, and 5th Maine under command of Col. Oliver O. Howard upon arrival in the Washington defences, and assigned to the division of Gen. Samuel P. Heintzleman. At Bull Run on July 21, 1861, the regiment lost two men (killed), one officer and thirty-four enlisted men wounded, and one officer and thirty men missing. Detached from Howard's brigade on August 12, it joined the 3rd Vermont, 6th Maine, and 33rd New York at "Camp Advance" in Virginia, about a mile west of the Chain Bridge, where it assisted in the construction of Fort Ethan Allen and performed reconnaissance and guard duty during the remainder of the year.

The rank of this fully equipped sergeant of either the 2nd or 3rd Vermont is indicated by light-colored chevrons on the sleeves of his "cadet mixed," gray frock coat. His waist belt is fastened by a regulation 1839-Pattern "US" oval plate and supports an 1845-Pattern cap pouch and 1835-Pattern bayonet in scabbard. Out of sight, his .69 caliber round ball cartridge box is suspended from a shoulder belt with the 1826-Pattern "eagle" plate attached. He holds his musket at "shoulder arms." *Carte de visite—Michael J. McAfee collection.*

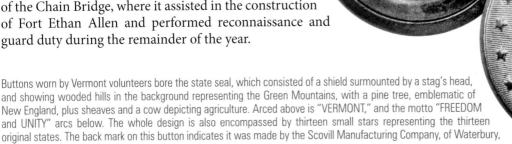

Buttons worn by Vermont volunteers bore the state seal, which consisted of a shield surmounted by a stag's head, and showing wooded hills in the background representing the Green Mountains, with a pine tree, emblematic of New England, plus sheaves and a cow depicting agriculture. Arced above is "VERMONT," and the motto "FREEDOM and UNITY" arcs below. The whole design is also encompassed by thirteen small stars representing the thirteen original states. The back mark on this button indicates it was made by the Scovill Manufacturing Company, of Waterbury, Connecticut. *The Civil War Relicman.*

Worn by Maj. Walter W. Cochran, 3rd Vermont Infantry, this high-crown chasseur cap bears the maker's mark "Bent & Bush/Corner of/Court & Washington St./Boston" on the leather covering on the underside of the crown. The distinctive peak at the front of the lower band is seen on caps worn by other Vermont volunteers in 1861. It has Vermont state seal buttons securing the chin-strap. Forty year-old Cochran received his major's commission in the 3rd Vermont on July 12, 1861, but resigned on August 6 due to disability caused by a severe attack of fever and ague. *Dr. Michael R. Cunningham collection.*

Encamped near St. Johnsbury in Caledonia County, the 3rd Vermont received their uniforms on July 4, 1861. The next day *The Caledonian* reported that several companies of the regiment marched by their office on their return from the Quartermaster General's office having been issued their uniforms.[38] Once again the state clothing was sub-standard. A letter from "Camp Baxter" published in the *Burlington Free Press* stated, "The uniforms are distributed and are not what the State of Vermont should furnish her soldiers... the cloth does not hold its color, and the light of the sun is fatal to its appearance. They are apparently well made with the exception of buttons, which are not half sewed on."[39] Breaking camp on July 31, 1861, the 3rd Vermont passed through Springfield en route for Washington, DC, on which occasion the local newspaper reported, "Their uniform consists of a gray suit throughout, very much like the uniform of the 10th Massachusetts regiment, only they have coats instead of jackets. They are armed with the Enfield rifle, and take with them camp stores and equipage complete. The regiment consists of ten companies of 84 men, and each company is attended by three women who will act as nurses."[40]

By the beginning of October, both the 2nd and 3rd Vermont were "suffering for want of clothing." Writing from "Camp Advance" near the Chain Bridge in DC, a member of the recently arrived 4th Vermont reported, "The 2nd do not look so neat and tidy as when in Camp Underwood. Their gray uniforms (which are being replaced by blue) are now dirty and dingy. They look as though they had seen service—and hard service, too."[41] Writing from "Camp Griffin," in Virginia, a man in the 3rd Vermont stated that the uniforms of his regiment were "dirty, rusty, too thin, [and] too shrunk."[42] By October 23, Governor Fairbanks had received a telegram from Brig. Gen. Smith, commanding the Vermont Brigade, stating, "They need immediately about 850 blue uniforms, and sixteen hundred pair of pants."[43] By November 14, 1861, these two regiments had received "new uniforms of army blue," plus blankets and overcoats, and a correspondent of the *Vermont Chronicle* commented, "These comforts must contribute something to health."[44]

The first regiment to be uniformed in blue by the state upon organization, the 4th Vermont was recruited from towns mostly in the southern part of the state and rendezvoused at Camp Holbrook, Brattleboro, by September 14, 1861. The coats and pants for both the 4th and 5th regiments were made in Boston, Massachusetts, and overcoats were produced in Rutland, Vermont.[45] Concerning clothing made for the former unit, a report in the *Vermont Phoenix* stated that they were "a great improvement over those of the preceding regiments...They are made of all wool cloth of the army blue color; and the hats are of the same style as is now worn in the regular service."[46] By October 31, a letter from a member of this regiment stated that it had received only "a partial supply of overcoats, and the shoes received at Brattleboro were already wearing out through the soles." The writer feared that the 4th Vermont would be "barefooted before new ones come."[47]

Living at Newbury, Vermont, William W. Heath enlisted as a private in Co. H, 4th Vermont on September 21, 1861. Photographed shortly after wearing his very crumpled state-issue blue uniform, he is surrounded by accoutrements, which consist of a black, rubberized knapsack with gray blanket roll; black, painted canvas haversack; and wool-covered 1858-Pattern canteen with white cotton sling. The M1841 rifle he is holding is probably a photographer's prop, as his regiment was armed with the Enfield rifle musket. *Eighth-plate tintype—Marius Peladeau collection.*

This unidentified infantryman wears an example of the frock coat with low, velvet collar issued to Vermont volunteers in 1861. His 1861-Pattern forage cap rests on the photographer's prop. He holds an M1861 rifle musket and has his .58 caliber cartridge box attached to his waist belt, rather than slung from a shoulder belt—a common practice in the Vermont Brigade. *Carte de Visite by "Richardson, St. Albans, Vt."—Marius Peladeau collection.*

Resident at Huntington, Vermont, George T. Morris enlisted in Co. K, 5th Vermont on August 14, 1861. He was wounded in 1862, detailed as a Sharpshooter in 1864, and re-enlisted as a Volunteer Veteran on October 12 of the same year, being promoted to corporal. He was finally mustered-out on June 29, 1865. He is armed with a pair of Pocket Colt revolvers and M1861 rifle musket, all of which were probably photographer's props. *Sixth-plate tintype—Marius Peladeau collection.*

Armed with the Enfield rifle musket, the 4th Vermont mustered-into federal service 1,048 men strong on September 21, and left that evening for Washington, DC, where it joined the 2nd, 3rd, and 5th regiments, and later the 6th Vermont, forming the Vermont Brigade. Both the 5th and 6th Vermont also received "blouses and pants, of army blue" supplied by the state.[48] The former regiment was hurried off to the front on September 23, 1861 only partly clothed and equipped. According to an account in the Brattleboro press, it did not receive overcoats until mid-October despite the cold and wet weather, and after having been informed that these would be waiting for them on arrival at Washington, DC.[49]

Although the 5th Vermont received the M1855 rifle muskets returned by the 1st Vermont at the end of that regiment's three-month period of service, there was not enough of this weapon to go 'round, and Governor Fairbanks made a requisition on the War Department for 280 rifle muskets to supplement the deficiency. Meanwhile, the regiment left for Washington on September 23, with three companies unarmed and was still not in receipt of the additional weapons when it marched into Virginia five days later. After participating in an advance toward Lewinsville, about four miles west of the Chain Bridge, a member of the unit wrote on October 12, "We have nothing to fight with but our hands, and the rebels are all around us." Another man commented, "Between two hundred and three hundred of our men are every night and day within hailing distance, not only of the enemy's picket, but of the enemy in force; and we have not six hundred guns that will bear inspection, and two hundred of our men have no guns at all, and not an officer has side arms...Company I of this regiment has not a gun, a dress or thick coat, or a pistol or overcoat. Two days ago there was not an overcoat in camp. Since then 400 have been received."[50] The 5th Vermont eventually received 280 Enfield rifles to supplement its lack of arms by the end of October 1861.

By the time the 6th Vermont was organized, the state had learned "a good deal in the business of equipping troops," and from the ampler supplies of army clothing then available the recruits were uniformed as fast as they arrived.[51] According to a report in *The Caledonian* of St. Johnsbury, Vermont, "Wm. B. Hatch of New York was authorized by Gov. Fairbanks to purchase the entire outfit for the sixth regiment, a duty which he performed with ability and strict fidelity to the interests of the state."[52] Mustered-into federal service at Camp Gregory Smith, Montpelier on October 15, 1861, the 6th Vermont left for Washington four days later, on which occasion the *Daily Messenger* of St. Albans reported that it was "fully uniformed and equipped, and leaves the State better appointed than any Regiment that has preceded it." [53] This regiment was completely armed with Enfield rifles.[54]

Recruiting began for the 7th and 8th Vermont, or "Butler Regiment," during the winter months of 1861, but neither of these regiments was fully organized and uniformed until the beginning of 1862. Efforts to raise a regiment of Vermont cavalry began in September 1861, when Lemuel B. Pratt, a wealthy farmer in Colchester, Chittenden County, was issued a commission and instructed to have the unit "ready as soon as possible."[55] Reported to "understand horses and men," and knowing "what kind are wanted for both," Pratt soon recruited the ranks to overflowing in all ten companies of what became the first full regiment of cavalry raised in New England. Going into camp at Burlington, the 1st Vermont Cavalry had received "stable jackets, haversacks, drawers, stockings and sacks [or sack coats]" by October 23, 1861.[56] When provided with the rest of their uniform clothing, about 300 troopers led by Col. Pratt paraded through the streets of Burlington on November 4, 1861, on which occasion it was reported by the *St. Albans Messenger* that "several of the companies wore their overcoats, and some only uniforms…" Described in the same journal, their full uniform consisted of "a blue-black regulation hat, and a fatigue cap: jacket of dark blue trimmed with yellow braid and brass buttons, and with brass scales on the shoulder; trousers of light blue; top boots; overcoat of brown cloth, made large and long, with a large cape; stable jacket; canteen; sabre and belt."[57]

The 1st Vermont Cavalry was the first full regiment of cavalry raised in New England. Commanded by Col. Lemuel B. Platt, this regiment was mustered-in on November 19, 1861, on which occasion twenty-year-old Harvey J. Bickford, of Danville, Vermont, enlisted in Co. D, which was recruited in Orange and Caledonia Counties. Issued his uniform at the beginning of that month, Bickford wears a twelve-button cavalry jacket complete with brass shoulder scales, and holds his fatigue cap, which has the brass company letter "D" and 1858-Pattern enlisted crossed saber insignia secured to its top. Probably due to inadequate studio lighting, his sky-blue trousers look dark blue. After hard service in Virginia, Bickford was discharged due to disability on October 11, 1862. Note the cavalry charge depicted in the very unusual studio back drop. *Carte de visite—Marius Peladeau collection.*

VERMONT Order of Battle, 1861		
Active Militia (Three-months' Service)	**Volunteer Infantry**	**Volunteer Cavalry**
1st Infantry (Green Mountain Boys)	2nd Regiment	1st Cavalry
	3rd Regiment	
	4th Regiment	
	5th Regiment	
	6th Regiment	

MAINE

MAINE

The lettering on the tent frontage indicates that some of these men may have belonged to Company A, 6th Maine. They wear a mixture of headgear including "Kossuth"-style hats and tasselled fezzes. Although some are in the gray frock coats made by Bangor tailors, others wear full-sleeved shirts with chest pockets. Two NCOs are distinguished by light-colored sleeve insignia. Four of the men seated in front are in the process of loading their percussion revolvers, which consist of two Navies and two pocket models. Others are armed with M1855 rifle muskets with the man at left loading his weapon. The first sergeant standing at center holds an M1840 non-commissioned officer's sword over his shoulder with a fife in the other hand. Stacked M1855 rifle muskets are visible in the tent in the background. *Albumen print—www.historicalimagebank.com.*

Six days after the fall of Fort Sumter, the legislature of the state of Maine met in extra session and on April 25, 1861, passed a bill to "receive, arm and equip immediately ten regiments of volunteers" to serve under a two-year enlistment. At the same time, another bill was passed to raise "a volunteer corps of militia of three regiments."[1] Meanwhile, in response to Lincoln's call for one three-month regiment from the Pine Tree State, the first of these regiments was mustered-into federal service for the shorter period only. Delayed from departure by an outbreak of measles, the 1st Maine Volunteer Militia was eventually ordered to Washington, DC, on June 1, where it remained until August 1, 1861, encamped on Meridian Hill.[2] Spending its entire service in the Washington defenses, it saw no combat and was mustered-out on August 5, 1861. This regiment was later reorganized for three years as the 10th Maine, and completed the war as the 29th regiment.

The recruitment of the 1st Maine, commanded by Col. Nathaniel J. Jackson, began within the 1st Division, Volunteer Militia of Maine on April 20, and in a week its ten companies were full and encamped around Portland. A total of 779 volunteers were mustered-into this regiment on May 3, 1861. A report in the *Bangor Daily Whig and Courier* on May 1, 1861, advised that each man was to be provided with "1 cap and pompon, 1 eagle and ring, 1 pair of trowsers, 1 coat, 2 pairs of grey flannel drawers and shirts, 1 pair of shoes, 1 overcoat, 1 blanket, 1 knapsack with straps, 1 canteen with straps and 1 haversack, and one sash is allowed to the orderly of each company."[3] Officers were to provide their own "uniform and equipments."[4] Much of the clothing for the enlisted men of

Working at the Machine Works of Ira Winn, on Union Street, Portland, in 1861, 23-year-old Enoch Westcott lived in nearby Westbrook when he enlisted on May 3 as a corporal in the second company of Portland Rifle Guards, which became Co. I, 1st Maine Volunteers. After nearly three-months' service defending the federal capital, he was taken ill with typhoid fever on July 29, and was carried home in the "sick car" when his regiment returned to Portland on August 3. He died nine days later, being the only man lost in his regiment. In this *carte de visite* copy of an original cased image, he wears the seven-button gray frock coat with tall standing collar hastily supplied to the 1st Maine by a Boston merchant tailor in April 1861. *Carte de visite inscribed on reverse "Enoch Wescott Saccarappa—A Member of the 1st Regt Main[e] vol. Co. I"—author's collection.*

the 1st Maine was acquired in Boston, Massachusetts. A report in the *Whig and Courier* stated that a delegation consisting of two Republicans and two Democrats was sent to that city to make the various purchases. It also dismissed claims that these men received a commission for contracts secured.[5]

Enlisting in the Portland Light Guards (Co. C), 1st Maine, Pvt. John M. Gould recorded in the regimental history, "We had our uniforms and clothing issued to us as fast as they could be made up or bought." An entry dated April 28, 1861, in a diary he kept stated, "we were marched to the new City Hall, where we each received a pair of woollen shirts, two pairs of woollen drawers, two pairs woollen stockings, and one pair of shoes with leather strings, the shoes being the great, wide kind you see in shops on the wharves, where fishermen trade."[6] Meanwhile, on April 30, the 1st Maine had more of its uniform distributed. A letter dated May 1, published in the *Lewiston Daily Evening Journal* stated, "Yesterday and today have been spent in the armory, and being marched down, in squads, to the Clothing rooms, to be fitted out with clothes and shoes."[7] Of this occasion Gould wrote, "We received our overcoats, pantaloons, haversacks and knapsacks—the last miserable thing of painted cloth which daubs everything it touches. The overcoat is gray with the Massachusetts brass button on it, and is not a bad coat; the pantaloons are of poorer stuff and made in a hurry; color a mixture of gray, red and brown." On May 9 he stated, "Our company had their under coats and rubber blankets distributed. This furnishes us completely, except in cartridges and caps. The coats are made of a very poor gray cloth and have the Maine buttons; the overcoats are being altered, receiving the Maine button in place of the Mass[achusetts]."[8] According to photographic evidence, the frock coats supplied to the 1st Maine were plain gray and had a tall, standing collar and seven-button front. Pattern-1858 caps had wide bands, and color and trim possibly varied between companies. Shirts were gray and either pullover or button front.

Footwear produced for the 1st Maine was of poor quality. Some were produced by Cobb, Robinson, Hill & Co., which was a shoe manufacturer in the Phoenix Block in Lewiston. According to the *Lewiston Daily Evening Journal* this firm had been "pushing the work along night and day for the past week," and on May 4 "sent 200 pairs to headquarters."[9] Ten days later, the same newspaper reported that a requisition had been made for "new shoes for the First Regiment—those furnished on the first requisition proving to be miserable slop-shop work."[10]

A national flag supplied by military goods dealer A. W. Pollard was presented to the 1st Maine as it passed through Boston on May 12, 1861, which was described as "an American flag, of silk, heavily tasseled and surmounted by an eagle." On a silver plate on the staff was the inscription, "Presented to the First Regiment Maine Volunteers, by Dresser, Stevens & Co. Boston, May 1861. *Ubi libertas, ibi patria* [where there is liberty, there is my country]."[11]

The 1st Maine was armed by the state with 728 M1855 Springfield rifle muskets with Maynard tape primer from the arsenal at Portland. The officers and "about half of the privates were furnished with Colt's revolvers" when the regiment left for the front.[12] Towards the end of their three-month term of service, on July 30, 1861, these weapons were given to the 6th Maine in exchange for "old flint-lock, smooth-bore [muskets], altered over to a percussion-lock and understood to be more dangerous to the user and his right-hand comrade, than to the enemy."[13]

The clothing received by the 1st Maine proved unsuitable. The pantaloons were cause for concern as soon as the regiment reached the heat of the federal capital in early June. Private Gould recalled, "The first thing we did after arriving at our quarters [on Meridian Hill] was to strip, or 'peel,' as the slang was, and most of us peeled down to shirt and drawers and fell to work ripping out the trowser lining." Regarding their heavy gray frock coats, Gould observed, "We had our usual drills by company and regiment, and dress parades every evening all in our shirt sleeves, which was the only comfortable rig we had." On June 4, 1861, the Washington *Evening Star* reporter Crosby S. Noyes, formerly of Lewiston, Maine, reported that the men of the regiment "complain with reason at the outrageous swindle perpetrated upon them by the Boston dealers who supplied their uniforms, the cloth and the workmanship being so inferior that the clothes are already falling to pieces."[14] In a letter to the *Bangor Daily Whig and Courier*, dated July 8, a member of the 2nd Maine commented regarding the condition of the 1st regiment that their clothing was in "such a state that they could not be moved properly as they are....A gentleman told me that fifty or sixty had no shoes to their feet, and there was great complaint in other respects."[15] On May 27, the *Lewiston Daily Evening Journal* reported, "We understand that the 'committee on military expenditure,' on the part of the State, have demanded, and obtained such a reduction on the bill for clothing purchased in Boston for the 1st Regiment, as to make the whole purchase of a character (as regards price) that they should satisfy all complaints from every quarter. The executive is evidently looking after these matters."[16]

Having been paid on July 11, 1861, many men bought "sutler-stuff" to replace their unsatisfactory state uniforms. Gould commented that the Lewiston Zouaves (Co. K) acquired "blue flannel coats and white gaiters." At the end of their three-month period of service, members of this regiment made an effigy representing a 1st Maine soldier as a mark of their "contempt for the

This fully equipped but unidentified volunteer may also have served in either the 1st or 2nd Maine. He wears a seven-button frock coat and high-crowned Pattern-1858 forage cap with lighter-colored band and darker top. He appears to be holding an M1855 rifle musket, and has a regulation pattern cap pouch attached to his waist belt, the latter being fastened by a small 1839-Pattern plate. A tin-drum canteen rests on his left hip. *Michael J. McAfee collection.*

WANTED, IMMEDIATELY! To Work for the Army, 100 COAT MAKERS! APPLY TO Wheelwright & Clark,

apr29 1w

Published in the *Bangor Daily Whig and Courier* on April 29, 1861, this request for "coat makers" coincides with the contract to make the uniforms for the 2nd Maine acquired by Wheelwright & Clark. *Author's collection.*

uniform," and, according to Gould, "putting it on a pole over the flames tried to burn it, but it 'stood fire' well."[17]

Upon return to Portland on August 3, the wear and tear on the uniforms of the 1st Maine was plain to see as the tired volunteers took off their knapsacks. Gould recorded, "This taking off of baggage revealed the weakness of shoddy, and Co. C will never forget the independence of an 'infant' named Phawkes, in whose pantaloons seat there were two holes, each eight inches square, inside of which there might have been seen a remnant of shirt trying to 'cover the law.' We were all of us nearly as badly off…"[18]

Ordered to the federal capital in place of the stricken 1st Maine, the 2nd Maine or "The Bangor Regiment" wore uniforms of improved quality, described as being "grey throughout, consisting of pants without stripes, a frock coat, a military fatigue cap and an overcoat" when the regiment passed through Boston on May 15, 1861.[19] On arrival in Washington, this was further reported as being made of "stout cadet grey," and composed of "grey frock coats, pants, and fatigue caps, with heavy overcoats of the same material."[20] This clothing was

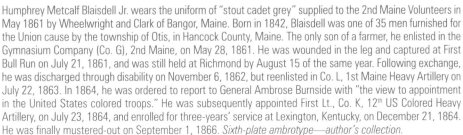

Humphrey Metcalf Blaisdell Jr. wears the uniform of "stout cadet grey" supplied to the 2nd Maine Volunteers in May 1861 by Wheelwright and Clark of Bangor, Maine. Born in 1842, Blaisdell was one of 35 men furnished for the Union cause by the township of Otis, in Hancock County, Maine. The only son of a farmer, he enlisted in the Gymnasium Company (Co. G), 2nd Maine, on May 28, 1861. He was wounded in the leg and captured at First Bull Run on July 21, 1861, and was still held at Richmond by August 15 of the same year. Following exchange, he was discharged through disability on November 6, 1862, but reenlisted in Co. L, 1st Maine Heavy Artillery on July 22, 1863. In 1864, he was ordered to report to General Ambrose Burnside with "the view to appointment in the United States colored troops." He was subsequently appointed First Lt., Co. K, 12th US Colored Heavy Artillery, on July 23, 1864, and enrolled for three-years' service at Lexington, Kentucky, on December 21, 1864. He was finally mustered-out on September 1, 1866. *Sixth-plate ambrotype—author's collection.*

Pvt. Greenlief Celdon Rogers was a 22-year-old lumberman when he enlisted with the Milo Artillery as part of Co. D, 2nd Maine Infantry on May 28, 1861. He was the only man from Dover, in Piscataquis County, Maine, to enlist in that regiment. He received a disability discharge on November 21, 1862, but re-enlisted in Co. K, 31st Maine Infantry on April 29, 1864. After the war, he moved to Mount Haley, near Midland, Michigan, where he died in 1872. In this 1861 image he wears a cadet gray frock coat with nine-button front and high-standing collar, matching trousers, and white-canvas gaiters. His Pattern-1858 forage cap of the same color rests on the photographer's prop. *Carte de visite by "D.C. Dinsmore, Dover, Maine" with pencil inscriptions on the reverse reading "Pvt. Greenlief C. Rogers/ Dover, Me/22 yrs/D—2nd Me—ANA Milo Art/Only man from Dover in 2nd Maine/D for D—11—21—62/31st M?"—author's collection.*

This coat was worn by 22-year-old Galen Worcester who was a cooper living in Bangor when he enlisted for two years in Co. E, 2nd Maine, on April 25, 1861. One of 66 men in this regiment who refused to be mustered-in when their term of enlistment was changed from two to three years on May 28, 1861, he was tried by court martial and found guilty of failure to do his duty, despite the fact he had fought at First Bull Run. Rather than face a prison sentence at Dry Tortugas on Key West, he agreed to transfer into Co. I, 2nd New York Infantry on October 4, 1861, and served in that regiment until August 8, 1862, when he transferred back into the 2nd Maine. Surviving the war, he returned to Bangor where he was listed as a carpenter in the 1880 Census. Made from a cadet gray cloth, which has acquired a brownish tinge with age, this coat was lined with linen and polished cotton cloth, and had nine state-seal buttons at its front, and three smaller buttons of the same type on each plain cuff. *Michael J. McAfee.*

supplied by Wheelwright and Clark, who "sub-let contracts to all the tailors in the city [of Bangor], hired all available help, and then gave the balance to the lady volunteers sewing at City Hall."[21] In order to recruit the necessary assistance to produce these uniforms, this Bangor-based firm placed a notice in the local press asking for "100 Coat Makers," and local merchant tailors such as Joseph P. Jackson, of 44 Main Street, and Irish immigrant Michael Gilligan, at 6 Smith's Block, Bangor, whose "Cutting Department" was managed by J. H. Larkin, most probably responded with help.[22] By May 3, 1861, the lady volunteers working under "professional" guidance in the City Hall and vestry of the Free Church had produced 900 of the 3,200 garments required, consisting of "shirts and drawers" as well as additional uniform clothing, such as coats and pants.[23] The womenfolk of Bangor also raised sufficient funds to purchase white linen to make "Havelocks" for the 2nd Maine,

Buttons worn by Volunteer Maine Militia bore the state arms adopted in 1820. This consisted of a shield emblazoned with a white pine, emblematic of New England since colonial times, with a moose below. A husbandman resting on a scythe supports the shield on the left, while a seaman leaning on an anchor braces the other. A crest above contains the North Star, adopted from the Massachusetts seal. The motto *Dirigo*, meaning "I direct" alludes to the North Star, and is symbolic of Maine helping mariners find their way. The back mark on this example of a staff button is "SCHUYLER H & G.—NEW YORK." *The Civil War Relicman.*

Mustered-into federal service as Co. A, plus providing officers and noncommissioned officers for Co. D, 3rd Maine Infantry, the Bath City Greys was the only company of that regiment that existed under antebellum militia laws of the state of Maine. Wearing a red fatigue cap, the rest of the uniform of this enlisted man of the Greys is prewar full dress. His dress cap, with pompon and elaborate wreathed plate, rests on the table. *Sixth-plate tintype—Anne S. K. Brown Military Collection, Brown University.*

and 800 of these were sent by express to Washington, DC, on June 6, 1861.[24]

The 2nd Maine received M1840 converted muskets from the general government, but was also supplied by the state with 195 Springfield muskets.[25] An accoutrement contract for "knapsacks, haversacks, cartridge boxes &c." for this regiment was given to James Littlefield, who was listed in the trade directory of the period as dealing in "Harnesses, Trunks, Wolf and Buffalo Robes" in Bangor, Maine.

Finally arriving in Washington, DC, on May 31, 1861, following a short period of quarantine at Willet's Point, New York, after an outbreak of measles, the 2nd Maine also found their uniforms uncomfortable. A member of the regiment wrote on July 8, "Our men do complain of one thing, that is their heavy clothing. They say they suffer with it, in this heat. If they had thin pantaloons, they would do very well. It is a pity they cannot be made more comfortable in this respect."[26] During the same period another volunteer stated, "We are soon to...adopt the United States uniform, consisting of a blue blouse, blue caps, or dark felt hats, &c."[27] However, the 2nd Maine did not begin to receive its state-issue blue clothing until toward the end of August, 1861.[28]

Encamped on the State Grounds at Augusta by May 20, 1861, the 3rd Maine, also known as "The Kennebec Regiment," was commanded by Col. O. O. Howard. Only the Bath City Greys (Co. A) were fully uniformed in gray suits, while the remainder of the regiment, which was composed of newly enlisted companies, received "1473 [grey] flannel shirts," "925 [grey] Trowsers," and "929 Woolen Overcoats" from the state during June 1861. The whole regiment also received "966 Red Woolen Blankets" at the same time.[29] Co. A was armed with M1816 smoothbore Springfield .69-caliber muskets with Belgian (cone-in-breech) conversion, while the rest of the unit was armed with M1842 "Springfield, smooth-bore, muzzle-loading muskets, fitted with the common bayonet." According to Cpl. Abner R. Small, Co. G, 3rd Maine, on July 3, 1861, this unit "gave up the grey regimentals...worn from home, and received new uniforms: loose blue flannel blouses, looser light-blue pantaloons, and baggy forage caps; not a fit in the lot."[30] Recalling his experience after Bull Run, Pvt. Page F. Francis of the Bath City Greys commented, "I finally got into camp safe and sound, but without anything but my clothes, gun and equipments; even my cap was gone."[31]

Mainly enlisted on the coast and composed principally of "ship-builders and those engaged in the coasting trade," the 4th Maine, under Col. Hiram G. Berry, were reported as wearing "substantial grey suits" and carrying "the Springfield musket of 1836" when they passed through Wilmington, Delaware, on June 20,

1861. When they arrived in Washington, DC, in mid-July they were described as being dressed in a "durable grey cloth, and... well made." This regiment was also provided with "full camp equipage, including fourteen wagons and fifty-four horses," and was accompanied by the Rockland Brass Band of seventeen pieces, and a drum corps of twenty men. Their banners consisted of a silk United States flag, heavily gold-fringed, regulation size, and a regimental flag of blue silk, heavily embroidered," plus "a large white standard inscribed in heavy letters, 'From the Home of Knox!'"[32]

By June 24, 1861, the firm of Storer & Cutler had made 980 "uniform coats" of "Hamilton Doeskin, all wool" for the 5th Maine. At the same time, 930 pairs of pantaloons of "Dexter Doeskin," made at Dexter, Maine, were produced by Chadbourn & Kendall for the same regiment.[33] Headgear consisted of drab or gray high-crowned "Kossuth"-style felt hats, turned up on one side. When this regiment passed through Wilmington, Delaware, en route for the capital, the *State Journal and Statesman* noted that its uniform was "gray throughout, with drab felt hats, regulation pattern. The officers are also uniformed in gray, with regulation hats. There is a band attached to the regiment, consisting of twenty-five performers. An efficient drum and fife corps is also attached to the regiment. They have fifteen baggage wagons and two ambulance wagons, drawn by sixty-four powerful horses. The regiment is fully supplied with tents and camp equipage, and have also a supply of over 16,000 ball cartridges."[34] When the 5th Maine arrived in Washington, DC, it was described as wearing "light grey pantaloons and coats, and high top, dark grey felt hats, turned up at the sides."[35]

While passing through New York, the "Sons of Maine" resident in the city presented the 5th Maine with a regimental banner of "blue silk, with a heavy yellow fringe, lancewood staff, silver spear, and blue and white tassels," which bore "the coat of arms of the state of Maine and the United States combined, surmounted by a star and the state motto: '*Dirigo* [I lead].'" Under the coat of arms were "the words 'Fifth Regiment Maine Volunteers,' in gold letters, and over it the Websterian motto: 'Liberty and Union now and forever—one and inseparable.'"[36]

After Bull Run, Cpl. Benjamin Given, Co. E, 5th Maine, wrote to his wife stating, "We had to leave behind us all our equipage, I left even my blanket and my coat, which in the intense heat was unendurable. My gun I bore off, though many threw theirs away."[37] Both the 4th and 5th Maine received M1842 muskets although these were subsequently replaced with M1841 (Windsor) rifles with saber bayonets and M1855 rifle muskets respectively.[38] The 5th Maine (three years) had "a new uniform throughout and new camp equipments" shortly after Col. Nathaniel Jackson was appointed to command on September 9, 1861.[39]

Commanded by Col. Abner Knowles, the 6th Maine received "Kossuth"-style hats, and wore "grey uniforms, like the other regiments from Maine."[40] Mostly recruited in Washington and Penobscot Counties, this regiment was mustered-in at Portland on July 15, 1861. Its gray uniforms were made by Bangor merchant tailors

Both of these men are identified as Maine volunteers by the "VMM" or "Volunteer Militia of Maine" plates that fasten their waist belts. The state contracted for these plates for belts and cartridge boxes for its militia during the late 1850s. Note the small tin-drum canteen carried by the man at top. The headgear of this man consists of a Pattern-1851 dress cap, while that of the man at bottom right is composed of a chasseur-pattern cap made of different cloth from his plain nine-button gray frock coat. *Anne S. K. Brown Military Collection, Brown University/ninth-plate tintype—Michael J. McAfee collection.*

Also identified to state by his "VMM" belt plate, which he wears upsidedown to compensate for the reversed photographic process, this volunteer possibly enlisted in the 6th Maine, many of which were photographed wearing the same style of fez. He also wears a Pattern-1856 dark-blue frock coat. He holds an M1855 Springfield rifle musket at "Shoulder Arms." *Sixth-plate tintype by S.L. Carleton, Portland, Maine—Library of Congress LC-DIG-ppmsca-33446.*

Wheelwright & Clark, plus Michael Gilligan, and Sargent & Davis, from "Cadet mixed" woollen cloth made by the Lewiston Falls Manufacturing Company, owned by Col. J.M. Frye.[41] Seemingly in anticipation of receiving this contract, Wheelwright & Clark advertised in the Bangor press for 100 each of "coat makers" and "pant makers" on July 3 and 9 respectively.[42] At the same time, contracts for 4,000 pairs of pants for "the Maine Regiments" were issued, with H. J. Libby & Co. producing 2,000 pairs, plus "Messrs. Storer & Cutler 1,000 pairs—at 81 [cents] per pair, to be made of the Bates mills goods—and Messrs. T. A. White & Co., of Bangor, 1,000 pairs at 87½ cents, to be made of the York mills goods."[43]

The 6th Maine left Portland on July 17 for duty in the defenses around the federal capital. According to a *New York Herald* report on its arrival at that city, each man in the 6th Maine also had "an extra fatigue uniform, consisting of gray pants and shirt, presented to them by various sewing societies."[44] Based on photographic evidence, many members of this regiment also wore tasseled fezzes.

Of the remaining nine Maine regiments enlisted in 1861, only the 7th through 9th Regiments continued to be issued with state-made uniforms of blue cloth. Initially, the 7th Maine, or Washburn Zouaves, was to "adopt the Zouave dress and drill," but nothing seems to have come of this.[45] When the regiment left the state en route for Baltimore on August 23, 1861, the *Augusta Age* reported that it was "clad in regulation blue" and carried M1841 "Windsor" rifles with sword bayonet supplied by the Massachusetts Ordnance Department, although it was "imperfectly drilled and not fully equipped," being "hurriedly made up in response to the summons of the War Department."[46] When the 8th Maine passed through

Composed almost entirely of the hardy lumbermen of the Penobscot Valley, most of these men of Co. B, 6th Maine, are wearing trimmed and tasselled fezzes, although one man in the back row has a stiffened fez of different pattern. Some have either a letter "B" or numeral "6" attached to its front. Many also wear what were probably some of the gray shirts presented by "sewing societies" before this regiment left for the war. Two men seated in the front row wear the regimental gray frock coats. Reclining second from left, smoking the long-stemmed clay pipe, is Private Dorephus, or Dorphis, L. Fields, of Ellsworth, in Hancock County, Maine, who was mustered-in on July 15, 1861. *Albumen print—Bedford Hayes collection.*

Boston on September 10, 1861, it was reported in the *Boston Herald* as dressed in "light blue pants and overcoats, with dark blue flannel blouses, and the regulation black hats."[47] When the 9th Maine arrived in the same city two weeks later, the *Daily Advertiser* commented that it was "neatly uniformed in the regular uniform, of dark and light blue, with good, substantial overcoats."[48]

Production of uniforms and clothing for these regiments had been initiated on July 25, when Acting Quartermaster Gen. John L. Hodson requested proposals for 1,000 to 2,000 each of blouses, pairs of trousers, and pairs of Brogans, to be delivered in Augusta, Maine, by August 20, 1861. Also required was from 2,000 to 4,000 shirts, "the State furnishing flannel." On the same occasion, the state requested 1,000 to 2,000 each of knapsacks, haversacks, canteens, "sets Equipments," and "sets Camp Utensils, French Pattern."[49] On August 14, 1861, the *Portland Daily Advertiser* advised that Chadbourn & Kendall were filling the contract for "one thousand pairs pantaloons, from the army regulation goods, manufactured at Dexter." Henry Darn & Son were "engaged on eight hundred sets of equipments."[50] By August 17, Longley & Garcelon, saddlers and harness makers at Lewiston, had nearly completed a state contract "to furnish 400 equipments and 20 harnesses" for the 7th Maine.[51]

Holding the distinction of having the highest battle casualties of any Union cavalry regiment in service having suffered 174 officers and men killed and wounded, the 1st Maine Cavalry was organized for three years' service in Augusta, Maine, on October 31, 1861. This regiment was not uniformed until the beginning of November, up to which time, according to the regimental history, it was "insufficiently clothed."[52] The day before organization, the *Lewiston Daily Evening Journal* advised that the 1st Maine Cavalry would be clothed in "a blue jacket and pants, trimmed with yellow."[53] Earlier, on October 2, 1861, the state had requested proposals from contractors for "1,200 pairs Sewed Boots for Cavalry," at the same time needing "Coats, Pants, Blouses, Shirts, Drawers, Camp-utensils, Knapsacks, Haversacks, Canteens and Shoes for Infantry Regiments."[54] The latter indicates that the remaining regiments recruited in 1861, consisting of the 10th through 15th Maine Infantry, also received uniforms issued by the state. Passing through Boston on October 6, 1861, the 10th Maine, the nucleus of which was composed of ex-three-month volunteers of the 1st Maine, wore a "substantial uniform of light blue," and were provided with neat, compact knapsacks, much more comfortable to march with than the baggy arrangements some of the Maine troops, and many other States, have carried."[55] The reference to light blue on this occasion may indicate that this regiment was wearing overcoats. Much of the clothing issued to the 12th Maine was too small. On November 29, 1861, the *Lewiston Journal* reported, "Gen. Butler seeing the men agonizing in too small fits, ordered a tailor who measured the immense shoulders of the men and will give them fits! General Butler says that the men shall be comfortably clad and accoutred before he leaves the shores of New England."[56]

With further regard to the cavalry regiment, Cobb, Robinson & Co. of Auburn, Maine, secured a contract to produce "200 or more pairs of sewed cavalry boots," and advertised for "ten good Bootmakers" on October 9, 1861.[57] The firm of Longley & Garcelon acquired a contract worth $4,000 to supply "cavalry and infantry equipments, harnesses, &c." to these regiments, which included 100 saddles and sets of equipment for the 1st Maine Cavalry.[58] A week later, the *Lewiston Journal* estimated that the cost of the cavalry equipment would be "no less than $50,000" and consisted of "One saddle, one bridle, one halter, one watering bridle, saddle bags, pistol holster, and belts for the men."[59] Towards the end of October, the same newspaper commented, "The band of the Maine Cavalry ride on grey horses. Most of the horses are of chestnut color, and nearly all have long black tails."[60]

MAINE
Order of Battle, 1861

Volunteer Infantry

1st Maine Volunteer Militia (three-months' service)	6th Regiment	11th Regiment
2nd Regiment	7th Regiment (Washburn Zouaves)	12th Regiment
3rd Regiment (The Kennebec Regiment)	8th Regiment	13th Regiment
4th Regiment	9th Regiment	14th Regiment
5th Regiment	10th Regiment	15th Regiment.

Volunteer Cavalry

1st Maine Cavalry

BIBLIOGRAPHY

GENERAL SOURCES

BOOKS

Bazelon, Bruce S. and William F. McGuinn. *A Directory of American Military Goods Dealers & Makers 1785-1885*. Manassas, Virginia: REF, 1987.

Campbell, J. Duncan and Michael J. O'Donnell. *American Military Headgear Insignia*. Alexandria, Virginia: O'Donnell, 2004.

Coates, Earl J. and John D. McAulay. *Civil War Sharps Carbines & Rifles*. Gettysburg, PA: Thomas, 1996.

Dornbusch, C. E. (compiler). *Military Bibliography of the Civil War*. vol. 1. "Regimental Publications and Personal Narratives: Northern States (in seven parts)." New York Public Library, New York: Arno Press, 1961-62.

Elting, John R., and Michael J. McAfee (ed.). *Military Uniforms in America*, vol. III, "Long Endure: The Civil War Period 1852-1867. Novato, CA: Presidio Press, 1982.

Hewett, Janet B., (ed.), et al. *Supplement to the Official Records of the Union and Confederate Armies*. 100 volumes. Wilmington, NC: Broadfoot, 1995-1999.

Langellier, John P. *Army Blue: The Uniform of Uncle Sam's Regulars 1848-1873*. Atglen, PA: Schiffer, 1998.

Langellier, John P. and C. Paul Loane. *Army Headgear 1812-1872*. Atglen, PA: Schiffer, 2002.

McAulay, John D. *Rifles of the U.S. Army 1861–1906*. Lincoln, RI: Andrew Mowbray, 2003.

O'Donnell, Michael J. and J. Duncan Campbell. *American Military Belt Plates*. 2nd Ed. Alexandria, VA: O'Donnell Publications, 2000.

Scott, Robert N.. *The War of the Rebellion: A Compilation of the Official Records of the Union and Confederate Armies*. 128 volumes. Washington: Government Printing Office, 1880–1901.

Tice, Warren K. *Uniform Buttons of the United States 1776-1865*. Gettysburg, PA: Thomas, 1997.

Todd, Frederick P., et al. *American Military Equipage 1851–1872*, vol. 1, Providence, RI: Company of Military Historians, 1974.

Todd, Frederick P., et al. *American Military Equipage 1851–1872*, vol. 2, Providence, RI: Company of Military Historians, 1977.

Todd, Frederick P., et al. *American Military Equipage 1851–1872*, vol. 2, "State Forces." Chatham Square Press, 1983.

Troiani, Don., et al. *Don Troiani's Regiments & Uniforms of the Civil War*, Mechanicsburg, PA: Stackpole, 2002.

Wilson, Mark R. *The Business of Civil War: Military Mobilization and the State, 1861–1865*. Baltimore, MD: The John Hopkins University Press, 2006.

JOURNALS AND MAGAZINES

Military Collector & Historian. A quarterly journal published by the Company of Military Collectors and Historians, 1951–1961; Company of Military Historians, 1962–present day.

North South Trader Civil War: The Magazine for Collectors & Historians. A quarterly magazine founded by William S. Mussenden, published by Stephen W. Sylvia, 1973–present day.

Military Images: Photographic history of the U.S. soldier and sailor 1839–1920. A bimonthly magazine founded by Harry Roach in 1979 and edited today by Ronald S. Coddington.

MASSACHUSETTS

PRIMARY SOURCES

"Bill of Dress of the Boston Light Artillery...Submitted by
the Officers and Members...Boston May 16/59," Adjutant
General's Files, War Records Section, Commonwealth
of Massachusetts Military Division, Adjutant General's
Office, Boston, MA.

*Public Documents of Massachusetts being the annual reports
of various Public Officers and Institutions for the year 1861.*
Boston, MA: Secretary of the Commonwealth, 1862.

*Sketches and Business Directory of Boston and its Vicinity
for 1860 and 1861.* Boston, MA: Darrell and Moore and
George Coolidge, 1861.

*The Boston Directory embracing the City Record: A General
Directory of the Citizens, and a Business Directory for
the year commencing July, 1861.* Boston, MA: Adams,
Sampson and Company, No. 91 Washington Street. 1861.

NEWSPAPERS:

Barre, Massachusetts, *Barre Gazette*
Boston, Massachusetts, *Boston Daily Advertiser*
Boston, Massachusetts, *Boston Daily Courier*
Boston, Massachusetts, *Daily Evening Journal*
Boston, Massachusetts, *Daily Evening Traveller*
Boston, Massachusetts, *Boston Evening Transcript*
Boston, Massachusetts, *Boston Herald*
Gloucester, Massachusetts, *Cape Ann Light
and Gloucester Telegraph*
Lowell, Massachusetts, *Lowell Daily Citizen & News*
Lowell, Massachusetts, *Lowell Daily Courier*
Pittsfield, Massachusetts, *Berkshire County Eagle*
Pittsfield, Massachusetts, *Pittsfield Sun*
Salem, Massachusetts, *Salem Register*
Springfield, Massachusetts, *Springfield Republican*

SECONDARY SOURCES

Adams, John G.B. *Reminiscences of the Nineteenth
Massachusetts regiment.* Boston, MA: Wright and Potter,
1899.

Albert, Alphaeus H. *Record of American Uniform and
Historical Buttons* (Bicentennial Ed.). Boyertown, PA:
Boyertown, 1977.

Adjutant General, Massachusetts, *Massachusetts Soldiers,
Sailors, and Marines in the Civil War.* 10 vols. 1931–1937.

Cook, Benjamin F. *History of the Twelfth Massachusetts
Volunteers (Webster Regiment).* Boston, MA: 12th
(Webster) Regiment Association, 1882.

Cowdin, Robert, *Gen. Cowdin and the First Massachusetts
Regiment of Volunteers.* Boston, MA: J. E. Farwell and
Company, 1864.

Cudworth, Warren H. *History of the First Regiment
(Massachusetts Infantry) from the 25th of May, 1861, to the
25th of May, 1864.* Boston, MA: 1866.

Cunningham, Dr. Michael R. "Sergeant Francis M. Kingman:
'the dauntless color-bearer' of the 29th Massachusetts,"
Civil War Historian (2008), vol. 4, No. 1.

Davis Jr., Charles E. *Three Years in the Army: The Story of the
Thirteenth Massachusetts Volunteers from July 16, 1861, to
August 1, 1864.* Boston, MA: Estes and Lauriat, 1894.

Derby, W. P. *Bearing Arms in the Twenty-Seventh
Massachusetts Regiment of Volunteer Infantry.* Boston, MA:
Wright and Potter, 1883.

Dollard, Robert. *Recollections of the Civil War and Going West to Grow Up in the Country.* Scotland, SD: 1906.

Emmerton, James A. *A Record of the Twenty-Third Regiment Mass. vol. Infantry in the War of the Rebellion.* Boston, MA: William War and Co., 1886.

Hanson, John W. *Historical Sketch of the Old Sixth Regiment of Massachusetts Volunteers.* Boston, MA: Lee and Shepard, 1866.

Hutchinson, Gustavus D. *A Narrative of the Formation and Services of the Eleventh Massachusetts Volunteers.* Boston, MA: Alfred Mudge and Son, 1893.

Johnson, Raymond, Roger Sturcke, and Michael J. Winey. "4th Battalion of Rifles, Massachusetts Volunteer Militia, 1860–1861," Plate No. 603, *Military Collector & Historian* (Spring 1987), vol. 39, No. 1.

Marvin, Abijah P. *History of Worcester in the War of the Rebellion.* Worcester, MA: Published by the Author, 1870.

McAfee, Michael J. "Massachusetts Men in Gray at Fort Monroe, 1861 (Reprised)," *Military Collector & Historian,* spring 2013, vol. 65, No. 1.

McAfee, Michael J. "Uniforms & History: 3rd Regiment, Massachusetts Volunteer Militia," *Military Images,* vol. 19, No. 2, September-October 1997.

McAfee, Michael J. "Uniforms & History: The 18th Massachusetts Volunteer Infantry Regt.," *Military Images,* vol. 20, No. 3, November–December 1998.

McAfee, Michael J. "Uniforms & History: The 19th Regiment Massachusetts Volunteer Infantry," *Military Images,* vol. 28, No. 3, November–December 2006.

McAfee, Michael J. "Uniforms & History: Boston Light Artillery, "Cook's Battery 1861," *Military Images,* vol. 27, No. 6, May–June 2006.

McAfee, Michael J. "Uniforms & History: Fourth Battalion of Rifles, Massachusetts Volunteer Militia, 1860–61," *Military Images,* vol. 11, No. 1, July–August 1989.

McAfee, Michael J. "Uniforms & History: The Minute Men of '61, 8th Regiment, Massachusetts Volunteer Militia," *Military Images,* vol. 18, No. 1, January–February 1997.

McAfee, Michael J. "Uniforms & History: The New England Guard—Company A, 4th Battalion of Infantry, Massachusetts Volunteer Militia," *Military Images,* vol. 18, No. 5, March–April 1997.

Moller, George D. *Massachusetts Military Shoulder Arms 1784–1877.* Lincoln, RI: Andrew Mowbray, 1988.

Nason, George W. *History and Complete Roster of the Massachusetts Regiments—Minute Men of 1861.* Boston, MA: Smith and McCance, 1910.

Newell, Capt. Joseph Keith (ed.). *"Ours." Annals of the 10th Regiment, Massachusetts Volunteers, in the Rebellion.* Springfield, MA: C. A. Nichols, 1875.

Osborne, William H. *The History of the Twenty-Ninth Regiment of Massachusetts Volunteer Infantry in the Late War of the Rebellion.* Boston, MA: Albert J. Wright, 1877.

Quint, Alonzo H. *Record of the Second Massachusetts Infantry, 1861-65.* Boston, MA: James P. Walker, 1867.

Roe, Alfred S. *The Fifth Regiment Massachusetts Volunteer Infantry.* Fifth Regiment Veteran Association: Boston, MA, 1911.

Roe, Alfred S. and Charles Nutt. *First Regiment of Heavy Artillery, Massachusetts Volunteers, Formerly the Fourteenth Regiment of Infantry, 1861–1865.* Worcester and Boston, Massachusetts—Regimental Association: Commonwealth Press, 1917.

Stamatelos, James. "Whipple's Patent Military Cap." *Military Images.* vol. 5, No. 6, May–June 1984.

Stephenson, Luther. "Three Months' Service in 1861, with the Fourth Regiment, MVM," Massachusetts Order Loyal Legion—Civil War Papers, vol. 2, Boston, MA: 1890.

Stone, James Madison. *Personal Recollections of the Civil War.* Boston, MA: published by the author, 1918.

Todd, Frederick P. *American Military Equipage 1851–1872.* vol. 2, "State Forces." New York City: Chatham Square Press, 1983.

Troiani, Don. "French Uniforms, Cloth & Equipage of the Union Army." Part 1, *North South Trader's Civil War*, vol. 26, No. 2.

Troiani, Don. "French Uniforms, Cloth & Equipage of the Union Army," Part 2, *North South Trader's Civil War*, vol. 26, No. 3.

Troiani, Don, et al. *Regiments & Uniforms of the Civil War*, Stackpole: Mechanicsburg, PA, 2002.

Warren, Richard. "Boston Light Artillery (Cook's Battery), Massachusetts, 1861," *Military Collector & Historian.* Summer 2002, vol. 54, No. 2.

Weddle, Ryan B., "Massachusetts Men in Gray at Fort Monroe, 1861," *Military Collector & Historian.* Winter 2011, vol. 63, No. 4.

RHODE ISLAND

PRIMARY SOURCES

Frederic Sackett Papers, Rhode Island Historical Society.

Purchase Vouchers, Rhode Island State Archives.

Scott, Robert N. (ed.). *The War of the Rebellion: A Compilation of the Official Records of the Union and Confederate Armies.* Washington: Government Printing Office,1899, Series 3, vol. 1.

William R. Arnold Papers, Rhode Island Historical Society.

NEWSPAPERS

Baltimore, Maryland, *The Sun*

Bristol, Rhode Island, *Bristol Phenix*

Chicago, Illinois, *Chicago Evening Journal*

Kansas City, Kansas, *Kansas City Star*

Lowell, Massachusetts, *Lowell Daily Courier*

Madison, Wisconsin, *Weekly Wisconsin Patriot*

Newport, Rhode Island, *Newport Mercury*

Pawtucket, Rhode Island, *Pawtucket Gazette & Chronicle*

Philadelphia, Pennsylvania, *Philadelphia Inquirer*

Providence, Rhode Island, *Providence Daily Journal*

Providence, Rhode Island, *Providence Daily Post*

Providence, Rhode Island, *Providence Evening Press*

SECONDARY SOURCES

Archambault, Alan H. "1st Light Infantry of Providence, Rhode Island, 1861," *Military Collector & Historian.* Fall 2003, vol. 55, No. 3.

Archambault, Alan H. "2nd Regiment, Rhode Island Volunteer Infantry, 1861–1865," *Military Collector & Historian.* Spring 1991, vol. 43, No. 1.

Archambault, Alan H. "The First Regiment Rhode Island Detached Militia, 1861," *Military Collector & Historian.* Fall 2001, vol. 53, No. 3.

Denison, Frederic. *Shot & Shell: the Third Rhode Island Heavy Artillery regiment in the War of the Rebellion.* Providence, RI: For the Third R. I. H. art. Vet. Association, by J. A. Reid, 1879.

Dennett, Tyler. *John Hay—From Poetry to Politics.* New York: Dodd, Mead and Company, 1933.

Gorges, Chris. "Kady Brownell: Lady of Combat," *North South Trader's Civil War*, vol. 35, No. 6.

Grandchamp, Robert, "Dirty, ragged, and with a full assortment of grayback: Rhode Island Uniforms in the Civil War," *Military Images*, vol. 28, No. 6, May–June 2007.

Grandchamp, Robert. "'The appearance of a gang of Chinamen:' A Study of the Uniforms Worn by Brown's Battery B, First Rhode Island Light Battery," *Military Collector & Historian*, vol. 59, No. 1, Spring 2007.

Hennessey, James. "The Burnside Zouaves of Providence, R.I., 1861–1870," *Military Collector & Historian*. Spring 1979, vol. 31, No. 1.

McAfee, Michael J. "Uniforms & History: 1st Regiment, Rhode Island Detached Militia, 1861." *Military Images*, vol. 10, No. 6, May–June 1989.

McAfee, Michael J. "Uniforms & History: The First Light Infantry of Providence, Rhode Island." *Military Images*, vol. 14, No. 3, November–December 1992.

Rhodes, Elisha H. *The First Campaign of the Second Rhode Island Infantry*. Providence, RI: Sidney S. Rider, 1878.

Rhodes, John H. *The History of Battery B, First Rhode Island Light Artillery*. Providence, RI: Snow and Farnham, 1892.

Rhodes, Robert H. (ed.). *All for the Union, a History of the 2nd Rhode Island Volunteer Infantry in the War of the Great Rebellion as told by the diary and letters of Elisha Hunt Rhodes who enlisted as a private in '61 and rose to the command of his regiment*. Lincoln, RI: Andrew Mowbray, 1985.

Severin, John and Frederick P. Todd. "1st Regiment of Rhode Island Detached Militia, 1861." *Military Collector & Historian*. Summer 1955, vol. 7, No. 2.

Spicer, William Arnold. *History of the 9th & 10th Rhode Island Volunteers, and the 10th Rhode Island Battery, in the Union Army in 1862*. Providence, RI: Snow and Franham, 1892.

Warren, Richard. *1st Rhode Island Detached Militia, 2nd Rhode Island Volunteer Infantry, 1st & 2nd Rhode Island Batteries*. Federal Data Series–No. 2, Confederate Historical Society, 1987.

Woodbury, Augustus, *Campaign of the First Rhode Island Regiment*. Providence, RI: Sidney S. Rider, 1862.

NEW HAMPSHIRE

PRIMARY SOURCES

Hewett, Janet B. (ed.), et al., *Supplement to the Official Records of the Union and Confederate Armies*. Part II, vol. 27, serial No. 39.

Scott, Robert N. *The War of the Rebellion: A Compilation of the Official Records of the Union and Confederate Armies*. series 3, vol. 1. Washington: Government Printing Office, 1899.

NEWSPAPERS

Amherst, New Hampshire, *Farmer's Cabinet*

Boston, Massachusetts, *Boston Evening Transcript*

Concord, New Hampshire, *New Hampshire Patriot & State Gazette*

Concord, New Hampshire, *New Hampshire Statesman*

Keene, New Hampshire, *New Hampshire Sentinel*

Manchester, New Hampshire, *Dollar Weekly Mirror*

Portsmouth, New Hampshire, *Portsmouth Journal*

Washington, D.C., *National Republican*

Wilmington, Delaware, *Delaware Republican*

SECONDARY SOURCES

A Minor War History compiled from a Soldier Boy's Letters to "The Girl I Left Behind Me, 1861–1864. Lakeport, NH: Private Print of Martin A. Haynes, 1916.

Abbott, Stephen G. *The First Regiment New Hampshire Volunteers in the Great Rebellion*. Keene, NHe: Sentinel, 1890.

Akers, Monte. "That Crazy Cap." *Military Images*, vol. 5, No. 4, January–February 1984.

Child M.D. William. *A History of the Fifth Regiment, New Hampshire Volunteers.* Bristol, NH: R.W. Musgrove, 1893.

Eldredge, Daniel. *The Third New Hampshire and All About It.* Boston, MA: E.B. Stillings, 1893.

Ellis, James A. (ed.). *History of New Hampshire.* vol. 5, American Historical Society, New York: n.d.

Field, Ron. The New Hampshire Volunteers of 1861, *Military Collector & Historian.* Winter 2012, vol. 64, No. 4.

Haynes, Martin A. *A History of the Second Regiment, New Hampshire Volunteer Infantry in the War of the Rebellion.* Lakeport, NH: 1896.

Jackman, Lyman. *History of the Sixth New Hampshire Regiment in the War for the Union.* Concord, NH: Republican Press Association, Railroad Square, 1894.

Langelier, John P. and C. Paul Loane. *U.S. Army Headgear 1812-1872.* Schiffer: Atglen, PA, 2002.

Little, Henry F.W. *The Seventh Regiment New Hampshire Volunteers in the War of the Rebellion.* Concord, NH: Ira C. Evans, 1896.

Livermore, Thomas L. *Days and Events, 1860-1866.* Boston and New York: Houghton Mifflin, 1920.

Lyford, James O. (editor), *History of Concord, New Hampshire.* Concord, NH: The Rumford Press, 1905.

McAfee, Michael J. "Uniforms & History: The 2nd New Hampshire Infantry," *Military Images,* vol. 24, No. 3, November–December 2002.

McAfee, Michael J. "Uniforms & History: The 7th New Hampshire Volunteer Infantry Regiment, 1861." *Military Collector & Historian.* Winter 1975, vol. 27, No. 4.

Merrill, R. Irving. *Merrill & Son's Concord City Directory for 1860-61.* Concord, NH: Rufus Merrill and Son, 1860.

Severin, John P. and Frederick P. Todd. "2d Regiment, New Hampshire Volunteer Militia, 1861." *Military Collector & Historian.* March 1953, vol. 5, No. 1.

Stanyan, John M. *A History of the Eighth Regiment of New Hampshire Volunteers.* Concord, NH: Ira C. Evans, 1892.

Waite, Maj. Otis F.W. *New Hampshire in the Great Rebellion.* Claremont, NH: Tracy, Chase and Company, 1870.

Warren, Richard, *1st to 5th New Hampshire Volunteer Infantry 1861–1862.* Federal Data Series–No. 1. Confederate Historical Society, 1987.

CONNECTICUT

PRIMARY SOURCES

Dear Transcript, Letters from Windham County Soldiers during the Civil War 1861–1865. Killingly Historical and Genealogical Society, 2009.

Geer's Hartford City Directory for 1861–1862. Hartford, CT: Elihu Geer, 16 State Street, 1861.

Report of the Quartermasters-General to the General Assembly, in *Public Documents of the Legislature of Connecticut, May Session, 1862.* Hartford, 1862.

NEWSPAPERS

Bridgeport, Connecticut, *Daily Advertiser and Farmer*

Charleston, South Carolina, *Charleston Daily Courier*

Hartford, Connecticut, *Daily Courant*

Hartford, Connecticut, *Hartford Weekly Times*

Middletown, Connecticut, *The Constitution*

Milwaukee, Wisconsin, *Milwaukee Morning Sentinel*

New Haven, Connecticut, *Columbian Weekly Register*

New Haven, Connecticut, *Daily Palladium*

New London, Connecticut, *Daily Chronicle*

New York City, New York, *New York Herald*

Norwich, Connecticut, *Morning Bulletin*

SECONDARY SOURCES

Andrews, E.B., *A Private's Reminiscences of the first Year of the War.* Providence, RI: n.p., 1886.

Bennett, E.B. (compiler). *First Connecticut Heavy Artillery: Historical Sketch and Present Addresses of Members.* East Berlin: Privately printed, 1889.

Croffut, W. A. and John M. Morris. *The Military and Civil History of Connecticut during the War of 1861–65.* New York: Ledyard Bill, 1869.

Frinkle Fry (pseudonymn for Elnathan B. Tyler). *Wooden Nutmegs at Bull Run. A Humorous Account of some of the Exploits and Experiences of the Three Months Connecticut Brigade.* Hartford, CT: George L. Coburn, 1872.

Marvin, Edwin E. *The Fifth Regiment Connecticut Volunteers.* Hartford, CT: Wiley, Waterman and Eaton, 1889.

Murray, Thomas H. *History of the Ninth Regiment, Connecticut Volunteer Infantry. "The Irish Regiment," in the War of the Rebellion, 1861–65.* New Haven, CT: Price, Lee and Adkins, 1908.

Sprague, Homer B. *History of the 13th Infantry Regiment of Connecticut Volunteers.* Hartford, CT: Case, Lockwood and Co., 1867.

Todd, Frederick P. "State of Connecticut Uniforms 1856," *Military Collector & Historian.* Spring 1958, vol. 10, No. 1.

VERMONT

PRIMARY SOURCES

Hewett, Janet B. (editor), et al. *Supplement to the Official Records of the Union and Confederate Armies.* Part 2, vol. 69 (Serial No. 81).

NEWSPAPERS

Boston, Massachusetts, *Boston Evening Transcript*

Boston, Massachusetts, *Boston Herald*

Brattleboro, Vermont, *Vermont Phoenix*

Burlington, Vermont, *Burlington Free Press*

Lowell, Massachusetts, *Lowell Daily Citizen & News*

Montpelier, Vermont, *Vermont Watchman* and *State Journal*

New York City, New York, *New York Herald*

New York City, *New York Illustrated News*

St. Albans, Vermont, *St. Albans Daily Messenger*

St. Johnsbury, Vermont, *The Caledonian*

Troy, New York, *Troy Daily Whig*

Windsor, Vermont, *Vermont Chronicle*

Windsor, Vermont, *Vermont Journal*

SECONDARY SOURCES

Benedict, G.G. *Vermont in the Civil War: A History of the part taken by the Vermont Soldiers and Sailors in the War for the Union.* Burlington, VT: The Free Press Association, 1886.

Cunningham, Dr. Michael R. "The Civil War Chasseur Cap: A study of wartime and postwar characteristics." *North South Trader's Civil War*, vol. 37, No. 3.

Davis, Gilbert A. *History of Reading. Windsor County, Vermont.* n.p., 1903.

McAfee, Michael J. "Uniforms & History: 2nd Regiment, Vermont Volunteer Infantry, 1861–1865," *Military Images,* vol. 13, No. 2, September–October 1991.

Peladeau, Marius. "The 1st Vermont Cavalry in the War: A Photo Gallery," *North South Trader's Civil War.* vol. 26, No. 4.

Peladeau, Marius. "Green Mountain Soldiers: Vermonters in the Civil War," *Military Images.* vol. 13, No. 2, September–October 1991.

Peladeau, Marius. "Vermont Civil War Insignia." *North South Trader's Civil War*. vol. 21, No. 4.

Waite, Otis F. R. *Vermont in the Great Rebellion.* Claremont, NH: Tracy, Chase and Company, 1869.

MAINE

PRIMARY SOURCES

A Business Directory of the Subscribers to the New Map of Maine. Portland, ME: J. Chace, Jr. and Co., n.d.

Annual Report of the Adjutant General of the State of Maine for the year ending December 31, 1861, Augusta: Stevens and Sayward, 1862.

NEWSPAPERS

Bangor, Maine, *Bangor Daily Whig and Courier*

Boston, Massachusetts, *Boston Daily Advertiser*

Boston, Massachusetts, *Boston Herald*

Lewiston, Maine, *Lewiston Daily Evening Journal*

New York City, New York, *New York Herald*

Portland, Maine, *Portland Daily Advertiser*

Washington, D.C., *Daily National Intelligencer*

Washington, D.C., *The Evening Star*

Wilmington, Delaware, *Delaware State Journal and Statesman*

SECONDARY SOURCES

Gould, Maj. John M. and Rev. Leonard G. Jordan. *History of the First-Tenth-Twenty-ninth Maine Regiment.* Portland, ME: Stephen Berry, 1871.

Haarmann, Albert W. (compiler). "The Blue and the Gray." *Military Images.* vol. VI, No. 6, May–June 1985.

McAfee, Michael J. "Uniforms & History: Maine Regiments of 1861." *Military Images.* vol. 22, No. 5, March–April 2001.

Small, Abner Ralph. *The Road to Richmond: The Civil War Letters of Major Abner R. Small of the 16th Maine Volunteers.* Fordham University Press: New York, 2000.

Stanley, R. H. and Geo. O. Hall. *Eastern Maine and the Rebellion.* Bangor, ME: R. H. Stanley and Co., 1887.

Tobie, Edward P. *History of the First Maine Cavalry.* Emory and Hughes: Boston, 1887.

ENDNOTES

INTRODUCTION

1. *Newport (RI) Mercury*, May 4, 1861, 2:3.
2. See "Gray Uniforms Prohibited," *Boston (MA) Herald*, August 22, 1861, 4:1.
3. "Proposals for Army Cloths," *North America and (PA) United States Gazette*, November 13, 1861, 2:3.

MASSACHUSETTS

1. See "Letter to the Governor [George S. Boutwell] from the Commanders of the Divisions, Brigades, Regiments & Battalions [Massachusetts Volunteer Militia]," March 25, 1852, Collection of the Massachusetts Adjutant General's Office, War Records Section. Much of the content of this letter was enacted in General Order No. 1 of the same date. See Frederick P. Todd, *American Military Equipage* 1851—1872, vol. II, "State Forces" (Chatham Square Press, Inc., 1983), 894. During August 1853, General Order No. 5 modified the dress regulations to specify the Pattern-1851 uniform minus branch service facing color, and with the state rather than Federal button.
2. "Troops for Fort Monroe," *New York Herald*, May 12, 1861, 8:5. The uniform of the Union Guards was given a slightly different description in the regimental history of the 29th Massachusetts, of which that unit became Co. I in December 1861: "The uniform consisted of gray frock coats, the gift of the 'Empire Fire Company' of Lynn, Kossuth hats, looped at one side, and light blue trousers. The hats and trousers were furnished by the state." See William H. Osborne, *The History of the Twenty-ninth Regiment of Massachusetts Volunteer Infantry in the late War of the Rebellion* (Boston, MA: Albert J. Wright, 1877), 42.
3. John W. Hanson, *Historical Sketch of the Old Sixth Regiment of Massachusetts Volunteers (Boston, MA: Lee and Shepard, 1866)*, 20. Regarding the clothing of the Watson Light Guard (Co. H), 6th Massachusetts MVM, the *Lowell Daily Courier* of April 20, 1861 (2:5) stated, "The uniform will probably be Cadet gray, and it is intended to have it made early in the coming week by different tailors." The *Lowell Daily Citizen & News* of April 24, 1861 (2:5) reported that it would be "trimmed with black." The *Daily Courier* dated April 22 (2:4) confirmed, "The uniforms of the company are to be made of the cadet cloth, from the Merrimack Woolen Manufacturing Company (at Dracut "Navy-Yard"). They are to be made up at once. Burbank & Chase make 30; Bennett, 10; Lancaster & Totman, 10, and the remainder by other tailors in the city." The next day the same journal added, "Capt. Davis and others visited Boston yesterday and purchased a revolver for each man of the company, and regulation swords for the officers, which will, when otherwise equipped, put them on a "war footing" suitable to meet the enemies of the stars and stripes. In our reference to the making of the uniforms for this company yesterday, we should have added to the tailors who were engaged on them, Hugh McEvoy, who makes fifteen." See "Capt. Davis's Company," *Lowell Daily (MA) Courier*, April 23, 1861, 2:3.
4. James Louis Sherman, "A School Boy Minute Man of '61" in George W. Nason, *History and Complete Roster of the Massachusetts Regiments—Minute Men of '61* (Boston, MA: Smith & McCance, 1910), 71.
5. Robert Dollard, *Recollections of the Civil War and Going West to Grow Up in the Country* (Scotland, SD: 1906), 17–18.
6. See "Supplies Furnished," *Boston Herald*, April 17, 1861, 4:4.
7. *Dollard, Recollections of the Civil War*, 20-21.

8. See "Military Movements. Arrival of Troops in Boston," *Boston Daily (MA) Advertiser*, April 17, 1861, 1:8; & "The Fourth Regiment via Fall River," *Boston Herald*, April 18, 1861, 2:1. The latter confirms that "guernsey frocks" were issued. The three-month volunteers received rifle muskets from the state commands not at once sent to the seat of war, which were probably M1855s of which 2,429 were acquired from the General Government in 1858.

9. Dollard, *Recollections of the Civil War*, 19. The clothing firm Whitten, Hopkins & Co. sold "Russia and Guernsey Frocks," which may have been the source for the over shirts issued to the 4th and 8th MVM. See *Sketches and Business Directory of Boston, 1861*, 376.

10. See "The Military in Boston—The Scene at Faneuil Hall," *Boston Herald*, April 17, 1861, 2:1; & "The Departure of the Fifth Regiment," *Boston Herald*, April 22, 1861, 2:1. The cloth for these overcoats was probably purchased from the Middlesex Company which supplied the state with 6,812 ¾ yards of cloth in 1861. See "Report of the Military Committee of the Council, December 27, 1861," Public Documents 7 in *Public Documents of Massachusetts...for the Year 1861*, 4. Hereafter referred to as "Report of the Military Committee."

11. "The Supply Department," *Boston Herald*, April 18, 1861, 4:1. Whitten, Hopkins & Co. was located at 32 Milk Street, Boston. See *Massachusetts City Directory*, 1861, 491. Owned by Charles V. Whitten, Samuel B. Hopkins and Horation S. Burdett, this firm supplied a total of 16,468 overcoats for Massachusetts volunteers during 1861. See "Report of the Military Committee," 4. It also made some of the uniforms for the 1st and 2nd New Hampshire Volunteers, for which see hereafter.

12. Luther Stephenson, "Three Months' service in 1861, with the Fourth Regiment, MVM," *Massachusetts Order Loyal Legion—Civil War Papers*, vol. II (Boston, MA: 1890), 540-41.

13. "The Lowell Troops," *Lowell Daily (MA) Courier*, May 13, 1861, 2:1. The citizen was J. A. Goodwin.

14. See "Fatigue Uniforms for the Sixth Regiment," *Lowell Daily Citizen (MA) & News*, May 14 1861, 2:4; & "New Fatigue Frocks for the Sixth," *Lowell Daily Courier*, May 14, 1861, 2:4. The latter source added, "The same kind of frocks will be furnished by Lawrence for the companies from that city, and measures will be at once taken to have the same frock for the Groton and Acton companies, so that the entire Sixth shall be dressed alike."

15. "The Sixth Massachusetts Regiment Receive Havelocks," *Evening (Washington, DC) Star*, May 5, 1861, 3:2.

16. *Pittsfield (MA) Sun*, April 25, 1861, 2:6 citing *New York Express*.

17. "The Massachusetts Troops," *Salem (MA) Register*, May 2, 1861, 2:4.

18. Alfred S. Roe, *The Fifth Regiment Massachusetts Volunteer Infantry* (Fifth Regiment Veteran Association: Boston, MA, 1911), 42.

19. See "Mustering of the Forces," *Daily Evening (MA) Traveller*, April 16, 1861, 2:4.

20. "Military Movements in Massachusetts—Soldiers' Shirts and Drawers," *Daily Evening Traveller*, April 22, 1861, 2:6. For the state issuance of "Blue Flannel Shirts" see "Schedule of Clothing, Camp and Garrison Equipage issued from the Quartermaster-General's Department of the State of Massachusetts, from April 22, 1861, to January 31, 1862," Document 7, *Public Documents of Massachusetts...for the Year 1861* (hereafter referred to as "Schedule of Clothing...April 22, 1861, to January 31, 1862".)

21. "Garments for the Soldiers," *Lowell Daily Citizen & News*, May 6 1861, 2:5.

22. Roe, *The Fifth Regiment Massachusetts Volunteer Infantry*, 19.

23. "Red Flannel Shirts," *Boston Herald*, April 29, 1861, 2:5.

24. See "Military," *Cape Ann Light and (MA) Gloucester Telegraph*, April 20, 1861, 1:1; & "Company G," *Cape Ann Light and Gloucester Telegraph*, April 27, 1861, 1:1.

25. *Ibid*, April 27, 1861, 2:4.

26. See "Capt. Center, of Co. G," *Cape Ann Light and Gloucester Telegraph*, May 11, 1861, 1:6.

27. "The Massachusetts Salem Zouaves," *Evening Star*, May 10, 1861, 3:1.

28. "Fred Smith's Journal. No. 13, Camp Andrew, Baltimore, July 28," *Berkshire County (MA) Eagle*, August 1, 1861, 2:5. See also Ron Field, Roger Sturcke, Richard J. Podsiadlo, and Michael J. Winey, "Salem Zouaves, Massachusetts Volunteer Militia, 1861, *Military Collector & Historian* 37, no. 2 (Summer 1985): 88-89.

29. "Military Matters," *Boston Daily Courier*, October 5, 1861, 1:8. See also James A. Emmerton, *A Record of the Twenty-Third Regiment Mass. vol. Infantry in the War of the Rebellion* (Boston, MA: William War & Co.), 1886, 2-3.

30. See "Military Movements," *Boston Daily (MA) Advertiser*, December 7, 1861, 1:7.

31. "The Salem Zouave Drill Corps," *Salem Register*, June 13, 1861, 2:2.

32. "Corporal Fred Smith's Journal. No. 4, Camp near Relay House, May 21, 1861," *Berkshire County Eagle*, May 30, 1861, 2:5. On May 20, 1861 (2:6) the *Salem Register* reported, "All the Regiment, with the exception of the Salem Zouaves, are uniformed alike in the U.S. Army fatigue dress …" At this time a volunteer in the American Guard (Co. G) commented, "The government uniforms…arrived yesterday afternoon—blue sack-jackets, pants, and caps—and Uncle Abraham must have taken our measure from his own. Nothing fits any but the six-foot men in the regiment. But it is a neat suit, and will immeasurably improve our appearance in the line. Being scarcely up to the army standard, your correspondent will find himself lost in one of them, and will be compelled to employ the services of several tailors to reduce it to his dimensions." See "Head-Quarters, 8th Reg't MVM, Camp Essex, (Relay House,) May 9, '61," *Cape Ann Light and Gloucester Telegraph*, May 18, 1861, 1:4.

33. "Fred Smith's Journal—No. 12, Camp Andrew, Baltimore, *Berkshire County Eagle*, July 21, 1861, 2:5.

34. "The Allen Guard," *Berkshire County Eagle*, May 23, 1861, 2:3; "Shavings from the Allen Guard," *Pittsfield (MA) Sun*, July 25, 1861, 2:7. See also "Muster-Out Roll of the Allen Guard," *Pittsfield Sun*, August 8, 1861, 2:5.

35. "Head-Quarters, 8th Reg't MVM, Camp Essex, (Relay House) June 4, '61," *Cape Ann Light and Gloucester Telegraph*, June 8, 1861, 2:4.

36. "The Departure of the Fifth Regiment," *Boston Herald*, April 22, 1861, 2:1.

37. *Ibid*, April 22, 1861, 2:1.

38. "Parades Yesterday," *Evening Star*, April 30, 1861, 2:2.

39. "From the Fifth Regiment," *Boston Evening (MA) Transcript*, June 1, 1861, 4:2.

40. William T. Eustis, "Sketch of the Fifth Massachusetts Regiment MVM," in Nason, *History and Complete Roster of the Massachusetts Regiments—Minute Men of '61*, 124 & 127.

41. "City Military Affairs," *Philadelphia (PA) Inquirer*, May 14, 1861, 2:6.

42. "Letter from Major E.B. Stannard, 3rd Battalion Rifles, MVM to Governor Nathaniel P. Banks, June 18, 1859," Adjutant General's Office, War Records Section, Secretary of the Commonwealth, Massachusetts Archives.

43. Abijah P. Marvin, *History of Worcester in the War of the Rebellion* (Worcester, MA: Published by the Author, 1870), 43.

44. "The Massachusetts Troops," *Boston Daily Advertiser*, June 15, 1861, 2:4.

45. See "Captain Dodd's Boston Rifle Company," *National (Washington, DC) Intelligencer*, May 13, 1861, 3:5; & "Captain Dodd's Boston Rifle Company," *Evening Star*, May 11, 1861, 3:1.

46. Charles E. Davis, Jr., *Three Years in the Army: The Story of the Thirteenth Massachusetts Volunteers from July 16, 1861, to August 1, 1864* (Boston, MA: Estes and Lauriat, 1894), p. xviii.

47. "Bill of Dress of the Boston Light Artillery…Submitted by the Officers and Members…Boston May 16/59," Adjutant General's Files, War Records Section, Commonwealth of Massachusetts Military Division, Adjutant General's Office, Boston.

48. Richard Warren, "Boston Light Artillery (Cook's Battery), Massachusetts, 1861," *Military Collector & Historian* 54, no. 2 (Summer 2002): 86-87. See also Michael J. McAfee, "Uniforms & History: Boston Light Artillery, "Cook's Battery" 1861," *Military Images* 27, no. 6 (May–June 2006): 30–31.

49. "Military Movements," *Boston Evening Transcript*, May 14, 1861, 4:2. See also "Affairs about Home—Parade of Major Cobb's Artillery," *Boston Herald*, June 15, 1861, 4:4, which mentions "a neat cap trimmed with red."

50. See "The City Appropriation of $100,000," *Boston Herald*, April 26, 1861, 2:6; & "The Volunteers," *Boston Herald*, May 11, 1861, 2:1.

51. "The New City Uniforms," *Boston Herald*, April 24, 1861, 4:4.

52. "Military Movements," *Daily Evening* (MA) *Traveller*, April 27, 1861, 2:3. In another column the same journal added, "The uniforms made from the 'Garibaldi tri-colored spots,' have made their appearance in our streets, and from their neatness have attracted general attention. As a change from the Regulation uniform they are only the more acceptable, being of a lighter weight, and from the fact that they are left without being 'teazled,' their strength is equal if not superior to the old style. They are made from finest wool and will bear the closest examination. It is the opinion of military men that the desideratum is obtained in this very popular make of goods, and we are glad to notice that several of our companies have adopted them."

53. See "Report of the Military Committee," p. 5. Whitten, Hopkins & Co. also produced 1,000 of "Basket" cloth of a more open weave; and 100 of "Cadet Doe[skin]" which was a compact twilled cloth. On May 5, 1861 the *Boston Daily Advertiser* inaccurately reported that George W. Simmons & Co., of Oak Hall, Boston, had received a contract to provide 1,000 uniforms for the "Committee of the City Council on Military Supplies" but the tender from that firm was not accepted. For this reportage see "Clothing for the Soldiers," *Boston Daily Advertiser*, May 5, 1861, 4:3; & "Clothing for the Volunteers," *Boston Herald*, April 29, 1861, 4:6.

54. "Military Matters in Boston and Vicinity," *Boston Daily Advertiser*, May 13, 1861, 4:2. This source added that the City Committee "also contributed handsomely to the fitting out of Capt. Clark's company, Capt. Dodd's Corps, Capt. Wardwell's, Capt. Read's, and have recently sent clothing and India rubber sheets to Capt. Sampson's Company, and to the Light Artillery, Major Cook."

55. "Military Movements," *Boston Evening Transcript*, May 15, 1861, 4:3.

56. Robert Cowdin, *Gen. Cowdin and the First Massachusetts Regiment of Volunteers* (Boston, MA: J.E. Farwell and Company, 1864), 6.

57. "Contract for Uniforms," *Boston Herald*, May 9, 1861, 4:2. According to the *Herald* of May 24, 1861, negotiations between the state and Boston City Council resulted in the 11th Massachusetts Volunteers being uniformed by the latter. Haughton, Sawyer & Co. produced 3,000 "Flannel" suits, while Pierce, Bros & Co. made 160 "Artillery" suits. See "Report of the Military Committee," 5.

58. See "Attention! Military! Army Equipments," *Pennsylvania Daily (PA) Telegraph*, May 14, 1861, 2:5.

59. *Pennsylvania Daily Telegraph*, May 18, 1861, 3:1. According to "Report of the Military Committee" (p. 5) Whitten, Hopkins & Co. supplied 5,165 "Uniform Suits" of "Army Blue."

60. See *Boston Daily Advertiser*, September 13, 1861, 2:2 where this accusation was refuted.

61. "Military Matters in Boston and vicinity," *Boston Daily Advertiser*, May 22, 1861, 1:8.

62. Luther Stephenson, "Three Months' service in 1861, with the Fourth Regiment, MVM," *Massachusetts Order Loyal Legion*, 540–41.

63. Osborne, *The History of the Twenty-ninth Regiment*, 17, 39. Following the expiration of the three month period of service of the 3rd MVM, the Plymouth Rock Guards re-organized as the Co. E of the Massachusetts Battalion on July 16, and were designated Co. E, 29th Massachusetts, when that regiment was organized on December 13, 1861. Similarly, when the 4th MVM ended its three months' service, the Greenough Guards became Co. K, Massachusetts Battalion, and Co. K, 29th Massachusetts. The Wightman Rifles re-organized as the Rifles of the Massachusetts Battalion, and were designated Co. A, 29th Massachusetts.

64. Ryan B. Weddle, "Massachusetts Men in Gray at Fort Monroe, 1861," *Military Collector & Historian* 63, no. 4 (Winter 2011): 291-292. See also Michael J. McAfee, "Massachusetts Men in Gray at Fort Monroe, 1861 (Reprised)," *Military Collector & Historian* 65, no 1 (Spring 2013): 88-89.

65. "Military Matters in Boston and Vicinity," *Boston Daily Advertiser*, August 2, 1861, 4:1.

66. Hanson, *Historical Sketch of the Old Sixth Regiment*, 21.

67. "Movements of the Military," *National Republican*, July 15, 1861, 3:1. The *Evening Star* of July 14 (3:1) also reported, "The men are uniformed in grey cloth with drab felt hats."

68. See "Uniforms, &c., Returned," *Lowell Daily Citizen & News*, June 2 1861, 2:4; & "More Uniforms Returned," *Lowell Daily Citizen & News*, June 4 1861, 2:4. In October 1860, the Watson Light Guard had paraded for their anniversary making "a fine appearance in their handsome [full-dress] grey uniform." See "The Watson's Anniversary," *Lowell Daily Citizen & News*, October 4, 1860, 2:5. See "Massachusetts Quota of Troops," *Boston Herald*, May 11, 1861, 4:2 for confirmation that the 8th MVM had received their state uniforms.

69. "The Rumor," *Lowell Daily Citizen & News*, May 22 1861, 2:5.

70. "The Massachusetts Regiments in Service," *Lowell Daily Courier*, May 29, 1861, 2:2.

71. See "War Items and Incidents," *Salem Register*, May 2, 1861, 2:5; & "Various War Items and Incidents," *Boston Evening Transcript*, April 30, 1861, 2:4. According to "Report of the Military Committee" (p. 7), Haughton, Sawyer & Co. produced 4,704 hats, while S.G. Taylor were paid for "coloring, trimming and repairing" a further 24,130 hats. Benjamin Franklin Edmands was a dry goods merchant and retired major general of the MVM. This headgear was confused with the Loomis or Whipple-style hat when it was inaccurately described in the *Boston Daily Advertiser*, of May 4, 1861, as being "a soft felt hat, in form not unlike the 'Kossuth' hat, the brim turned up on three sides, leaving a portion to form a visor in front; while within there is an arrangement for securing a moist napkin by elastic bands, to keep the head cool; and this or another napkin of linen may be attached, to be spread open behind, making a cape for the protection of the neck." See "New Military Hat," *Boston Daily Advertiser*, May 4, 1861.

72. Capt. Joseph Keith Newell (editor), *"Ours." Annals of the 10th Regiment, Massachusetts Volunteers, in the Rebellion* (Springfield, MA: C. A. Nichols & Co., 1875), 28.

73. "Military Matters," *Boston Daily Advertiser*, August 2, 1861, 4:1.

74. Dollard, *Recollections of the Civil War*, 20. The "Report of the Military Committee" (p. 7) states that G. P. Sawin supplied 12,130 "Fatigue Caps." Hatters Sawin & Wyeth were located at 288 Washington Street, Boston.

75. "Camp Ellsworth," *Boston Herald*, June 8, 1861, 2:2.

76. Cowdin, *Gen. Cowdin and the First Massachusetts Regiment*, 8.

77. "Overcoats in Hot Weather," *Boston Daily Advertiser*, June 22, 1861, 2:2.

78. "The Massachusetts Troops. Report on their Condition," *Boston Daily Advertiser*, June 15, 1861, 2:3. Rev. G. H. Hepworth may have prepared the report—see "The War. Preparations in New England," *Springfield* (MA) *Republican*, 4:1. Also see a much earlier mention of the unsatisfactory production of cloth in the *Boston Evening Transcript*, May 6, 1861, 2:3, which states, "Mr. Green, one of Governor Andrew's Council, was not verdant enough to purchase cotton flannel for the Massachusetts volunteers, although the threads were encased in wool, and the bogus article was defended by the eloquence of a salesman whose name we suppress out of regard to the opulent and high-minded firm he misrepresented in this case."

79. "Badly Shod," *Boston Daily Advertiser*, June 26, 1861, 2:2. See Mark R. Wilson, *The Business of Civil War: Military Mobilization and the State, 1861–1865* (Baltimore, MD: The John Hopkins University Press, 2006), 14. The main producer of "Army Shoes" for Massachusetts troops was Clement, Colburn & Co. who supplied 16,649 pairs. See "Report of the Military Committee," p. 7.

80. "Camp of the Sixth Mass. Reg't, Relay House, July 13, 1861," *Lowell Daily Citizen & News*, July 16 1861, 2:2.

81. Hanson, *Historical Sketch of the Old Sixth Regiment*, 71.

82. Warren H. Cudworth, *History of the First Regiment (Massachusetts Infantry) from the 25th of May, 1861, to the 25th of May, 1864* (Boston, MA: 1866), 42-44.

83. Gustavus D. Hutchinson, *A Narrative of the Formation and Services of the Eleventh Massachusetts Volunteers* (Boston, MA: Alfred Mudge & Son., 1893), 22. The 11th Massachusetts had received their gray uniforms from the Committee of the City Council on Military Supplies on May 24, 1861. See "Uniforms for Three Regiments," *Boston Herald*, May 24, 1861, 4:1.

84. "The 11th Mass. Regiment in the Fight," *Boston Herald*, July 30, 1861, 4:3.

85. "Military Matters," *Boston Daily Advertiser*, July 31, 1861, 4:2.

86. Alonzo H. Quint, *Record of the Second Massachusetts Infantry, 1861-65* (Boston, MA: James P. Walker, 1867), 23. See also "Military Matters," *Boston Daily Advertiser*, July 9, 1861, 1:8; & "The Second Regiment," *Boston Herald*, July 8, 1861, 4:5. Hatter Samuel O. Aborn was listed at 95 Washington Street in *Sketches and Business Directory of Boston and its Vicinity for 1860 and 1861* (Boston, MA: Darrell & Moore and George Coolidge, 1861), 447. As Aborn is not listed as a supplier of hats in "Report of the Military Committee," p. 7, the work was probably contracted out to him by either S.G. Taylor who supplied 12,000 hats or Haughton, Sawyer & Co., who supplied 4,704 hats.

87. "Arrival and Departure of the Second Regiment of Massachusetts Volunteers," *New York Herald*, July 10, 1861, 5:3.

88. "Camp Wightman," *Boston Herald*, May 24, 1861, 2:1.

89. "The Cass Regiment," *Boston Herald*, June 22, 1861, 2:2.

90. "Parade of the Ninth Regiment," *Boston Evening Transcript*, June 24, 1861, 2:5.

91. "The Twelfth Regiment," *Boston Herald*, May 13, 1861, 4:5. The 12th Massachusetts was named "The Webster Regiment" because it was organized and commanded by Fletcher Webster, the son of Daniel Webster, a leading statesman and senator from Massachusetts during the antebellum period. Whitten, Hopkins & Co. probably contracted the work out to Isaac Fenno & Co., as the latter is not listed in the "Report of the Military Committee."

92. "Military Matters in Boston and Vicinity," *Boston Daily Advertiser*, July 13, 1861, 4:1; & "The Webster Regiment in Boston," *Boston Daily Advertiser,* July 19, 1861, 4:1.

93. Benjamin F. Cook, *History of the Twelfth Massachusetts Volunteers* (Webster) (Regiment Association, 1882), 22.

94. "Clothing for 'Little Rhody's' Troops," *Boston Evening Transcript*, April 18, 1861, 2:6. Listed at 192 Washington Street, Boston, this "Clothing & Gents Furnishing store" was owned by Addison Macullar, George B. Williams, and Charles W. Parker.

95. Davis, *Three Years in the Army*, p. xvii. See Raymond Johnson, Roger Sturcke and Michael J. Winey, "4th Battalion of Rifles, Massachusetts Volunteer Militia, 1860–1861," Plate No. 603, *Military Collector & Historian* 39, no. 1 (Spring 1987): 34–35.

96. See "Uniforms for Three Regiments," *Boston Herald*, May 24, 1861, 4:1; & "Military Matters," *Boston Daily Courier*, July 29, 1861, 4:1. The *New York Tribune* of July 31, 1861 (6:6) reported that this regiment wore "dark blue loose jackets, light blue pants and army caps."

97. Michael J. McAfee, "Uniforms & History: Fourth Battalion of Rifles, Massachusetts Volunteer Militia, 1860–61," *Military Images 11, no. 1* (July–August 1989): 28–29. Also see "The Thirteenth Regiment Newly Uniformed," *Boston Herald*, July 27, 1861, 2:2.

98. "The Thirteenth Regiment," *Boston Herald*, July 30, 1861, 2:1. Also see "Tabular Statement—Ordnance and Ordnance Stores furnished by the Commonwealth of Massachusetts to Troops, (Infantry,) enlisted for Three Years and mustered-into the Service of the United States. December 24, 1861," Public Documents 7 in *Public Documents of Massachusetts...for the Year 1861*, 4.

99. John G.B. Adams, *Reminiscences of the Nineteenth Massachusetts regiment* (Boston, MA: Wright & Potter, 1899), 2.

100. "Military Matters in Boston and Vicinity," *Boston Daily Advertiser*, June 17, 1861, 4:3.

101. See "The Fourth," *Boston Evening Transcript*, July 5, 1861, 2:2; & "Parade and Review of the Second Battalion of Infantry," *Boston Herald*, July 17, 1861, 2:1. Visiting New York City in celebration of General Winfield Scott's 72nd birthday on June 14, 1858, the Boston Light Infantry were described as wearing "black coats and pants with white facings, and bearskin caps—see "The Military Display Yesterday," *New York Herald*, June 15, 1858, 5:3.

102. See "Military Movements," *Boston Daily Advertiser*, August 10, 1861, 1:8; *Boston Daily Advertiser*, August 13, 1861, 1:8; *Boston Daily Advertiser*, August 29, 1861, 4:1; & "The Massachusetts Nineteenth," *New York Tribune*, August 30, 1861, 5:5. Also see Michael J. McAfee, "Uniforms & History: The 19th Regiment Massachusetts Volunteer Infantry," *Military Images* 28, no. 3 (November/December 2006): 32–33. On September 9, 1861, the *Boston Herald* reported, "The jacket and pants are of light blue kersey, trimmed with light [*sic*], with russet leggings, and light blue sashes; the cap is a full fez of dark blue, with a long tassel."

103. Todd, *American Military Equipage*, 905. See also Michael J. McAfee, "Uniforms & History: The New England Guard—Company A, 4th Battalion of Infantry, Massachusetts Volunteer Militia," *Military Images* 18, no. 5 (March–April 1997): 37–38.

104. An advertisement for patriotic envelopes in the *Boston Daily Evening Transcript* of August 20, 1861 (3:4) stated that this was the "present uniform" of the New England Guards.

105. See "Military Matters," *Boston Herald*, September 23, 1861, 1:7.

106. See "Various Matters," *Boston Herald*, June 3, 1861, 2:3; & "Military Matters," *Boston Evening Transcript*, June 3, 1861, 4:2. The initial impetus for raising this company came from Chief Engineer Bird during mid-July, 1861, who recommended "to members and ex-members of the Department to enlist in a company of Fire Zouaves." See *Boston Daily Advertiser*, July 18, 1861, 4:1.

107. "Local Intelligence," *Pittsfield Sun*, July 25, 1861, 3:2.

108. "Return of the Allen Guard," *Berkshire County Eagle*, August 8, 1861, 2:4.

109. "Fourth Battalion of Rifles," *Boston Herald*, April 16, 1861, 2:4.

110. "Tenth Regiment in Camp at Medford," *Boston Herald*, July 17, 1861, 2:1.

111. Capt. Joseph Keith Newell (editor), *"Ours." Annals of the 10th Regiment, Massachusetts Volunteers, in the Rebellion* (Springfield, MA: C. A. Nicholls & Co., 1875), 362, 393, & 477.

112. "The Pollock Guard," *Berkshire County Eagle*, May 2, 1861, 2:8; & "Local Intelligence—The Pollock Guard," *Pittsfield Sun*, May 16, 1861, 2:7.

113. "The Pollock Guard," *Pittsfield Sun*, August 29, 1861, 2:7. See also "From the Tenth Regiment," *Springfield Republican*, August 17, 1861, 4:1.

114. Alfred S. Roe, *The Tenth Regiment Massachusetts Volunteer Infantry 1861–1864: A Western Massachusetts Regiment* (Springfield, MA: Tenth Regiment Veterans Association, 1909), 31.

115. Alfred Seelye Roe & Charles Nutt, *First Regiment of Heavy Artillery, Massachusetts Volunteers, Formerly the Fourteenth Regiment of Infantry, 1861–1865* (Worcester & Boston, MA—Regimental Association: Commonwealth Press, 1917), 12.

116. Roe & Nutt, *First Regiment of Heavy Artillery,* 60, 68 & 92.

117. James Madison Stone, *Personal Recollections of the Civil War* (Boston, MA: published by the author, 1918), 14.

118. "Barre Items," *Barre (MA) Gazette*, July 19, 1861, 2:8.

119 "Military Matters," *Boston Daily Advertiser*, July 29, 1861, 4:1; & "Uniforms for Three Regiments," *Boston Herald*, May 24, 1861, 4:1.

120. "The Fifteenth Regiment, M.V.," *Boston Herald*, August 7, 1861, 4:4. See a photograph of Pvt. Martin A. Eames, Co. B, 15th Massachusetts, in *Military Images* 6, no. 2 (September–October 1984): 14.

121. "Seventeenth Regiment of Massachusetts," *New York Tribune*, August 25, 1861, 5:2.

122. "Military Items," *Boston Herald*, July 31, 1861, 2:1. As they departed for the front on August 24, 1861 (1:8), the 17th Massachusetts was reported in the *Boston Daily Advertiser* to be wearing "the U.S. uniform."

123. "Military Movements," *Boston Daily Advertiser*, November 22, 1861, 1:8.

124. "More Troops En-Route," *Providence Daily (RI) Post*, August 27, 1861, 3:1.

125. See Don Troiani, "French Uniforms, Cloth & Equipage of the Union Army," Part I, *North South Trader's Civil War* 26, no. 2 (2003): 38-50; & Don Troiani, "French Uniforms, Cloth & Equipage of the Union Army," Part II, *North South Trader's Civil War* 26, no. 3 (2003): 24-32. As early as 1855 the US Army considered adopting a French *chasseurs á pied de la ligne* uniform for all of its foot troops.

126. Cited in "Ten Thousand French Uniforms," *Portsmouth (NH) Journal*, December 7, 1861, 1:5.

127. See "A Compliment to Massachusetts Soldiers," *Boston Evening Transcript*, November 23, 1861, 4:1.

128. *Boston Evening (MA) Journal*, December 26, 1861, 2:3.

129. Michael J. McAfee, "Uniforms & History: The 18th Massachusetts Volunteer Infantry Regt.," *Military Images* 20, no. 3 (November–December 1998): 40–41.

130. "Military Movements—Departure of the Nineteenth Regiment," *Boston Daily Advertiser*, August 29, 1861, 4:1.

131. Adams, *Reminiscences of the Nineteenth Massachusetts Regiment*, 13.

132. "20th Massachusetts Regiment," *Pittsfield Sun*, August 1, 1861, 3:3.

133. See "Arrival of the 22d Regiment," *Boston Herald*, October 8, 1861, 4:2; "The Departure of Colonel Wilson's Regiment," *Boston Herald*, September 25, 1861, 2:2; & "Military Movements—Departure of the Wilson Regiment," *Boston Daily Advertiser*, October 9, 1861, 1:8.

134. W. P. Derby, *Bearing Arms in the Twenty-Seventh Massachusetts Regiment of Volunteer Infantry* (Boston, MA: Wright & Potter Printing Company, 1883), 16.

135. "Military Supplies," *Boston Herald*, October 3, 1861, 3:1.

136. "Report of the Military Committee," p. 5.

137. "First Massachusetts Light Battery," *Boston Herald*, August 28, 1861, 2:2 & 4:5.

138. See Richard Warren, "Ben Butler and 'Friend Whipple' in 1861," *Military Collector & Historian 54, no. 3* (Fall 2002): 132–133. See also James Stamatelos, "Whipple's Patent Military Cap," *Military Images* 5, no. 6 (May–June 1984): 13-15.

139. "Military Movements," *Boston Daily Advertiser*, November 29, 1861, 1:8.

140. Cited in Don Troiani *et al, Regiments & Uniforms of the Civil War* (Stackpole Books: Mechanicsburg, PA, 2002), 189. Charles W., George, and Carlos Pierce, B. McLaughlin, George W. Shannon & William J. Keegan ran a dry goods business at "30 & 32 Franklin, house 4 Brookline;" see *The Boston Directory embracing the City Record: A General Directory of the Citizens, and a Business Directory for the year commencing July, 1861* (Boston, MA: Adams, Sampson & Company, No. 91 Washington Street. 1861), 355. Dealing in "dry goods," this company was probably only the supplier of this uniform, rather than the manufacturer.

141. See "Military Movements," *Boston Daily Advertiser*, November 29, 1861, 1:8; & "Gen. Butler's Expedition," *New York Times*, January 14, 1862, 1:5; & Nason, *History and Complete Roster of the Massachusetts Regiments—Minute Men of '61*, 318.

142. "From the 10th Regiment," *Berkshire County Eagle*, December 18, 1861, 2:3.

143. "Army Clothing," *Berkshire County Eagle*, November 14, 1861, 2:3. Dexter H. Brigham was listed in the *Springfield City Directory* from 1854 as owning a clothing store, later "clothing house," on Main Street, Springfield. Although neither Brigham or Tagert are listed as makers of clothing in "Report of the Military Committee," they may have been sub-contracted by Whitten, Hopkins & Co. who produced 5,150 "Infantry Coats," or Pierce Bros. & Co. who made 5,210 of the same item.

144. "Proposition to Organize a Coast Guard," *Daily Evening Traveller*, April 17, 1861, 2:2.

145. See "The Coast Guard," *Cape Ann Light and Gloucester Telegraph*, June 29, 1861, 2:3; & "Military Matters," *Boston Daily Advertiser*, June 15, 1861, 4:8.

146. "Parade of the Coast Guard," *Boston Herald*, June 17, 1861, 2:3.

147. "The Coast Guard," *Cape Ann Light and Gloucester Telegraph*, June 29, 1861, 2:3.

148. "Parade of the Coast Guard," *Boston Herald*, June 17, 1861, 2:3.

149. See "Military Matters in Boston and Vicinity," *Boston Daily Advertiser*, June 17, 1861, 4:2; & "Military Matters in Boston and Vicinity," *Boston Daily Advertiser*, July 13, 1861, 4:1. In his farewell address to his men Forbes hoped that "when some one of the new gun-boats were built the Coast Guard would be employed in it."

RHODE ISLAND

1. Robert N. Scott (editor), *The War of the Rebellion: A Compilation of the Official Records of the Union and Confederate Armies* (Washington: Government Printing Office,1899), Series III, vol. 1, 68–69, 82 & 84.

2. See Alan H. Archambault, "1st Light Infantry of Providence, Rhode Island, 1861," *Military Collector & Historian* 55, no. 3 (Fall 2003): 180–181; & Michael J. McAfee, "Uniforms & History: The First Light Infantry of Providence, Rhode Island," *Military Images* 14, no. 3 (November–December 1992): 28-29.

3. Tyler Dennett, *John Hay—From Poetry to Politics* (NY: Dodd, Mead and Company, Inc., 1933), 40.

4. "To the Ladies," *Providence Daily* (RI) *Journal*, April 18, 1861, 2:3. The clothing store of Massachusetts-born Henry A. Prescott was located at 27 and 29 Weybosset Street in Providence.

5. "Local Intelligence—The Rhode Island Infantry," *Providence Daily (RI) Post*, April 20, 1861, 3:1. See also John Severin and Frederick P. Todd, "1st Regiment of Rhode Island Detached Militia, 1861," *Military Collector & Historian* 7, no. 2 (Summer 1955): 49-51; Alan H. Archambault, "The First Regiment Rhode Island Detached Militia, 1861," *Military Collector & Historian* 53, no. 3 (Fall 2001): 98–109; & Michael J. McAfee, "Uniforms & History: 1st Regiment, Rhode Island Detached Militia, 1861," *Military Images* 10, no. 6 (May–June 1989): 28.

6. "Letter from a Mother," *Providence Daily Evening (RI) Press*, April 25, 1861, 3:6. The same letter, dated April 19, 1861, continued, "Bishop [Thomas March] Clark [rector of Grace Episcopal Church, Providence] was responsible for fifty tunics, and they were done at eight o'clock this morning. Ten were made in this house. J— went down with them this morning, with her needle and thread to sew on some buttons which were lacking. She is a good soldier."

7. "More Work for the Ladies," *Providence Daily Journal*, April 23, 1861, 2:5.

8. "Clothing for 'Little Rhody's' Troops," *Providence Daily Journal*, April 19, 1861, 2:4. According to a purchase voucher dated April 27, 1861, 1,276 of these garments were cut and trimmed at a further cost of $255.20. At the same time, 2,276 calico shirts were purchased from the same firm at a cost of $820. See "Purchase Voucher, State of Rhode Island to Macullar, Williams and Parker," April 27, 1861—Rhode Island State Archives.

9. Purchase Voucher, State of Rhode Island to Bowen and Pabodie, April 18, 1861. RI State Archives. According to "Stores and Equipments," *Providence Daily Evening Press*, April 20, 1861, 2:4, the order for hats was received on April 16, 1861.

10. "Local Intelligence—The Rhode Island Infantry," *Providence Daily Post*, April 20, 1861, 3:1.

11. "Stores and Equipments," *Providence Daily Post*, April 22, 1861, 3:2.

12. "The Uniform," *Providence Daily Journal*, April 17, 1861, 2:4.

13. *Newport (RI) Mercury*, May 4, 1861, 2:3.

14. "Local Matters," *The (MD) Sun*, June 11, 1861, 1:6.

15. "Our Regiment at Washington," *The Sun*, May 11, 1861, 2:7.

16. See "The Rhode Island troops," *The Sun*, May 4, 1861, 2:3; & "Our Regiment at Washington," *The Sun*, May 11, 1861, 2:7.

17. "Letter from Washington, (Correspondence of the Chicago Journal), May 1, 1861, *Chicago Evening* (IL) *Journal*, May 6, 1861, 2:4. According to "Governor Sprague's Charger," *Providence Daily Evening Press*, April 20, 1861, 2:3, his "chosen steed" was "a sorrel horse, appropriately named UNION."

18. "Warlike Appearances in Washington," *Providence Daily Evening Press*, May 10, 1861, 2:3—citing *The Press* of Philadelphia.

19. Purchase Voucher, State of Rhode Island, April 18, 1861. Rhode Island State Archives. Also see notes on reverse of A.R. Waud drawing in the Library of Congress. See DRWG/US - Waud, no. 201.

20. "The Ladies," *Providence Daily Journal*, April 20, 1861, 2:5.

21. "Letter from a Mother," *Providence Daily Evening Press*, April 25, 1861, 3:6.

22. Cited in "The R.I. Regiment," *Providence Daily Evening Press*, May 11, 1861, 2:3.

23. "The Rhode Island Troops in the Field," *Providence Evening Press*, April 23, 1861, 2:2, citing the *New York Times*.

24. "Correspondence of the Mercury, Washington, D.C. May 14th, 1861," *Newport Mercury*, May 18, 1861, 2:5.

25. "Stores and Equipments," *Providence Evening Press*, April 20, 1861, 2:4.

26. "The Ladies," *Providence Daily Journal*, April 20, 1861, 2:5.

27. "The Departure of the Troops," *Providence Evening Press*, April 25, 1861, 2:3.

28. "The Rhode Island troops," *Newport Mercury*, May 4, 1861, 2:3. See also "The Latest from Washington," *Philadelphia Inquirer*, May 1, 1861, 1:4. Maria F. Strahan was named in a report published in the *National Republican*, May 1, 1861, 3:2.

29. "Letter from Washington, (Correspondence of the Chicago Journal), May 1, 1861, *Chicago Evening Journal*, May 6, 1861, 2:4.

30. "Our Washington Correspondence, Camp Sprague, Washington, DC June 10, 1861," *Pawtucket Gazette & (RI) Chronicle*, June 14, 1861, 2:5.

31. "The Rhode Island Regiment at Washington," *Providence Evening Press*, May 7, 1861, 2:3 citing the *Boston Journal* of May 3. See also *Lowell Daily Courier*, May 4, 1861, 2:1. A report in the *Weekly Wisconsin Patriot* dated May 18, 1861 (4:3) stated, "The vivandiere who was married to a member of one of the Rhode Island regiments in Washington, the other day, was dressed in the Turkish costume, and wore a blouse of cherry-colored satin, pants of blue, and a felt hat with white plumes—the national colors."

32. "War Items," *Providence Daily Evening Press*, May 17, 1861, 2:4—citing the *Philadelphia Press*.

33. "The Return Home," *Providence Daily Journal*, July 30, 1861, 2:3.

34. "Reception of the First Regiment," *Providence Daily Post*, July 29, 1861, 3:1.

35. Robert Brownell in "Women Soldier Veteran Kady C. Brownell Appointed on the New York Park Board," *Kansas City Star*, December 26, 1895, 5. See also Chris Gorges, "Kady Brownell: Lady of Combat," *North South Trader's Civil War* 35, no. 6 (2012): 40–45, 62.

36. 0"The Muskets Have Come," *Providence Daily Journal*, April 24, 1861, 2:3.

37. "Letter from Volunteer. Washington, April 30, 1861," *Providence Daily Post*, May 4, 1861, 3:2.

38. "Revolvers and Bowie Knifes to be Laid by," *Providence Daily Evening Press*, May 22, 1861, 2:5.

39. Augustus Woodbury, *Campaign of the First Rhode Island Regiment* (Providence, RI: Sidney S. Rider, 1862) 225-231. Also see National Archives Record Group 217–759 State Claims Rhode Island.

40. "Letter to Mother," dated April 27, 1861. Frederic M. Sackett Papers (MSS 695), Rhode Island Historical Society.

41. "Stores and Equipment," *Providence Evening Press*, April 20, 1861, 2:4.

42. "From the First Regiment," *Providence Daily Post*, June 17, 1861, 2:2.

43. William R. Arnold Papers (MSS 9001-A), Rhode Island Historical Society.

44. *Providence Daily Journal*, April 23, 1861, 2:4.

45. According to the regimental history, "The caissons, forges, guns, &c., passed through the summer campaign; were transferred to Capt. [William H.] Reynolds' company after the Battle of Bull Run; were engaged at Poolesville, Harper's Ferry, Bolivar and vicinity, during the spring and summer of 1862. This severe usage they have borne, with scarcely a necessity for repair, so thoroughly was the labor performed before they left Rhode Island." (Woodbury, 9 fn).

46. "The Patriotic Movement," *Providence Daily Journal*, April 19, 1861, 2:2.

47. F. Stansbury Haydon, *Military Ballooning During the Early Civil War* (Baltimore, MD: The John Hopkins University Press, 1968), 39–48.

48. "The Marines in New York," *Providence Evening Express*, April 20, 1861, 2:4.

49. *Newport Mercury*, June 15, 1861, 2:1—citing the *New York Tribune*.

50. "The Rhode Island Troops in the Field," *Providence Evening Press*, April 23, 1861, 2:1. Reeder was born in Easton, Pennsylvania, in 1807.

51. See "The Marine Artillery," *Newport Mercury*, April 24, 1861, 2:3.

52. "The Ladies," *Providence Daily Evening News*, May 16, 1861, 2:4.

53. See "Preparing for the New Regiment," *Providence Daily Post*, May 14, 1861, 3:1; "Work for the Ladies," *Providence Daily Evening News*, May 13, 1861, 2:6; & "The Second Regiment," *Providence Daily Post*, June 1, 1861, 3:2.

54. "Visit of the Volunteers," *Bristol (RI) Phenix*, June 15, 1861, 2:2.

55. Elisha H. Rhodes, *The First Campaign of the Second Rhode Island Infantry* (Providence, RI: Sidney S. Rider, 1878), 9.

56. "The Second Regiment," *Providence Daily Post*, June 6, 1861, 3:1.

57. "Camp Burnside," *Providence Daily Post*, June 15, 1861, 3:1.

58. Rhodes, *The First Campaign,* 12.

59. "Correspondence of the Journal. The Return Home," *Providence Daily Journal*, July 30, 1861, 2:3. See also the Arnold diary, July 25, 1861, Rhode Island Historical Society.

60. "Departure of the Second Regiment," *Newport Mercury*, June 22, 1861, 2:6: also see "The New Regiment," *Newport Mercury*, May 18, 1861, 3:1.

61. "Correspondence of the Journal. Camp Brightwood, Aug. 29, 1861," *Providence Daily Journal*, September 2, 1861, 2:3.

62. Robert H. Rhodes (editor), *All for the Union, a History of the 2nd Rhode Island Volunteer Infantry in the War of the Great Rebellion as told by the diary and letters of Elisha Hunt Rhodes who enlisted as a private in '61 and rose to the command of his regiment. (*Lincoln, RI: Andrew Mowbray Incorporated, 1985), 47. See also Alan H. Archambault, "2nd Regiment, Rhode Island Volunteer Infantry, 1861–1865," *Military Collector & Historian* 43, no. 1 (Spring 1991): 32-35.

63. Frederic Denison, *Shot & Shell: the Third Rhode Island Heavy Artillery regiment in the War of the Rebellion* (Providence, RI: For the Third R.I.H. art. Vet. Association, by J.A. Reid, 1879), 38–39.

64. "Camp Greene," *Providence Daily Post*, September 14, 1861, 2:6.

65. *Newport Mercury*, October 19, 1861, 2:1.

66. "Military," *Newport Mercury*, November 23, 1861, 3:3.

67. "Departure of the Burnside Battalion," *Providence Evening Press*, December 27, 1861, 3:7.

68. John H. Rhodes, *The History of Battery B, First Rhode Island Light Artillery* (Providence, RI: Snow & Farnham, 1892), 1–3, 12 & 18.

69. See Robert Grandchamp, "'The appearance of a gang of Chinamen:' A Study of the Uniforms Worn by Brown's Battery B, First Rhode Island Light Battery," *Military Collector & Historian* 59, no. 1 (Spring 2007): 58.

70. *Ibid,* 58–59.

71. "New England Cavalry!" *Farmer's* (Amherst, NH) *Cabinet*, December 26, 1861, 3:6.

72. See *Newport Mercury*, May 18, 1861, 2:3; & June 1, 1861, 2:3. The *Providence Daily Post* described this unit as wearing "gray frock-coats and capes, gray forage caps and dark pants" on June 3, 1861.

73. "The Providence Horse Guards," *Providence Daily Post*, July 3, 1861, 3:1.

74. "Pawtucket—Military Display," *Providence Daily Post*, June 1, 1861, 3:1. See also "Pawtucket," *Providence Daily Evening Press*, May 25, 1861, 2:4.

75. See "Zouaves," *Providence Daily Journal*, April 22, 1861, 2:2.

76. "The Burnside Zouaves," *Providence Daily Post*, July 18, 1861, 3:1.

77. "Arrival of the First Regiment," *Providence Daily Post*, July 29, 1861, 2:2.

78. William Arnold Spicer, *History of the 9th & 10th Rhode Island Volunteers, and the 10th Rhode Island Battery, in the Union Army in 1862* (Providence, RI: Snow & Franham, 1892), 40. See also James Hennessey, "The Burnside Zouaves of Providence, R.I., 1861-1870," *Military Collector & Historian* 31, no. 1 (Spring 1979): 25, 24–25.

NEW HAMPSHIRE

1. "Local Military Movements," *New Hampshire* (NH) *Statesman*, May 11, 1861, 2:5.

2. "The Ladies for the War," *New Hampshire* (NH) *Sentinel*, April 25, 1861, 2:6.

3. "See to our Soldiers," *New Hampshire Sentinel*, May 2, 1861, 2:4.

4. "From Concord," *New Hampshire Sentinel*, April 26, 1861, 2:1. See also "The New Hampshire Troops," *Portsmouth* (NH) *Journal*, May 4, 1861, 2:1.

5. "N. H. Legislature," *New Hampshire Patriot & State (NH) Gazette*, July 3, 1861, 3:1; & "More Troops," *Evening Star*, May 28, 1861, 3:1. Whiting, Galloupe, Bliss & Co. was a clothing store at 14 Federal & 95 Congress, Boston. Whitten, Hopkins & Co., was located in the same section at 32 Milk Street. See *Massachusetts City Directory*, 1861, p. 491. As Whiting, Kehoe & Galloupe, the former firm had supplied uniform clothing for ratings and enlisted men of the entire US Navy in 1851. One of the partners in the second firm may have been George Hopkins, listed as a tailor in 1856. The latter firm also made some of the overcoats for the Massachusetts three month volunteers.

6. "Advices from our camps," *Farmer's Cabinet*, May 24, 1861, 2:6.

7. "The New Hampshire Troops," *Boston Evening Transcript*, May 8, 1861, 2:3.

8. Letter written from "Camp Constitution, Portsmouth, May 10, 1861," *A Minor War History compiled from a Soldier Boy's Letters to "The Girl I Left Behind Me, 1861–1864* (Lakeport, NH: Private Print of Martin A. Haynes, 1916), 5. See also John P. Severin and Frederick P. Todd, "2d Regiment, New Hampshire Volunteer Militia, 1861," *Military Collector & Historian* 5, no. 1 (March 1953): 16–18.

9. Martin A. Haynes, *A History of the Second Regiment, New Hampshire Volunteer Infantry in the War of the Rebellion* (Lakeport, NH: 1896), 7.

10. "Advice from our camps—Friday May 17," *Farmer's Cabinet*, May 24, 1861, 2:6.

11. See Receipt dated May 3, 1861, Box marked 2nd New Hampshire, State Archives, Concord, New Hampshire.

12. "Correspondence of the Statesman, III. Washington, June 14, 1861," *New Hampshire Statesman*, June 22, 1861, 3:4.

13. Receipts dated May 4, 1861, signed Lt. Joseph A. Hubbard, Abbot Guards, & Capt. William P. Austin, Claremont Volunteers, Box marked 2nd New Hampshire, State Archives, Concord, New Hampshire. The latter company eventually did not enlist in the 2nd New Hampshire.

14. "N. H. Legislature," *New Hampshire Patriot*, July 3, 1861, 3:1. See also "War Expenses," *Portsmouth Journal*, July 6, 1861, 2:5; & "More Troops," *Evening Star*, May 28, 1861, 3:1. B. F. & D. Holden was established in Concord, New Hampshire, by Benjamin F. Holden circa 1842 when he converted a "flouring mill" into a woolen mill and began "the manufacturing of woollen goods." He was joined by his brother Daniel in 1847, and by 1861 this firm had grown into "large proportions under the joint management." James O. Lyford, *History of Concord, New Hampshire* (Concord, NH: The History Commission Of Concord, 1903), 652.

Massachusetts-born George M. Herring was a 48 year-old trader and shoe maker who employed two "shoe cutters" at his premises in Farmington, New Hampshire in 1860—see 1860 Census: Roll: M653_680; Page: 409. Forty-four-year-old Charles C. Mooney was listed as a "Shoe Manufacturer" at Alton, New Hampshire—see *1860 Census*: Roll: M653_666; Page: 287. George L. Thayer was a thirty-five-year-old "shoe maker" working with his father and listed as resident at Plympton, Plymouth, about thirty-five miles south of Boston, Massachusetts—see *1860 Census*; Roll: M653_518; Page: 487. The contractor for the "Shoe Shop" at the State Prison, Concord, was William F. Savory.

15. According to a business broadside dated June 5, 1861, James R. Hill had an "immense Harness Manufactory" on Main Street in Concord, which had "just completed …an order for the State of New Hampshire, for sixteen hundred full sets of leather equipments for the NH Volunteers—consisting, we believe, of gun-belts, cartridge boxes, cap-boxes, knapsack straps, bayonet scabbards, &c."

James Haughton and Samuel E. Sawyer were well established suppliers of military goods with branches at Boston, New York and Philadelphia. Their premises in Boston were situated at 26 & 28 Pearl Street. Horace H. Day advertised for sale in the *New York Times* on April 26, 1861 (p. 6) "1,000 rejected Government knapsacks with straps complete." Some, if not all, of these were purchased by Abbott for the 1st New Hampshire.

Evidence that the first two regiments received rubberized haversacks is found in a report on the 3rd New Hampshire, published in the *Statesman*, which stated, "The Haversacks are of white canvas, as those hitherto in use are found to impart a taste of rubber to their contents." See "Military Affairs. The Third Regiment," *New Hampshire Statesman*, August 24, 1861, 2:3.

16. "State of New Hampshire," *New Hampshire Statesman*, May 18, 1861, 2:4.

17. Thomas L. Livermore, *Days and Events, 1860–1866* (Boston & New York City: Houghton Mifflin Company, 1920), 9.

18. "The Cheshire Light Guard," *New Hampshire Sentinel*, June 27, 1861, 2:5. The reference to a brass shoulder belt plate bearing the "New Hampshire arms" is unusual, as there is no record of such a plate having survived.

19. "Military Movements in the City," *National Republican*, June 24, 1861, 3:1. See also "The Troops," *Evening Star*, June 24, 1861, 3:2.)

20. "Pay of the Troops," *Portsmouth Journal*, May 4, 1861, 2:1.

21. "2d N.H. Regiment in Boston," *New Hampshire Sentinel*, June 27, 1861, 2:5.

22. See "Departure of the First Regiment," *New Hampshire Patriot*, May 29, 1861, 2:1.

23. *ORs*, Series III, vol. 1, 103.

24. Haynes, *A History of the Second Regiment*, 7-8; see also "New Hampshire Legislature, June Session, 1861," *New Hampshire Statesman*, June 8, 1861, 2:7; & "General Court—Governor Goodwin's Closing Message," *Portsmouth Journal*, June 8, 1861, 2:7.

25. "The First New-Hampshire Regiment," *New Hampshire Sentinel*, May 30, 1861, 2:5.

26. *ibid.*

27. See "Fife Major of the First," *New Hampshire Statesman*, May 25, 1861, 2:5.

28. Livermore, *Days and Events, 1860–1866*, 20-21.

29. Janet B. Hewett (editor) et al, *Supplement to the Official Records of the Union and Confederate Armies,* Part II, vol. 39 (Serial No. 51) (Wilmington, NC: Broadfoot Publishing Company, 1996), 109. Hereafter referred to as *SORs*.

30. Stephen G. Abbott, *The First Regiment New Hampshire Volunteers in the Great Rebellion* (Keene, NH: Sentinel Printing Company, 1890), 165.

31. "Letter from Col. Tappan, Martinsburg, Va., July 13, 1861," *Farmer's Cabinet*, July 26, 1861, 3:2.

32. "The New Hampshire Soldiers," *Farmer's Cabinet*, August 9, 1861, 3:1, citing a *Mirror* reporter "who was with them."

33. "The Cheshire Light Guard," *New Hampshire Sentinel*, June 6, 1861, 2:2.

34. "Letter from the Second Regiment. Camp Sullivan, Washington, DC, July 7, 1861," *New Hampshire Statesman*, July 13, 1861, 2:6.

35. "The Payment of the 2nd N.H. Regiment," *New Hampshire Patriot*, July 24, 1861, 2:5.

36. "The Second Regiment," *New Hampshire Statesman*, September 7, 1861, 2:6.

37. See *New Hampshire Statesman*, August 2, 1861, 3:2 & *New Hampshire Statesman*, July 27, 1861, 3:5 for reference to blue uniforms; and Daniel Eldredge, *The Third New Hampshire and All About It* (Boston, MA: press of E. B. Stillings & Co., 1893), 15 for supply of gray uniforms.

38. "The Third Regiment," *New Hampshire Patriot*, August 7, 1861, 2:1; see also "Soldiers' Equipment," *New Hampshire Statesman*, August 3, 1861, 2:1. See Eldredge, *The Third New Hampshire,* 21, for the cost of clothing and equipage for this regiment. Founded by Milan Harris, the Harris Mill was one of the first woolen mills in New England.

39. Born in Maine circa 1821, John G. Lincoln was listed as a "Tailor" in the 1860 census, and lived at 33 School Street, Concord, with his wife Catherine and four children. Wentworth G. Shaw was born in New Hampshire circa 1829; he was listed as a "Merchant Tailor" in 1860, and lived at 44 School with his wife Mary and two children. He was also a member of the Governor's Horse Guards—see Lyford, *History of Concord*, vii.

40. See Eldredge, *The Third New Hampshire,* 15; and "Fall Clothing," *Dollar Weekly* (NH) *Mirror*, April 13, 1861, 4:5. Listed in the 1860 census as a "Merchant," Cumner was born in Maine circa 1830.

41. Born in England in 1799, tailor Abraham Thorpe migrated to the US with his family aboard the ship *Meteor* in 1829 settling in New York City, and then moving to Weare, New Hampshire, where, with his son Joseph W., he engaged in "the manufacture of men's clothing for the Boston and New York markets." See James A. Ellis (editor), *History of New Hampshire,* Vol. V (New York: The American Historical Society, n.d.), 238–9.

42. Amos D. Purinton established a "hat, cap and fur store" on Morrill's Block at Dover, New Hampshire, circa 1839, and first employed John T. W. Ham on September 4, 1854. The partnership of Purinton and Ham began in 1859 and lasted until the death of the senior partner in 1877, after which the business was known as "Ham the Hatter" until 1890, when it became John T. W. Ham & Company. See Ellis, *History of New Hampshire,* 82–84.

43. "Military Affairs. The Third Regiment," *New Hampshire Statesman*, August 24, 1861, 2:3. A farmer of Westmoreland, New Hampshire, Charles F. Brooks had served in the state senate 9th District from 1857–59, and was a member of the Military Committee of the Governor's Council from 1861–63.

44. See John P. Langelier & C. Paul Loane, *U.S. Army Headgear 1812–1872* (Atglen, PA: Schiffer Military History, 2002), 66.

45. "Camp Sherman," *Farmer's Cabinet*, September 13, 1861, 2:3.

46. "Third Regiment," *New Hampshire Patriot*, August 28, 1861, 2:4.

47. "Passage of Troops," *Delaware Republican*, September 19, 1861, 3:4.

48. Eldredge, *The Third New Hampshire*, 21.

49. "Departure of the 3rd N.H. Regiment," *Portsmouth Journal*, September 7, 1861, 2:4.

50. Eldredge, *The Third New Hampshire*, 78, 89, 94 & 973.

51. "The Third Regiment Full," *New Hampshire Sentinel*, August 22, 1861, 3:1.

52. State of New Hampshire Executive Department, September 20, 1861.

53. "Military Affairs. The Third Regiment," *New Hampshire Statesman*, August 24, 1861, 2:3.

54. See Eldredge, *The Third New Hampshire*, 21 & Maj. Otis F.W. Waite, *New Hampshire in the Great Rebellion* (Claremont, NH: Tracy, Chase & Company, 1870), 184. The former source states "Enfield rifles," but the latter more accurately states "Enfield rifle muskets."

55. "Departure of the Fourth Regiment," *New Hampshire Patriot*, October 2, 1861, 2:1.

56. "The Fourth Regiment," *New Hampshire Statesman*, September 7, 1861, 2:5. Adams B. Cook was born in Massachusetts circa 1830 and was listed as a tailor at Weare in Hillsborough County, New Hampshire, in the 1860 Census. Joseph W. Thorpe was the son of Abraham Thorpe, who supplied the overcoats for the 3rd New Hampshire—see fn 35. David A. Warde, of Warde & Humphrey, was listed as a hardware dealer on 180 Main Street in *Merrill & Son's Concord City Directory* for 1860–61—see p. 90. Thirty-five-year-old John Pepper was the "agent" for the Holderness Woollen Mill. See Receipt from "N.H. State Prison John Foss Warden," dated September 16, 1861, for "5 cases Shoes... from Lawrence to Manchester [for the] 4th Regt.," State Archives, Concord, NH.

57. "Departure of the Fourth Regiment," *New Hampshire Patriot*, October 2, 1861, 2:1; & "The Fourth Regiment," *New Hampshire Statesman*, September 7, 1861, 2:5.

58. "The Fifth Regiment," *New Hampshire Statesman*, August 31, 1861, 3:1.

59. "Uniforms Rejected," *New Hampshire Patriot*, October 9, 1861, 2:4.

60. Livermore, *Days and Events, 1860–1866*, 27.

61. "Home and State Affairs," *New Hampshire Sentinel*, October 17, 1861, 2:6.

62. Receipt dated October 28, 1861, from James B. Gove, Keeper of Military Stores for the State of New Hampshire to E.M. Webber, Quartermaster, 5th New Hampshire, in collection of David Nelson.

63. "Splendid Military Goods," *New Hampshire Patriot*, October 16, 1861, 2:5. The Enfield rifle muskets were carried until November 1863 when replaced by M1863 Springfield rifle muskets—see William Child M.D., *A History of the Fifth Regiment, New Hampshire Volunteers* (Bristol, NH: R.W. Musgrove, Printer, 1893), 239.

64. "Officers' Uniforms," *New Hampshire Patriot*, September 11, 1861, 2:1.

65. See "Military," *New Hampshire Statesman*, November 9, 1861, 2:7; *Farmers' Cabinet*, November 15, 1861, 2:5; & "Camp Brooke," *New Hampshire Sentinel*, November 21, 1861, 2:6.

66. "Another Letter from Camp Brooks," *New Hampshire Sentinel*, December 12, 1861, 3:1.

67. See "Sharp's Rifles for the Sixth," *New Hampshire Statesman*, November 16, 1862, 2:3; & Lyman Jackman, *History of the Sixth New Hampshire Regiment in the War for the Union* (Concord, NH: Republican Press Association, Railroad Square, 1894), 18.

68. "New-Hampshire Regiments," *New Hampshire Statesman*, December 14, 1861, 2:3.

69. Henry F. W. Little, *The Seventh Regiment New Hampshire Volunteers in the War of the Rebellion* (Concord, NH: Ira C. Evans, Printer, 1896), 14–15. See also Michael J. McAfee, "The 7th New Hampshire Volunteer Infantry Regiment, 1861," *Military Collector & Historian* 27, no. 4 (Winter 1975): 168–169.

70. John M. Stanyan, *A History of the Eighth Regiment of New Hampshire Volunteers* (Concord, NH: Ira C. Evans, Printer, 1892), 36.

71. "Military," *New Hampshire Statesman*, November 9, 1862, 2:7.

72. Stanyan, *A History of the Eighth Regiment*, 53.

73. *Ibid.*, 39, 42.

CONNECTICUT

1. See Frederick P. Todd, "State of Connecticut Uniforms 1856," *Military Collector & Historian* 10, no. 1 (Spring 1958): 15-16.

2. "City Intelligence," *Hartford Daily* (CT) *Courant*, April 20, 1861, 2:4.

3. "City Intelligence," *Hartford Daily Courant*, April 22, 1861, 2:4. See *Geer's Hartford City Directory for 1861–62*, pp 109 & 215 for merchant tailors Fisher & Co. and Henry Schulze.

4. W. A. Croffut and John M. Morris, *History of Connecticut during the War of 1861–65* (New York: Ledyard Bill, 75 Fulton Street, 1869), 59 & 60-61.

5. "The Uniform Question before the Legislative Committee," *Hartford Daily Courant*, May 22, 1861, 2:6. For clothing issuance to the first five regiments see "Articles Purchased or Received, and Issued from April 1st to September 1st, 1861," *Report of the Quartermasters-General to the General Assembly*, in *Public Documents of the Legislature of Connecticut, May Session, 1862*. (Hereafter referred to as "Articles Purchased or Received.")

6. See *Geer's Hartford City Directory for 1861–62* (Hartford, CT: Elihu Geer, 16 State Street, 1861), 66 & 94 for reference to Theodore H. Bunce and Charles G. Day.

7. "City Intelligence," *Hartford Daily Courant,* May 3, 1861, 2:5. This would have been more than enough to supply the first three regiments. According to "Articles Purchased or Received," the 1st through 3rd Connecticut received 609, 709, and 548 "Uniform Coats" respectively.

8. "Military Matters," *New London Daily* (CT) *Chronicle*, May 21, 1861, 2:1.

9. "Hartford," *Providence Daily Evening Press*, May 10, 1861, 2:4. According to "Articles Purchased or Received," the 1st through 3rd Connecticut received 488, 754, and 523 "Over Coats" respectively.

10. "The Legislative Committee," *Hartford Daily Courant*, May 20, 1861, 2:4.

11. The dry goods business of Calvin Day, brother of Charles G. Day, and Elijah H. Owen was situated at 73 Asylum Street, Hartford. See *Geer's Hartford City Directory for 1861–62*, 270.

12. "Those Pantaloons," *Hartford Daily Courant*, May 23, 1861, 2:4. See also "The Ladies Protest," *Hartford Weekly* (CT) *Times*, May 25, 1861, 2:5, which was written in response to inaccurate accusations that the ladies were responsible for the shoddy clothing.

13. "Articles Purchased or Received."

14. "Editorial War Correspondence—Camp Buckingham, 1st Reg't, C.V., Washington, May 31, 1861," *The Connecticut Press*, June 8, 1861, 1:4.

15. "Articles Purchased or Received."

16. "Falstaff's Ragged Regiment—The New Haven Register says," *Charleston Daily* (SC) *Courier*, May 15, 1861, 1:5.

17. "Hartford," *Providence Daily Evening Press*, May 18, 1861, 2:2.

18. See "The Second Regiment on Ship-board," *Hartford Weekly Times*, May 18, 1861, 3:4.

19. "Explanatory," *Columbian Weekly* (CT) *Register*, June 8, 1861, 2:8. According to "Articles Purchased or Received," the state quartermaster department supplied 5,630 pairs of shoes for the first five regiments.

20. "Arrival of the Connecticut Second Regiment," *Evening Star*, May 14, 1861, 3:3.

21. "Arrival of the Second Regiment," *Columbian Weekly Register*, August 10, 1861, 2:5.

22. "Connecticut War Items," *Norwich Morning* (CT) *Bulletin*, May 14, 1861, 2:6.

23. "The Third Connecticut Regiment," *Evening Star*, May 25, 1861, 3:2.

24. *"Departure of Bridgeport Volunteers," Daily Advertiser and* (CT) *Farmer*, April 30, 1861, 2:1.

25. "Military Matters," *New London Daily Chronicle*, May 21, 1861, 2:1 citing "Hartford Daily Courant Monday."

26. "Connecticut War Items," *Norwich Morning Bulletin*, April 26, 1861, 2:2.

27. "State News," *Norwich Morning Bulletin*, May 21, 1861, 2:2.

28. See "Recall of Arms," *Norwich Morning Bulletin*, May 4, 1861, 2:4.

29. See Earl J. Coates & John D. McAulay, *Civil War Sharps Carbines & Rifles* (Gettysburg, PA: Thomas Publications, 1996), 13.

30. "State News," *Norwich Morning Bulletin*, May 21, 1861, 2:2.

31. Frinkle Fry, *Wooden Nutmegs at Bull Run. A Humorous Account of some of the Exploits and Experiences of the Three Months Connecticut Brigade* (Hartford, CT: George L. Coburn, Steam Print, 1872), 28.

32. "Letter from Captain John C. Comstock, of the 1st Regiment, C.V.," *Hartford Daily Courant*, July 1, 1861, 2:3.

33. "Correspondence of the Times, Washington City, Camp Welles, June 2d, 1861," *Hartford Weekly Times*, June 8, 1861, 2:7 & 8.

34. "Falls Village, Camp Mansfield, July 8th, 1861," *Hartford Daily Courant*, July 11, 1861, 2:4.

35. "Return Home of the First Regiment," *Hartford Daily Courant*, July 29, 1861, 2:2.

36. "First Regt. C.V.," *Columbian Weekly Register*, August 3, 1861, 1:7 & 3:5.

37. See "Military Items," *Connecticut Press*, June 8, 1861, 2:7; & "Articles Purchased or Received."

38. "Military," *Hartford Weekly Times*, June 8, 1861, 3:1. When they went on home on several days leave prior to departure for "the seat of war," the Garibaldi Rifles (Infantry Co. F) 4th Connecticut wore "a gray uniform of pants and jackets, with a gray felt hat."

39. E.B. Andrews, *A Private's Reminiscences of the First Year of the War of the Rebellion* (Providence, RI: 1886), no page number.

40. "Municipal War Movements. Arrival and Departure of the Fourth Regiment Connecticut Troops at Jersey City," *New York Herald*, June 12, 1861, 8:5.

41. "Camp McClure, June 13, 1861," *Milwaukee Morning* (WI) *Sentinel*, June 19, 1861, 1:2.

42. See "Military Matters," *Hartford Daily Courant*, June 5, 1861, 2:5; & "Articles Purchased or Received."

43. E.B. Bennett (compiler), *First Connecticut Heavy Artillery: Historical Sketch and Present Addresses of Members* (East Berlin, CT: Privately printed, 1889), 15; & "Military Matters," *Hartford Daily Courant,* September 21, 1861, 2:4.

44. "Military Matters," *Hartford Daily Courant,* October 8, 1861, 2:3.

45. Coates & McAulay, *Civil War Sharps Carbines & Rifles,* 13.

46. "City Intelligence," *Hartford Daily Courant,* April 20, 1861, 2:3.

47. "Colt's Armory Guard," *The (CT) Constitution,* June 23, 1858, 2:4.

48. Edwin E. Marvin, *The Fifth Regiment Connecticut Volunteers* (Hartford, CT: Wiley, Waterman & Eaton, 1889), 8.

49. "Patriotism of the Ladies," *Windham County (CT) Transcript,* May 2, 1861, 2:1 & "Union Guards of Windham County," *ibid,* May 2, 1861, 2:4.

50. Croffut and Morris, *History of Connecticut,* 73–74.

51. "Fifth Regiment Connecticut Volunteer Rifles," *New York Herald,* July 7, 1861, 8:2.

52. "City Intelligence," *Hartford Daily Courant,* July 31, 1861, 2:4.

53. "The Fifth Regiment," *Connecticut Press,* July 13, 1861, 2:7.

54. "Annual Report of the Adjutant General of the State of Connecticut, for the Year 1861," in *Public Documents of the Legislature of Connecticut, May Session, 1862* (Hartford, CT: J.R. Hawley & Co., 1862), 36.

55. "Arrival and Departure of Volunteers," *New York Tribune,* September 20, 1861, 8:5.

56. *Hartford Daily Courant,* September 24, 1861, 2:4. A paramilitary campaign organization affiliated with the Republican Party during the presidential election of 1860, the Wide Awakes wore capes, sashes and black glazed hats during their torch-lit rallies and parades.

57. "Military Affairs," *Hartford Daily Courant,* October 7, 1861, 2:5.

58. Croffut & Morris, *History of Connecticut,* 140. Ordered by authority of the state, the flag of the 9th Connecticut was described thus, "The State motto, 'Qui Transulit Sust,' appears on one side, while on the other appears on a green ground 'Erin Go Bragh,' as an indelible evidence of true Irish patriotism." See "Military," *Hartford Weekly Times,* November 23, 1861, 3:1.

59. "Military," *Hartford Daily Courant,* November 12, 1861, 2:3.

60. Thomas H. Murray, *History of the Ninth Regiment, Connecticut Volunteer Infantry, "The Irish Regiment," in the War of the Rebellion, 1861–65* (New Haven, CT: The Price, Lee & Adkins Co. 1908), 63–64.

61. *Ibid,* 47.

62. Homer B. Sprague, *History of the 13th Infantry Regiment of Connecticut Volunteers* (Hartford, CT: Case, Lockwood & Co. 1867), 31.

63. "Military Affairs," *Hartford Daily Courant,* November 5, 1861, 2:4.

64. See "Military," *Hartford Daily Courant,* October 16, 1861, 2:5; & "Military," *Hartford Daily Courant,* November 12, 1861, 2:3.

65. "A Fine Exhibition," *Hartford Daily Courant,* July 7, 1861, 2:3. See also "The Ellsworth Zouaves," *Hartford Daily Courant,* July 15, 1861, 2:3; & "The Deming Zouaves," *Hartford Daily Courant,* July 17, 1861, 2:3.

VERMONT

1. *St. Albans Daily (VT) Messenger,* April 30, 1861, 2:5.

2. See *The (VT) Caledonian,* September 7, 1860, 2:2. An undated report on the 1st Vermont in *Rebellion Record,* vol. 1, p. 65, states, "One or two companies have a blue uniform instead of the gray." This may have been a reference to the New England Guards (Co. F) 1st Vermont.

3. "The Muster of the First Regiment," *Burlington Free (VT) Press,* May 3, 1861, 2:1. See also *St. Albans Daily Messenger,* May 8, 1861, 2:5.

4. See "The Vermont Militia," *Vermont (VT) Phoenix,* April 25, 1861, 2:6; "Vermont Items," *Vermont Watchman & State (VT) Journal,* April 26, 1861, 2:2; & "Patriotic Movements of Massachusetts," *Boston Evening Transcript,* April 23, 1861, 2:3. Isaac Fenno & Co. were "Manufacturers and Dealers in Men's and Boy's Clothing" at 80 Federal Street, Boston.

5. "Local Intelligence. The Brattleboro Company," *Vermont Phoenix,* May 9, 1861, 2:5.

6. "Military Movements in St. Albans," *St. Albans Daily Messenger,* April 29, 1861, 2:1.

7. "Merrill & Co.'s cloth," *Vermont (VT) Journal,* June 15, 1861, 8:2. Citing a report in the *Rutland Courier,* the Journal stated that Governor Fairbanks met with several cloth manufacturers, also including Andrew P. Carpenter, of Pownal; George Perry & Co., of Rockingham; and chose to grant the contract to Prosper Merrill having decided that his samples of cloth were "the cheapest and the best." Born in Connecticut about 1812, Prosper Merrill opened his Felchville factory in 1861, but it fell silent when "army blue" replaced gray cloth. This mill burned down in 1868.

8. See "The Vermont Regiment," *Vermont (VT) Chronicle*, May 14, 1861, 79:6; & "Daughters of the Regiment," *Vermont Watchman & State Journal*, May 24, 1861, 1:5. Following the departure of the 1st Vermont from the New York, an observer commented, "I hope they may have a chance to put the green sprigs along side the Palmetto, and try toughness with them," see "The Departure of the Vt. Volunteers from New York," *Burlington Free Press*, May 17, 1861, 2:3.

9. See Marius Peladeau, "Vermont Civil War Insignia," *North South Trader's Civil War* 21 no. 4 (1998): 34–38.

10. "The Vermont Regiment in Troy," *Troy Daily (NY) Whig*, May 10, 1861, 3:3.

11. "The Armament of the First Regiment," *Burlington Free Press*, May 3, 1861, 1:5.

12. "The Vermont Regiment," *St. Albans Daily Messenger*, May 16, 1861, 2:3.

13. "The Vermont Regiment," *Vermont Phoenix*, May 16, 1861, 2:2 citing the *New York Tribune*.

14. "Vermont," *Lowell Daily Citizen & News*, May 22 1861, 2:3.

15. "1st Vermont Regiment," *Vermont Phoenix*, May 30, 1861, 2:5.

16. "Letter from Camp Butler," *St. Albans Daily Messenger*, June 3, 1861, 2:4.

17. *Burlington Free Press*, June 7, 1861, 2:2.

18. See "Vermont Items," *Vermont Phoenix*, May 23, 1861, 2:6; & *Vermont Phoenix*, June 13, 1861, 2:7.

19. "Havelock Caps," *Vermont Chronicle*, May 21, 1861, 83:4.

20. "State of Vermont," *The Caledonian*, May 10, 1861, 2:6.

21. "Vermont Uniform," *ibid*, May 10, 1861, 2:6, citing the *Rutland Herald*. This would have been a reference to the dress uniform worn by this company before it donned the clothing provided for the 1st Vermont.

22. "Camp Underwood," *Burlington Free Press*, June 14, 1861, 2:2 & 3.

23. "Camp Underwood," *Burlington Free Press*, June 21, 1861, 2:3.

24. "The Second Vermont Regiment," *Vermont Watchman & State Journal*, June 21, 1:3.

25. "Vermont Items," *Vermont Phoenix*, May 23, 1861, 2:7.

26. Gilbert A. Davis, *History of Reading* (Windsor County, VT: n.p., 1903), 234.

27. "Local Intelligence," *Vermont Phoenix*, June 6, 1861, 2:5.

28. "A Screw Loose," *ibid,* June 6, 1861, 2:5 & 6—citing *Woodstock Standard*.

29. "Those Uniforms," *Vermont Phoenix*, June 13, 1861, 2:1.

30. See *St. Alban's Daily Messenger*, May 18, 1861, 2:2; "Vermont Items," *Vermont Watchman & State Journal*, May 31, 1861, 1:4; & "Overcoats," *St. Albans Daily Messenger*, May 23, 1861, 2:1.

31. "Vermont," *Vermont Chronicle*, May 28, 1861, 87:4.

32. "Departure of the 2nd Regiment," *Vermont Phoenix*, June 27, 1861, 2:1.

33. "Arrival and departure of the Second Regiment of Vermont," *New York Herald*, June 26, 1861, 4:6.

34. "Those Uniforms," *Vermont Phoenix*, July 4, 1861, 2:7.

35. *SORs*, Part II, vol. 69, 239; & "Arrival of the Second Vermont Regiment at New York," *Vermont Phoenix*, July 4, 1861, 1:3.

36. See "Military Matters in Boston and vicinity," *Boston Daily Advertiser*, June 22, 1861, 4:1; & "Equipments for Vermont Troops," *Boston Herald*, June 21, 1861, 4:5.

37. "The Vermont Volunteers," *Vermont Chronicle*, June 11, 1861, 95:1.

38. "Camp Baxter," *The Caledonian*, July 5, 1861, 2:4.

39. "From the Third Regiment. Camp Baxter, St. Johnsbury, July 5th, 1861," *Burlington Free Press*, July 12, 1861, 2:3 & 4.

40. See "From Camp Baxter," *Vermont Journal*, July 6, 1861, 4:5; & "From the Springfield Republican. The Passage of the Third Vermont Regiment through Springfield," *St. Albans Daily Messenger*, August 1, 1861, 2:5.

41. "From the Fourth Regiment. Camp Advance (Chain Bridge), Oct. 4th, 1861," *Burlington Free Press*, October 11, 1861, 2:3.

42. "The Wants of Our Troops," *Burlington Free Press*, November 8, 1861, 2:2.

43. "The Wants of the Vermont Troops," *St. Albans Daily Messenger*, October 23, 1861, 2:1.

44. G.G. Benedict, *Vermont in the Civil War: a History of the part taken by the Vermont Soldiers and Sailors in the War for the Union*, vol. 1 (Burlington, VT: Free Press Association, 1886), 137; & "The Vermont Brigade," *Vermont Chronicle*, November 19, 1861, 187:4.

45. "Response of Gov. Fairbanks," *St. Albans Daily Messenger*, October 25, 1861, 2:2.

46. "The Fourth Regiment," *Vermont Phoenix*, September 19, 1861, 2:2.

47. "Vermont," *Vermont Chronicle*, November 5, 1861, 179:4.

48. See "Governor Fairbanks' Address," *St. Albans Daily Messenger*, October 14, 1861, 2:3. The *Boston Herald* of October 5, 1861, also reported that the 6th Vermont received "uniforms of the army regulation blue."

49. "The Fifth Regiment Again," *St. Albans Daily Messenger*, October 18, 1861, 2:1.

50. Vermont in the Civil War, 182; "The Fifth Regiment Again," *St. Albans Daily Messenger*, October 18, 1861, 2:1; & *St. Albans Daily Messenger*, October 23, 1861, 2:1.

51. G.G. Benedict, *Vermont in the Civil War*, 209-210.

52. "Honor to whom Homer," *The Caledonian*, December 6, 1861, 2:7.

53. "The Sixth Regiment," *St. Albans Daily Messenger*, October 21, 1861, 2:1.

54. "The Sixth Regiment," *St. Albans Daily Messenger*, October 5, 1861, 2:5.

55. "The Cavalry Regiment," *St. Albans Daily Messenger*, September 12, 1861, 1:5.

56. "The Cavalry Regiment," *St. Albans Daily Messenger*, October 23, 1861, 3:4.

57. "The Cavalry Regiment," *St. Albans Daily Messenger*, November 7, 1861, 2:1 & 4:3.

MAINE

1. "The Extra Session Closed," *Lewiston Daily Evening (ME) Journal*, May 2, 1861, 2:1.

2. See "The Maine Volunteers," *Lewiston Daily Evening Journal*, May 14, 1861, 2:3. According to this source, the number of sick was "about twenty—all mild cases." It continued, "As the orders of Gen. Scott are imperative against bringing on the Regiment while there is the least danger of infecting the army, it will be impossible for the whole force to leave at present."

3. "Soldiers' Uniforms," *Bangor Daily Whig and (ME) Courier*, May 1, 1861, 2:3.

4. "Editorial and News Items," *Lewiston Daily Evening Journal*, May 2, 1861, 2:2.

5. "Unfounded and ungenerous complaints," *Bangor Daily Whig and Courier*, May 13, 1861, 2:1. The delegation consisted of James G. Blane, editor of the *Kennebec Journal*, and chair of the Lower House of the state legislature; and Otis Cutler, a merchant of Portland, both of whom were Republicans; and William H. Chisam, a farmer of Augusta, and Michael Gilligan, a forty-nine-year-old Irishman listed as a "Merchant Taylor" in Bangor in the 1860 census, both of whom were Democrats. In a letter published on May 15, Governor Israel Washburn, Jr. defended Blane's "management of the contract for the outfits for the Maine 1st Regiment," and exonerated him from "charges made against him." See "Matters in Maine," *Lewiston Daily Evening Journal*, May 15, 1861, 2:3.

6. Maj. John M. Gould & Rev. Leonard G. Jordan, *History of the First-Tenth-Twenty-ninth Maine Regiment* (Portland, ME: Stephen Berry, 1871), 20. This clothing issuance is substantiated by a letter dated April 29 in the *Lewiston Daily Evening Journal*, May 3, 1861, 2:1, which stated that the 1st Maine was "formed in line and marched to the City Buildings, on Congress St., where they were quartered, and have had their woollen shirts, drawers and stockings dealt out to them—each man receiving two pairs of each, and one towel, one handkerchief and several small articles."

7. "Letter from a Soldier," *Lewiston Daily Evening Journal*, May 6, 1861, 2:1.

8. Gould & Jordan, *History of the First-Tenth-Twenty-ninth Maine Regiment*, 21. According to "Local and State News," *Lewiston Daily Evening Journal*, April 30, 1861, 2:3, the uniforms arrived on April 29 but "were found to have on them the Massachusetts coat of arms; so they have been returned."

9. "Local Items in Brief," *Lewiston Daily Evening Journal*, May 6, 1861, 2:3.

10. "Matters in Maine," *Lewiston Daily Evening Journal*, May 14, 1861, 2:3.

11. "Color for the First Maine Regiment," *Lewiston Daily Evening Journal*, May 8, 1861, 2:3.

12. "Affairs about Home—The First Maine Regiment in Boston," *Boston Herald*, June 3, 1861, 2:2.

13. *Annual Report of the Adjutant General of the State of Maine for the year ending December 31, 1861*, Appendix G, Exhibit 4, Augusta: Stevens and Sayward Printers to the state, 7—hereafter referred to as *Annual Report of the Adjutant General*. See also Gould & Jordan, *History of the First-Tenth-Twenty-ninth Maine Regiment*, 62.

14. "Arrival of the First Maine Regiment," *Evening Star*, June 4, 1861, 3:2. See also "Local and State News—First Maine Regiment in Washington," *Lewiston Daily Evening Journal*, June 7, 1861, 2:2.

15. "From the Bangor Regiment, Washington, 8th," *Bangor Daily Whig and Courier*, July 18, 1861, 2:2.

16. "Matters in Maine," *Lewiston Daily Evening Journal*, May 27, 1861, 2:5.

17. Gould & Jordan, *History of the First-Tenth-Twenty-ninth Maine Regiment*, 63.

18. See Gould & Jordan, *History of the First-Tenth-Twenty-ninth Maine Regiment*, 64. Gould must have referred to a pseudonym, as "Phawkes" is not listed in the muster roll for Co. C.

19. "The Maine Troops in Boston," *Boston Herald*, May 15, 1861, 2:1.

20. R.H. Stanley & Geo. O. Hall, *Eastern Maine and the Rebellion*, (Bangor, ME: R.H. Stanley & Co., 1887), 47; & "Second Maine Regiment," *Evening Star*, June 1, 1861, 3:1.

21. Stanley & Hall, *Eastern Maine and the Rebellion*, 47–48 & 90. Joseph S. Wheelwright was a 40 year-old ex-seaman who had become a successful merchant in the late 1850s, while Greenleaf J. Clark was fifty-four-year-old cotton mill owner originally from Dover City, New Hampshire, in 1860. By 1861, Wheelwright & Clark occupied "the lower story and the whole of the back of the building [in Bangor known as the Wheelwright & Clark block] as a store, for their merchandise."

22. See *Bangor Daily Whig and Courier*, April 29, 1861, 2:5; & July 9, 1861, 2:5 & 7.

23. See "The Ladies at Work," *Bangor Daily Whig and Courier*, April 30, 1861, 2:4; & "The Sewing Battalion," *Bangor Daily Whig and Courier*, May 3, 1861, 2:1.

24. "Havelocks for the Bangor Regiment," *Bangor Daily Whig and Courier*, May 31, 1861, 2:3; & *Bangor Daily Whig and Courier*, June 7, 1861, 2:3.

25. *Annual Report of the Adjutant General*, 7.

26. "From the Bangor Regiment, Washington, 8th," *Bangor Daily Whig and Courier*, July 18, 1861, 2:1.

27. "Letter from the Regiment, Headquarters, 2d Reg't V.M.M. Camp Hamlin, Falls Church, Fairfax Co., Va., July 4th" *Bangor Daily Whig and Courier*, July 11, 1861, 2:2 from "Stephen."

28. "Local and Maine Items," *Bangor Daily Whig and Courier*, August 26, 1861, 2:4.

29. *Annual Report of the Adjutant General*, 7. A report in the *New York Tribune* dated June 7, 1861 (8:1), stated, "The uniform is Canada gray throughout."

30. *Ibid*; & Abner Ralph Small, *The Road to Richmond: The Civil War Letters of Major Abner R. Small of the 16th Maine Volunteers* (Fordham University Press: NY, 2000), 8 & 14.

31. "Letter from a Member of the Maine 3d." *Lewiston Daily Evening Journal*, August 7, 1861, 2:2.

32. See "Still They Come," *Delaware State Journal and Statesman*, June 21, 1861, 2:6; "More Troops," *Evening Star*, June 21, 1861, 3:2; & "Affairs about Home," *Boston Herald*, June 18, 1861, 4:3.

33. "Clothing Contracts," *Bangor Daily Whig and Courier*, June 18, 1861, 2:4, citing the *Portland Advertiser*. Storer & Cutler were listed as "Importers and Wholesale Dry Goods, and Jobbers of Clothing" at 58 and 60 Middle Street. Chadbourn & Kendall were listed as "Manuf's Wholesale and Retail Clothing, Cloths, Trimmings, and Furnishing Goods" at 66 Middle Street—see the *Portland Directory*, 37 & 38.

34. "Local Affairs—Movement of Troops," *Delaware State Journal and Statesman*, July 2, 1861, 2:5.

35. "Arrival of the Fifth Maine Regiment," *National Republican*, June 29, 1861, 3:2.

36. "More Troops," *Evening Star*, June 29, 1861, 3:1.

37. "From the 5th Regiment," *Lewiston Daily Evening Journal*, July 27, 1861, 3:1.

38. *Annual Report of the Adjutant General*, 7.

39. *Lewiston Daily Evening Journal*, November 2, 1861, 3:2.

40. "Local Items," *Daily National Intelligencer*, July 20, 1861, 3:4.

41. *Bangor Daily Whig and Courier*, June 4, 1861, 2:3; & June 20, 1861, 2:5. On June 20, Gilligan advertised in the local press for 300 "coat makers."—The firm of Sargent & Davis was run by sixty year-old John Sargent and 40-year old Sidney Davis. See "The Woolen Mill," *Lewiston Daily Evening Journal*, June 5, 1861, 2:3 for a report on the Lewiston Falls Manufacturing Company.

42. See *Bangor Daily Whig and Courier*, July 3, 1861, 2:6; & July 9, 1861, 2:6.

43. "Clothing and Equipments," *Bangor Daily Whig and Courier*, July 11, 1861, 2:6.

44. "The Sixth Regiment of Maine," *New York Herald*, July 19, 1861, 8:5. See also "Arrival of the Sixth Maine Regiment," *National Republican*, July 20, 1861, 3:1.

45. "Local Items in Brief," *Lewiston Daily Evening Journal*, August 12, 1861, 3:2. See also "The Washburn Zouaves," *Portland (ME) Advertiser*, July 29, 1861, 2:4. This issue also reported the formation of "a company of Fire Zouaves" at Gardiner, Maine, under Capt. George W. Smith, formerly of the Fire King Eagles Company, which eventually enlisted in the 24th Maine Infantry in 1862.

46. See "The Maine Seventh Regiment," *The (ME) Age*, August 29, 1861, 3:2; & "Regiments Going to the War," *Boston Herald*, August 23, 1861, 2:2. For a record of the sale of 1,000 M1841 "Windsor" rifles with sword bayonets to the State of Maine by the Massachusetts Ordnance Department on August 21, 1861, see George D. Moller, *Massachusetts Military Shoulder Arms 1784–1877*, 87.

47. "The Eighth Maine Regiment," *Boston Herald*, September 11, 1861, 2:1.

48. *"The Ninth Maine Regiment," Boston Daily Advertiser*, September 25, 1861, 1:8.

49. "State of Maine, Headquarters, Adjutant General's Office, Augusta, July 25, 1861," *Lewiston Daily Evening Journal*, July 31, 1861, 2:4. One of the mills running "night and day in the manufacture of blue army cloth" in Maine at this time was Lang's Woolen factory at North Vassalboro. See "Matters in Maine," *Lewiston Daily Evening Journal*, July 23, 1861, 3:1. On August 14, 1861, the *Journal* further reported, "The woolen mills at Oxford, hitherto engaged in the manufacture of flannels, are now employed in the manufacture of 'government blue.'"

50. "Army Contracts," *Portland Daily Advertiser*, August 14, 1861, 2:4.

51. "Local Items in Brief," *Lewiston Daily Evening Journal*, August 17, 1861, 3:2.

52. Edward P. Tobie, *History of the First Maine Cavalry* (Boston, MA: Press of Emory & Hughes, 1887), 13.

53. "The Cavalry Regiment," *Lewiston Daily Evening Journal*, October 31, 1861, 3:2.

54. "Notice to Contractors for Cavalry and Infantry Uniforms and Equipments," *Lewiston Daily Evening Journal*, October 4, 1861, 3:3.

55. "The 10th Maine Regiment Off to the War," *Boston Herald*, October 7, 1861, 2:2.

56. "The 12th Maine," *Lewiston Daily Evening Journal*, November 29, 1861, 3:1.

57. "Wanted," *Lewiston Daily Evening Journal*, October 4, 1861, 3:3.

58. *Lewiston Daily Evening Journal*, October 9, 1861, 3:3; & "Cavalry Equipments," *Lewiston Daily Evening Journal*, October 17, 1861, 3:1.

59. "Cavalry Matters," *Lewiston Daily Evening Journal*, October 16, 1861, 3:1. Also see "Cavalry Equipments," *Lewiston Daily Evening Journal*, October 17, 1861, 3:1 for fuller description.

60. *Lewiston Daily Evening Journal*, October 25, 1861, 3:2.

INDEX

A

Abbott, Adjutant General Joseph Carter (NH), 67.
Abbott, Stephen (NH), 70.
Aborn, S.O. (hatter), 34.
Alabama (steamer), 100.
Allen, James (RI), 57.
Andrews, Private Elisha Benjamin (CT), 90.
Andrew, Governor John A. (MA), 25.
Andrews, Brigadier General Samuel, 34.
Army of Northeastern Virginia, 70.
Army of the Shenandoah, 70.
Arnold, Colonel John (CT), 88.
Astor House, (NY), 27, 29.

B

Balch, Major Joseph P. (RI), 48, 51, 52.
Baldwin's Cornet Band (NH), 70.
Balmoral boot, 27.
Barnes, George A. (merchant), 34.
Baxter, Adjutant and Inspector General H. Henry (VT), 101.
bayonet scabbard, 15, 88, 140 n15.
bearskin cap, 20, 45, 49, 93, 95, 135 n101.
Beasley, Sarah (RI), 56.
Beckwith, Captain J.G. (CT), 91.
Beecher, Rev. H. Ward, 16.
Belcher, Captain George A. (CT), 93.
Benedict & Burnham (button makers), 17.
Berry, Governor Nathaniel S. (NH), 74.
Berry, Colonel Hiram G. (ME), 117.
Bienville (steamer), 55.
Big Bethel, 9, 28, 101.
blanket, 8, 15, 22, 25, 29, 35, 53, 54, 55, 57, 58, 60, 67, 69, 88, 90, 91, 100, 105, 106, 112, 113, 117, 118; (poncho-style) 9, 73, 74, 75.

blouse, 9, 25, 26, 29, 35, 39, 41, 42, 50, 51, 53, 54, 56, 57, 59, 60, 61, 69, 71, 73, 74, 75, 77, 78, 79, 85, 87, 89, 90, 92, 107, 117, 120, 138 n31.
blue uniforms, 15, 22, 34, 43, 49, 58, 94, 86, 105, 106, 141 n37, 144 n2; (army blue); 9, 105, 107, 133 n59, 144 n7.
boots, 15, 22, 34, 91, 108, 120.
bonnet de police (French fatigue cap), 40, 41.
Boston Committee on Military Supplies, 30.
Bowen & Pabodie (hatters), 51, 53, 137 n9.
Bowers, Captain William Lloyd (RI), 51.
bowie knife, 56, 57, 71, 72, 77, 138 n38.
breeches, 92, 93.
Brewster, Captain E.A.P. (MA), 23, 24.
Brigham, D.H., & Co. (military outfitters), 42, 137 n143.
Briggs, Captain Henry S. (MA), 25.
Briggs House (Chicago), 27, 29.
Brogans (shoes), 75, 120.
Brooks, Charles F. (NH), 73, 141 n43.
Brown, Colonel Nathaniel W. (RI), 60.
Brown. David F. (clothier), 79.
Brownell, Kady F. (RI), 55, 56, 138 n35.
Buckingham, Governor William A. (CT), 84, 91.
Bunce, Theodore H. (tailor), 86, 143 n6.
Burnside, Major General Ambrose (RI), 15, 48, 50, 51, 52, 53, 54, 55, 57, 58, 70, 115.
Butler, Major General Benjamin, 29, 42, 100, 120, 136 n138 & 141.
buttons, 16, 20, 21, 22, 24, 26, 27, 30, 35, 36, 37, 39, 40, 41, 43, 52, 59, 61, 70, 71, 75, 76, 77, 85, 86, 87, 88, 89, 99, 100, 103, 108, 114, 115, 118, 137 n6; (ball buttons) 36, 38, 53; (pewter) 40, 41; (Connecticut) 90, 91; (Maine) 113, 116; (Massachusetts) 17, 28, 34, 113, 130 n1; (New Hampshire) 68, 69; (Rhode Island) 50, 54; (Vermont) 102, 104, 105.

C

Cadet grey, 26, 67, 68, 98, 115; (Cadet Mixed) 27, 34, 91, 101, 104, 119.

Cahill, Colonel Thomas W. (CT), 93.

Cameron, Secretary of War Simon

Camps (military)

Camp Advance (VA), 104, 105, 146 n41.

Camp Ames (RI), 60.

Camp Andrew (MA), 17, 132 n28 & 33.

Camp Baxter (VT), 105, 145 n38, 39 & 40.

Camp Burnside (RI), 59, 139 n57.

Camp Chase (MA), 92.

Camp Douglas (DC), 84.

Camp Fairbanks (VT), 98.

Camp Greene (RI), 61, 139 n64.

Camp Gregory Smith (VT), 107.

Camp Griffin (VA), 105.

Camp Holbrook (VT), 105.

Camp Mansfield (CT), 90, 143 n34.

Camp McClure (CT), 91, 143 n41.

Camp Sprague (RI), 56, 138 n30.

Camp Tyler (CT), 93.

Camp Underwood (VT), 101, 105, 145 n22 & 23.

Camp Union (NH), 66.

camp utensils, French pattern, 120.

canteens 15, 26, 33, 34, 60, 67, 90, 100, 101, 108, 112, 120; (gutta percha) 69, 71, 104; (oblate spheroid or "bullseye") 57, 60, 95, 103, 106; (tin drum) 54, 57, 114, 118.

canvas shoes, 93.

cap pouch, 52, 69, 75, 77, 100, 103, 104, 114.

cartridge box, 15, 28, 29, 53, 58, 59, 67, 69, 75, 88, 100, 101, 103, 104, 106, 117, 118, 140 n15,

Center, Captain Addison (MA), 22, 132 n26.

Chadbourn & Kendall (military suppliers), 118, 120, 147 n33.

Chain Bridge, 104, 105, 107, 145 n41.

Chamberlain, Captain William D. (MA), 14.

Chandler, Captain Charles G. (VT), 101.

Chappell, Second Lieutenant James H. (RI), 53, 55.

chasseur uniforms, 20, 21, 29, 35, 37, 38, 40, 41, 91; (chasseur pattern cap) 52, 53, 54, 67, 69, 65, 86, 88, 92, 102, 105, 118, 136 n125; (semi-chasseur uniforms) 9, 27, 28, 30, 32.

Clark Jr., Colonel George (MA), 16, 20.

Coatzacoalcos (steamer), 55.

Cobb, Robinson & Co. (leather goods), 113, 120.

Cochran, Major Walter W. (VT), 105.

cocked hat, 92.

Colt, Samuel, 64, 89, 91.

Commodore (steamer), 34.

Committee of the City Council on Military Supplies (MA), 27, 29, 30, 131 n10 & 11, 133 n53, 54, 57 & 59; 134 n71, 74, 79, 83 & 86; 135 n91, 136 n136, 137 n143.

Comstock, Captain John C. (CT), 89, 143 n32.

Connecticut volunteer infantry

1st Connecticut, 85, 86, 87, 88, 89, 90, 91, 94.

1st Connecticut Cavalry Battalion, 93, 94.

1st Connecticut Heavy Artillery, 91, 94.

2nd Connecticut, 87, 88, 89, 90, 94.

3rd Connecticut, 84, 86, 88, 89, 90, 92, 94, 143 n7 & 9.

4th Connecticut (1st Connecticut Heavy Artillery), 90, 91, 94, 143 n38.

5th Connecticut ("First Connecticut Revolving Rifles"), 84, 91, 92, 94.

6th Connecticut, 92, 93, 94.

7th Connecticut, 92, 94.

8th Connecticut, 92, 94.

9th Connecticut ("Irish Regiment"), 92, 93, 94, 144 n58.

10th Connecticut, 94.

11th Connecticut, 89, 93, 94.

27th Connecticut, 88.

Connecticut militia and volunteer companies
 Brewster Rifles (Rifle Co. C), 3rd Connecticut, 84, 88.
 Captain Dean's Zouaves, 93.
 City Guard (Co. A), 4th Connecticut, 91, 94.
 Clinton Guard (Rifle Co. D), 2nd Connecticut, 87, 90.
 Colt Guard, 91.
 Deming Zouaves, 93, 144 n65.
 Ellsworth's Zouaves, 93.
 Emmett Guard, 92.
 Governor's Foot Guard, 93.
 Hartford Invincibles (Rifle Co. E), 3rd Connecticut, 89.
 Hartford Horse Guards, 95.
 Hartford Rifle Company aka Light Guard (Rifle Co. A), 1st
 Connecticut, 87.
 Mansfield Guard (Rifle Co. A), 2nd Connecticut, 95.
 Mechanic Rifles (Rifle Co. A), 3rd Connecticut, 92.
 New Haven Grays, Co. C, 2nd Connecticut, 87, 88.
 Norwich Light Guard, 89.
 Putnam Phalanx, 92.
 Smith Guard, 91.
 Union Guards, 89, 91, 144 n49.
Continental House (PA), 27, 29.
Continental-style uniform, 92.
Cook, Adams B. (clothier), 75, 77, 142 n56.
Cook, Major Asa (MA), 26.
Cook, William H. (MA), 20.
Cowdin, Colonel Robert (MA), 29. 33, 133 n56. 134 n76.
Cudworth, Rev. Warren H., (MA), 33, 134 n82.
Cumner, Nathaniel W., (clothier), 71, 141 n40.
Cune & Brackett (tailors), 102.
Cunningham, First Lieutenant William G. (CT), 86.

D

Dahlgren howitzer, 43.
Darn & Son, Henry (leather equipage), 120.

Davis, State Quartermaster General George F. (VT), 100,
 101, 102, 104.
Day & Co., Charles G. (clothier), 86, 91, 92.
Day, Horace H. (military supplier), 69.
Devereux, Captain Charles U. (MA), 8, 24.
Dickinson, Captain L.A. (CT), 93.
Dodd, Captain Albert (MA), 26, 132 n45, 133 n54.
doeskin cloth, 15, 25, 26, 27, 71, 101, 118, 133 n53.
dress cap, 19, 37, 88, 117, 118.
dress hat, 30, (pattern 1858 hat) 34, 52, 53, 55, 58, 59; ("keg"
 hat) 7; ("Kossuth" hat) 14, 30, 34, 51, 53, 55, 69, 112, 118,
 130 n2, 134 n71.
Drew & Co., George W. (supplier), 160.
Dyer, Cyrus G. (RI), 52.

E

Edmands, General Benjamin F., 27, 30, 134 n71.
Edmands hat, 30, 31, 32.
Eldredge, Daniel (NH), 73, 141 n37, 38 & 40; 142 n48, 50 & 54.
Empire State (steamer), 48, 57.
Epaulet, 15, 17, 26, 27, 31, 40, 41, 55, 77, 88.

F

Fairbanks, Governor Erastus (VT), 98, 100, 102, 105, 107,
 144 n7, 145 n45 & 48.
Faneuil Hall (MA), 15, 131 n10.
Fatigue cap, 22, 24, 25, 26, 33, 40, 42, 49, 53, 58, 59, 61, 67,
 68, 77, 78, 79, 87, 88, 91, 95, 100, 108, 115, 117, 134 n74;
 (forage cap) 17, 26, 34, 37, 38, 41, 52, 53, 54, 57, 60, 61,
 62, 68, 69, 72, 73, 87, 88, 91, 93, 100, 106, 117, 139 fn72;
 (185 pattern cap) 106, 114, 115; (1861-pattern cap) 106;
 (chasseur pattern cap) 105, 67, 85, 86, 118; (McDowell-
 style) 53, 57; (Mexican War-style) 92.

fatigue shirts, 20, 21.

Felchville Mill (VT), 102.

Fenno, Isaac, & Co., 34, 100, 135 n91, 144 n4.

Ferry , Colonel Orris S. (CT), 91.

fez cap, 8, 24, 29, 32, 33, 38, 60, 62, 112, 119, 135 n102.

First Bull Run (First Manassas), 9, 24, 50, 52, 54, 60, 70, 71, 95, 115, 116.

First New England Regiment of Cavalry, 57, 61, 63, 80.

Fisher & Co. (tailor), 85, 142 n3.

Forbes, Robert B., 43, 137 n149.

forts (Fort Ethan Allen), 104; (Fort Independence) 37; (Fort McHenry) 26, 33; (Fortress Monroe) 14, 26, 28, 29, 33, 60, 100; (Fort Sumter) 34, 112; (Fort Warren) 34, 36, 39.

Francis, Private Page F. (ME), 117.

frock coat, 14, 15, 16, 17, 26, 27, 29, 30, 34, 35, 39, 42, 60, 61, 71, 74, 75, 76, 77, 78, 79, 81, 86, 87, 88, 92, 98, 101, 102, 104, 106, 112, 113, 114, 115, 118, 119, 130 n2, 131 n8, 9 & 14; 139 n72.

Frye, Captain Frederick (CT), 89,

Frye, Colonel J.M. (ME), 119.

G

Gaiters, 20, 24, 35, 37, 38, 40, 41, 62, 114, 115.

Garibaldi clothing, 27, 29, 30, 33, 133 n 52, 143 n38.

Gloucester, MA, 20, 21, 22.

Gilligan, Michael (tailor), 116, 119, 146 n5, 147 n41.

Given, Corporal Benjamin (ME), 118.

Godillot, Alexis (French uniform manufacturer), 41.

Goodwin, Governor Ichabod (NH), 66, 141 n24.

Gordon, Colonel George H. (MA), 34.

Gore, Capt. James W. (CT), 87.

Gould, Private John M. (ME), 113, 114, 115.

Gove, James B. (NH), 77, 142 n62.

Guernsey frock, 15, 131 n8 & 9.

H

habit-veste (French fatigue jacket), 40, 41.

Harpers Ferry, 56.

Harris Mill (NH), 71, 141 n38.

Hatch, William B. (purchasing agent), 107.

Hathaway, Major J.M. (CT), 85.

Haughton, James, 29.

Haughton, Sawyer, & Co. (military suppliers), 8, 27, 28, 29, 30, 69, 133 n57, 134 n71 & 86, 140 n15.

Havelock, 8, 16, 34, 39, 53, 59, 88, 101, 116, 131 n15, 147 n24.

Havelock hat (or cap), 42, 43, 71, 72, 73, 74, 75, 77, 79, 81, 145 n19.

haversack, 15, 26, 34, 54, 57, 60, 67, 69, 71, 74, 79, 90, 92, 100, 101, 104, 106, 108, 112, 113, 117, 120, 140 n15.

Hawley, Captain Joseph R. (RI), 87.

Hay, Private Secretary John, 10, 49.

Haley's Tailoring Establishment, Samuel A. & Benjamin F., 73, 75, 77, 79.

Ham, John T.W., 141 n42.

Haynes, Martin A. (NH), 68, 140 n8.

Heintzleman, Brigadier General Samuel P., 104.

Helm, William H. (RI), 58.

Herring, George M. (shoe supplier), 69, 140 n14.

Hill, James R. (leather goods), 69, 75, 79, 140 n15.

Hilliard & Spencer (textile mill), 86.

Hodson, Acting Quartermaster General John L. (ME), 120.

Holden, B.F. & D. (textile mill), 69, 75, 140 n14.

Holderness Woollen Mill (NH), 75, 79, 142 n56.

Howard, Colonel Oliver O. (VT), 104, 117.

hunting shirt, 9, 50, 51, 52, 53, 54, 58, 59, 61.

Hutchinson, Sergeant Gustavus D. (MA), 33.

J

Jacket (roundabout), 8, 9, 20, 21, 22, 24, 26, 27, 28, 29, 30, 33, 34, 35, 36, 38, 39, 40, 41, 42, 43, 56, 61, 62, 69, 87, 90, 91, 98, 101, 105, 108, 120, 132 n32, 135 n96 & 102, 143 n38.
Jackson, Joseph P. (tailor), 116.
Jackson, Colonel Nathaniel J. (ME), 112, 118.
Joslyn Fire Arms Company, 89.

K

Kelley & Edmunds (tailors), 77.
Keyes, Colonel Erasmus D., 84, 90.
Klouse & Co., S. (hatter), 69.
Koffman, M. (tailor), 91.
knapsacks, 15, 17, 25, 33, 34, 41, 57, 60, 74, 75, 79, 88, 90, 91, 92, 100, 101, 112, 113, 115, 117, 120, 140 n15; (militia pattern) 36, 49; (Pattern 1855) 35; (rubberized) 67, 69, 106.
Knowles, Colonel Abner (ME), 118.

L

Ladd, Luther C. (MA), 14.
Lane, George (clothier), 20.
Lawton, Pvt. Charles E. (RI), 55.
Lawton, Colonel Robert B. (RI), 61.
Leggings, 21, 35, 36, 38, 40, 93, 135 n102.
Leslie, Edwin C. (tailor), 18.
Lewiston Falls Manufacturing Company, 119, 147 n41.
Libby & Co., H.J. (merchant tailors), 119.
Lincoln & Shaw (clothier), 71, 74, 75, 76, 77, 79, 81.
Lincoln, President Abraham, 17, 21, 24, 25, 26, 48, 59, 112.
lindsey woolsey, 101.
Liscomb, Nathaniel S. (hatter), 25.

Little, Henry (NH), 78.
Littlefield, James (leather goods), 117.
Livermore, Pvt. Thomas L. (NH), 69, 70, 75.
Longley & Garcelon (saddles & harness), 120.
Loomis, James M. (hatter), 43, 73, 134 n71.
long arms
muskets
US Model 1816 flintlock or conversion musket, 60, 67, 79, 117.
US M1842 smoothbore percussion musket, 61, 67, 69, 72, 74, 84, 89, 91, 103, 104, 117, 118.
rifle muskets, rifles & carbines
Austrian M1854 rifle musket, 78.
Burnside carbine, 57, 61.
Colt M1855 revolving rifle, 91.
Enfield rifles, 72, 74, 92, 93, 105, 107, 142 n54.
Enfield Pattern 1853 rifle musket, 35, 42, 70, 74, 75, 77, 78, 106, 107, 142 n54 & 63.
Sharps carbine, 42, 61.
Sharps New Model 1859 breech loading rifle, 78.
Short Enfield rifle with sword bayonet, 61,
Springfield M1855 rifle musket, 54, 57, 59, 88, 89, 99, 104, 107, 112, 114, 118, 119, 131 n8.
Springfield M1861 rifle musket, 106, 107.
U.S. M1841 Rifle (Mississippi rifle), 35, 106.
Whitney M1841 contract rifle, 26.
Windsor M1841 rifle, 35.
Lounsbury, Bissell & Co. (mill owner), 92.
Lyon, Major Jordan M. (CT), 93.

M

Macullar, Williams and Parker (clothiers), 34, 51, 137 n8.
Maine militia and volunteer artillery, infantry & cavalry
1st Maine Cavalry, 120, 121.
1st Maine Heavy Artillery, 115.

1st Maine Volunteer Militia, 112, 121.

2nd Maine Inf.("The Bangor Regiment"), 84, 90, 114, 115, 116, 117, 121, 146 n15, 147 n24 & 26.

3rd Maine Inf. ("The Kennebec Regiment"), 117, 121.

4th Maine Inf., 117, 121.

5th Maine Inf., 104, 118, 121.

5th Maine Light Artillery Battery, 50.

6th Maine Inf., 104, 122, 114, 118, 119, 121.

7th Maine Inf. ("Washburn Zouaves"), 119, 120, 121.

8th Maine Inf., 119, 121.

9th Maine Inf., 120, 121.

10th Maine Inf., 112, 120, 121, 148 n55.

15th Maine Inf., 120.

Maine volunteer companies

Bath City Greys (Co. A), 3rd Maine Inf., 117.

Gymnasium Company (Co. G), 2nd Maine Inf., 115.

Lewiston Zouaves (Co. K), 1st Maine Inf., 114.

Milo Artillery (Co. D), 2nd Maine Inf., 115.

Portland Light Guards (Co. C), 1st Maine Inf., 113.

Portland Rifle Guards (Co. I), 1st Maine Inf., 113.

Manning, Captain Charles H. (MA), 42.

Marston, Colonel Gilman (NH), 71.

Massachusetts Ordnance Department, 119, 147 n46.

Massachusetts State Prison, 33, 140 n14.

Massachusetts State uniform (officers), 29.

Massachusetts Volunteer artillery, cavalry & infantry

1st Inf., 27, 28, 30, 34, 44.

1st Battery, Massachusetts Light Artillery, 42, 44.

2nd Massachusetts Independent Battery, 26, 44.

2nd Inf., ("Gordon's Regulars"), 34, 44.

3rd Cavalry, 42, 44.

4th Massachusetts Independent Battery, 43, 44.

7th Inf., 29, 44.

8th Inf., 44.

9th Inf., (1st Irish Regiment), 34, 44.

10th Inf., (Western Regiment), 29, 30, 38, 42, 44, 105.

11th Inf., (Boston Volunteers), 20, 29, 30, 44, 33, 34, 133

n57, 134 n83.

12th Inf., (Webster Regiment), 34, 44, 135 n91.

13th Inf., 29, 34, 35, 44.

14th Inf., 29, 39, 44.

15th Inf., 29, 39, 44, 136 n120.

17th Inf., 39, 41, 44, 136 n122.

18th Inf., 30, 40, 41, 44, 136 n129.

19th Inf., 24, 35, 38, 41, 44.

20th Inf., 42, 44.

22nd Inf., (Senator Wilson's Regiment), 42, 44.

23rd Inf., 23, 24, 44.

24th Inf., (New England Guards), 37, 38, 44.

27th Inf., 42, 44.

30th Inf., (Eastern Bay State Regiment), 38, 42, 44.

31st Inf., 38, 39, 44.

32nd Inf., 24, 44.

38th Inf., 28, 44.

44th Inf., (2nd New England Guards), 37, 44.

60th Inf., 44.

Massachusetts Volunteer Militia

1st Regiment of Light Infantry (Tiger First), 35.

1st MVM, 18, 28, 33, 34, 44.

1st Battalion Riflemen (Poore's Battalion), 35, 44.

2nd Battalion Riflemen (Boston Light Infantry), 35, 44.

3rd MVM, 14, 29, 30, 33, 44, 133 n63.

3rd Battalion of Riflemen (Deven's Battalion), 25, 44.

4th Battalion, 35, 37, 44.

4th Battalion of Rifles, 34, 44.

4th MVM, 15, 16, 28, 29, 30, 31, 32, 44, 133 n63.

5th MVM, 17, 19, 20, 24, 25, 26, 34, 44.

6th MVM, 14, 15, 16, 17, 18, 29, 30, 32, 33, 44.

7th MVM, 22, 25, 30, 33.

8th MVM, 8, 15, 16, 17, 20, 21, 22, 24, 25, 29, 33, 35, 38, 44, 45, 131 n9, 134 n68.

10th MVM, 38.

43rd MVM (Tiger Regiment), 35, 44.

Massachusetts volunteer and militia companies

Allen Guard (Co. K), 8th MVM, 16, 17, 24, 25, 38, 132 n34, 135 n108.

American Guard (Co. G), 8th MVM, 20, 21, 25, 132 n32.

Barre Volunteers (Co. K), 21st Massachusetts Volunteers, 39.

Barton Roughs (Co. E), 10th Massachusetts Volunteers, 38.

Beverly Light Infantry (Co. E), 8th MVM, 17, 20.

Boston Cabot Zouave Cadets, 38.

Boston City Guard, 34.

Boston Fire Zouaves (Co. I), 30th Massachusetts Volunteers, 38.

Boston Light Artillery, MVM, 25, 26, 42, 44.

Boston Light Infantry, MVM, 35, 36, 38, 135 n101.

Boston Tiger Fire Zouaves, Co. K, 19th Massachusetts Volunteers, 38.

Brewster's Zouaves (Co. A), 23rd Massachusetts Volunteers, 23, 24.

Chadwick Light Infantry (Co. K), 1st MVM, 28, 30.

Charlestown Artillery (Co. D), 5th MVM, 24.

City Guards (Co. K), 14th Massachusetts Volunteers, 39.

Coast Guard, 43, 137 n144 & 149.

Cobb's Light Battery, 26.

Cushing Guards (Co. A), 8th MVM, 20.

Dodd's Rifles (Co. D), 3rd Bn. Riflemen, MVM, 26.

Easton Light Infantry (Co. B), 4th MVM, 15.

Emmett Guards (Co. C), 3rd Bn. Riflemen, MVM, 26.

Foster Guard, Co. B, 17th Massachusetts Volunteers, 39.

Glover Light Guards (Co. H), 8th MVM, 25.

Great Barrington Company (Co. A), 10th Massachusetts Volunteers, 38.

Greenough Guards (Co. K), 4th MVM, 29, 133 n63.

Hancock Light Infantry (Co. H), 4th MVM, 132.

Independent Zouaves, 38.

Johnson Grays (Co. B), 10th Massachusetts Volunteers, 38.

Lawrence Light Infantry (Co. I), 6th MVM, 45.

Lincoln Light Infantry (Co. I), 4th MVM, 16.

Lowell City Guard (Co. D), 6th MVM, 14.

Lynn Light Infantry (Co. D), 8th MVM, 20.

Mechanic Phalanx (Co. C), 6th MVM, 17, 18, 30.

Methuen Light Infantry (Co. B), 14th Massachusetts Volunteers, 39.

Mounted Rifle Rangers, 42, 44.

National Greys, Co. A, 6th MVM, 14, 32.

New England Guard battalion, MVM, 37, 44.

New England Guard (Co. A), 4th Battalion Infantry, MVM, 37, 135 n103 & 104.

Plymouth Rock Guards (Co. E), 3rd MVM, 29, 133 n63.

Pollock Guard (Co. D), 10th Massachusetts Volunteers, 38, 42, 136 n112,

Poore's Savages (Co. A), 1st Battalion, MVM, 35.

Putnam Guards (Co. I), 14th Massachusetts Volunteers, 39.

Richardson Light Guard (Co. B), 5th MVM, 17, 19.

Roxbury City Guards (Co. D), 1st Massachusetts Volunteers, 29.

Salem Light Infantry, or Salem Zouaves, (Co. I/J), 8th MVM, 8, 22, 23, 24, 25, 132 n32.

Salem Zouave Drill Corps, 24.

Scott Grays (Co. F), 14th Massachusetts Volunteers, 39.

South Abington Light Infantry (Co. E), 4th MVM, 28.

Summerville Light Infantry (Co. I), 5th MVM, 17, 19.

Sutton Light Infantry (Co. C), 8th MVM, 25.

Taunton Light Infantry (Co. G), 4th MVM, 32.

Union Guards, (Co. I), 3rd MVM, 14, 130 n2.

Wardwell's Tigers (Co. F), 5th MVM, 20.

Warren Light Guards (Co. F), 4th MVM, 15.

Washington Light Guard (Co. K), 6th MVM, 17, 18, 29.

Watson Light Guard (Co. H), 6th MVM, 30, 130 n3, 134 n68.

Wightman Rifles (Co. M), 4th MVM, 29, 133 n63.

Worcester City Guard (Co. A), 3rd Battalion of Riflemen, 25.

McClellan cap, 39.

McClellan, General George Brinton, 9, 41, 73.

Meigs, Quartermaster General Montgomery C., 9, 41.

Merrill, Prosper, 100, 102, 104, 144 n7.

Military Equipment Depot (Boston), 27.

Mooney, Charles C. (shoe supplier), 69, 140 n14.

N

National Guard (7th New York State Militia), 16.

Naval Academy, 8, 20.

Neil House (Columbus, Ohio), 27, 29.

Nevins, David, 39.

Newell, Lieutenant Joseph K. (MA), 30, 134 n72, 135 n111.

New Hampshire State Prison, 69, 70, 73, 75, 140 n14, 142 n56.

New Hampshire Volunteer infantry

    1st New Hampshire (three months), 66, 67, 68, 69, 70, 71, 74, 79, 80, 81, 140 n15,

    2nd New Hampshire, 67, 68, 69, 70, 71, 80, 81, 131 n11, 140 n11 & 13.

    3rd New Hampshire, 71, 72, 73, 74, 77, 80, 140 n15, 142 n56.

    4th New Hampshire, 72, 74, 75, 78, 80, 81.

    5th New Hampshire, 72, 74, 75, 77, 78, 80, 81.

    6th New Hampshire, 71, 75, 76, 77, 78, 79, 80, 81.

    7th New Hampshire, 78, 80.

    8th New Hampshire, 75, 77, 79, 80.

New Hampshire militia and volunteer companies

    Cheshire Light Guards (Co. A), 2nd New Hampshire, 68, 70.

    Goodwin Rifles or Guards (Co. B), 2nd New Hampshire Infantry, 70, 71.

New Haven Arms Company, 89.

New York City, 8, 16, 20, 29, 39, 42, 70, 100, 104, 135 n101, 141 n41.

New York regiments

    2nd New York Cavalry, 84, 94.

    33rd New York Infantry, 104.

    49th New York Infantry, 41.

    72nd New York Infantry, 41.

    Norwalk Felt cloth, 91.

O

observation balloon, 57.

Osborne, Captain E. Walter (CT), 88.

overalls, 87, 101.

overcoat, 8, 9, 15, 16, 17, 25, 26, 29, 31, 32, 33, 34, 35, 37, 39, 42, 49, 55, 61, 67, 68, 71, 72, 73, 74, 75, 77, 78, 79, 86, 87, 88, 89, 90, 91, 92, 100, 101, 104, 105, 107, 108,112, 113, 115, 117, 120, 131 n10 & 11, 134 n77, 140 n5, 142 n56, 145 n30.

P

Paine, Allen, Pond & Co. (military suppliers), 104.

pantaloons, 14, 18, 27, 30, 36, 37, 38, 40, 41, 42, 49, 53, 56, 61, 62, 71, 85, 86, 87, 89, 90, 91, 92, 98, 101, 113, 114, 115, 117, 118, 120, 143 n12.

pants, 8, 14, 16, 17, 20, 21, 22, 24, 25, 26, 27, 29, 30, 34, 37, 38, 39, 41, 42, 43, 49, 51, 53, 56, 59, 60, 61, 62, 67, 68, 69, 70, 71, 73, 74, 75, 77, 79, 85, 86, 87, 88, 89, 90, 91, 92, 93, 95, 98, 100, 101, 105, 107, 115, 116, 119, 120, 132 n32, 135 n96, 101 & 102; 138 n31, 139 n72, 143 n38.

Patterson, Major General Robert, 70.

Perkins, J.J. (supplier), 29.

Pemberton Mills, 39.

Pennsylvania regiments

    62nd Pennsylvania Infantry, 41.

    83rd Pennsylvania Infantry, 41.

Pepper, John (clothier), 75, 142 n56.

Phelps, Colonel J. Wolcott (VT), 98.

Pierce Bros. & Co. (military outfitters), 42, 69, 133 n57, 137 n143.

Pierce, Colonel Thomas P. (NH), 71.

Pike, Fife Major Francis "Saxie," (NH), 70.

Pitman, Lieutenant Colonel Joseph S. (RI), 48.

Pittsfield (MA), 16, 17, 18, 25, 38, 42.

Platt, Colonel Lemuel B. (VT), 108.

Pollard, A.W. (military goods dealer), 114.

pompon, 14, 15, 19, 26, 35, 37, 38, 88, 112, 117.

poncho rubber blanket, 73.

Pontocrac Mill, 38.

Poore, Major Ben Perley (MA), 35.

Porter, General Fitz-John, 41.

Pratt, Colonel Lemuel B. (VT), 108.

Pratt, Wright & Co. (tailors), 102.

Prescott, Henry A. (clothier), 51, 53, 137 n4.

Prosper Merrill & Co. (cloth mill), 102.

Purinton, Amos D., 141 n42,

Purinton & Ham (hatters), 71, 73, 74, 75, 77, 79, 81, 141 n42.

Putnam, Colonel Haldimand S. (NH), 78.

R

Read, Captain S. Tyler (MA), 42.

Reed, Lieutenant Colonel John H. (MA), 29.

Reeder, Governor Andrew H. (KS), 58, 139 n50.

Relay House, 16, 18, 24, 25, 33, 132 n32 & 35, 134 n80.

Regiment of Boston Volunteers (MA), 20, 44.

revolver, 18, 21, 26, 35, 42, 52, 53, 54, 57, 59, 61, 66, 70, 71, 72, 86, 100, 107, 112, 114,

130 n3, 138 n38.

Reynolds, Joseph R. (textile mill), 86.

Reynolds, Captain William H. (RI), 61, 138 n45.

Rhode Island blouse, 59, 60.

Rhode Island regiments and batteries
    1st Regiment, Detached Militia, 48, 49, 50, 52, 53, 54, 55, 56, 57, 58, 59, 63, 137 n5.
    1st Rhode Island Light Artillery, 58, 61, 63.
    2nd Rhode Island Infantry, 52, 58, 59, 60, 61, 63, 139 n62.
    3rd Rhode Island Infantry, 60.
    3rd Rhode Island Heavy Artillery, 57, 61, 63.
    4th Rhode Island Infantry, 61, 63.
    5th Rhode Island Infantry, 61, 63.
    5th Rhode Island Heavy Artillery, 55.
    10th Rhode Island Infantry, 54, 62.
    12th Rhode Island Infantry, 52.
    Battery A, 1st Regiment Rhode Island Light Artillery
    Burnside Rifle Battalion, 61, 63.
    Providence Marine Corps of Artillery, 57, 63.
Rhode Island militia and volunteer companies
    Burnside Zouaves, 62.
    Bristol County Volunteers (Co. G), 2nd Rhode Island, 59.
    Emmett Guards, 3rd Rhode Island Infantry, 60.
    First Light Infantry, 49, 59.
    Jackson Guards, 3rd Rhode Island Infantry, 60.
    Mechanic Rifles, No. 1 (Co. G), 1st Rhode Island Detached Militia, 56.
    Mechanic Rifles, No. 2 (Co. H), 1st Rhode Island Detached Militia, 54, 56.
    Montgomery Guards, 3rd Rhode Island Infantry, 60.
    Newport Artillery (Co. F), 1st Rhode Island Detached Militia, 49, 53, 61.
    Providence Artillery (Co. B), 1st Rhode Island Detached Militia, 57.
    Providence Horse Guards, 61.
    Warren and Bristol Company (Co. G), 2nd Rhode Island Infantry, 59.
    Woonsocket Guards (Co. J), 1st Rhode Island Detached Militia, 49.
Rhodes, Corporal Elisha Hunt (RI), 59, 60.

Rhodes, Sergeant John H. (RI), 61.

Richards, W.A. (supplier), 29.
Rockland Brass Band (ME), 118.
Roe, Alfred S. (MA), 39.
Rogers & Raymond (supplier), 92.

S

sack coats, 24, 25, 30, 69, 78, 85, 86, 87, 89, 91, 92, 108, 132 n32.
saddle, 120.
Sargent & Davis (tailors), 119, 147 n41.
satinet cloth, 25, 86, 87, 90.
Savage Revolving Fire Arms Company, 89.
Sawyer, Samuel E. (merchant), 29, 140 n15.
Schulze, Henry (tailor), 85, 86, 142 n3.
Scovill Manufacturing Company, 68, 76, 104.
Seamless Clothing Manufacturing Company, 42, 43, 73.
Second Bull Run (Second Manassas), 40.
sewing societies, 16, 20, 59, 85, 116, 119, 147 n23.
shako, 19, 26, 40, 70.
Sherman, General Thomas W., 73.
Sherman, Private James L. (MA), 15.
Ship Island, MS, 93.
Shoddy, 9, 39, 75, 76, 77, 101, 102, 104, 115, 143 n12.
shoes, 33, 38, 42, 49, 56, 67, 69, 70, 71, 73, 74, 77, 65, 87, 89, 90, 92, 93, 100, 101, 105, 112, 113, 114, 120, 134 n79, 142 n56, 143 n19; brogans, 75, 120; (canvas) 93.
Short, Joseph (patent knapsack), 74, 75, 79.
shoulder knots, 35, 37, 38.
shoulder scales, 20, 21, 25, 26, 27, 39, 41, 76, 108.
Slocum, Colonel John S. (RI), 59, 60.
Small, Corporal Abner R. (ME), 117.
Smith, Corporal Frederick W. (MA), 24, 25, 132 n28, 32 & 33.

Smith, Quartermaster George H. (RI), 57.
Sprague, Governor William (RI), 48, 53, 55, 56, 61, 138 n17.
"stag's head" cartridge box plate, 100.
stable jacket, 108.
Stark, Brigadier General George (NH), 71.
Stephenson, Captain Luther (MA), 16, 29.
Storer & Cutler (tailors), 118, 119, 147 n33.
Strahan, Maria F. (RI), 56, 138 n28.
Strong, Corporal Charles R. (MA), 25.
Sturtevant, Major Edward E. (NH), 74.
swords and sabers
    Foot Officer's sword (M1850), 24, 57.
    Light Artillery saber (M1840), 26, 58, 95.
    Non-commissioned officer's sword (M1840), 112.

T

Tagert & Wilson (tailors), 38.
tail-coat, spiketail coat, or swallow-tail coat, 17, 20, 25, 26, 37, 49, 67, 68, 71, 73, 81, 87, 88, 92, 93, 95, 98, 100.
Tappan, Colonel Mason W. (NH), 69, 71.
Terry, Colonel Alfred H. (CT), 87.
Thayer & Co, George L. (shoe supplier), 69.
Thorpe, Abram, or Abraham (clothier), 73, 141 n41.
Thorpe, Joseph W. (clothier), 75, 79, 142 n56.
Tibbets, Charles (RI), 56.
Tompkins, Captain Charles H. (RI), 57.
trousers 9, 14, 15, 16, 24, 25, 26, 28, 29, 30, 35, 39, 41, 50, 51, 56, 57, 62, 67, 69, 70, 73, 74, 75, 78, 85, 86, 87, 88, 90, 93, 99, 102, 108, 115, 120, 130 n2; (chasseur-pattern) 20; (light artillery) 61; (infantry) 42, 50.
turban, 35, 36.
Tyler, Colonel Daniel (CT), 87.

U

Union Manufacturing Company, 91.
United States Zouave Cadets, 38.
U.S. Army hat, pattern 1858, 34, 39, 51, 55, 78.
US Corps of Cadets, 26.
USS *Constitution*, 8, 20.

V

Vermont regiments & batteries
    1st Vermont Infantry ("Green Mountain Boys"), 68, 98, 99,
      100, 101, 104, 107, 109, 144 n2, 145 n8 & 21.
    1st Vermont Cavalry, 108, 109.
    2nd Vermont Inf., 101, 102, 104, 109.
    3rd Vermont Inf., 102, 103, 104, 105, 109.
    4th Vermont Inf., 105, 106, 107, 109.
    5th Vermont Inf., 107, 109.
    6th Vermont Inf., 107, 109, 145 n48,
    7th Vermont Inf., 108, 109.
    8th Vermont Inf. ("Butler Regiment"), 108, 109.
    9th Vermont Inf., 30, 109.
Vermont volunteer companies
    Bradford Guard, 2nd Vermont Inf., 101.
    Burlington Light Guard (Co. H), 1st Vermont Inf., 98.
    Capital Guards (Co. F), 2nd Vermont, 101.
    Green Mountain Guards (Co. A), 1st Vermont, 99.
    New England Guards (Co. F), 1st Vermont, 98, 99, 144 n2.
    Ransom Guards (Co. C), 1st Vermont, 98, 101.
vivandieres & nurses, 55, 56, 100, 105, 138 n31.

W

Ward, C.T. (tailor), 91.
Wardrop, Colonel David W. (MA), 33.
Warde, Humphrey & Co. (blankets), 75, 142 n56.
Wass, Captain Ansel D. (MA), 38.
Welles, Secretary of the Navy Gideon, 43.
Wheaton, Surgeon Francis L. (RI), 52.
Wheelwright and Clark (merchant tailors), 115, 116.
Whelden, Charles M. (MA), 38.
Whipple hat, 43, 134 n71, 136 n138.
Whipple, Jonathan F. (clothier & hatter), 42, 73.
White & Co., T.A. (merchant tailors), 119.
Whiting, Galloupe, Bliss & Co. (clothiers), 8, 34, 67, 68, 69,
    140 n5.
Whitney, Jr.,Eli (arms manufacturer), 89.
Whitten, Hopkins & Co. (clothiers), 16, 25, 27, 29, 42, 67, 68,
    131 n9 & 11, 133 n53 & 59, 135 n91, 137 n143, 140 n5.
wide-awake capes, 92.
Wilkinson, Solon S. (leather equipment), 77.
Williams, Lieutenant Horace P. (MA), 20.
Winthrop, Theodore (MA), 29.
Wisconsin volunteer infantry
    1st Wisconsin, 91.
Woodbury, Chaplain Augustus V. (RI), 52, 56.
Woodbury, Captain Isaiah (MA), 24.
Woods, J.W. (merchant), 29.
Woodward, Solomon (clothier), 102, 104.
Wright, Captain Ira (CT), 85, 86.

Z

Zouave or zouave-style uniforms, 8, 20, 21, 22, 23, 24, 25, 26,
    27, 29, 30, 33, 34, 35, 36, 38, 39, 61, 62, 90, 91, 93, 114, 119,
    121, 132 n32, 135 n106, 147 n45.